Essential Writings of
Karl Marx

Economic and Philosophic Manuscripts, Communist Manifesto, Wage Labor and Capital, Critique of the Gotha Program

by Karl Marx

Red and Black Publishers, St Petersburg, Florida

Introduction copyright © 2010 by Red and Black Publishers. All Rights Reserved.

Library of Congress Cataloging-in-Publication Data

Marx, Karl, 1818-1883.
  [Selections. English. 2010]
  Essential writings of Karl Marx : Economic and philosophic manuscripts, Communist manifesto, Wage labor and capital, Critique of the Gotha Program / by Karl Marx.
    p. cm.
  ISBN 978-1-934941-86-7
1. Communism. 2. Socialism. I. Title.
  HX39.5.A224 2010
  335.4--dc22

                                                    2010011557

Red and Black Publishers, PO Box 7542, St Petersburg, Florida, 33734
Contact us at: info@RedandBlackPublishers.com
          Printed and manufactured in the United States of America

Contents

Editor's Preface

A Quick and Dirty Introduction to Marxism

Ever since humans had the capacity to fathom the unknown, they have attempted to understand and explain the Ultimate Reality, the source from which springs all that is, was or will ever be. One of the earliest such attempts in the West was made in the 6th century BCE by the Miletian philosphers of Greece. Led by the philosophers Thales and Anaximander, the Miletians decided that all things, whether animate or inanimate, material or spiritual, were merely differing manifestations of some unifying "thing", which they called Physis. This Physis, Anaximander explained, was driven into a cycle of constant change by the interaction of opposing but unified poles.

Some time later, the Greek philosopher Heraclitus embellished upon the ideas of the Miletians. Reality, concluded Heraclitus, was not an eternal unchanging entity, but was in a constant state of flux and change. "No one ever steps twice into the same river," he declared, "for what occurs in the next instant is never the same as the first."

This constant state of "Becoming" was, he said, brought about by the periodic interplay of opposites. Each pair of opposites conflicts to provoke change, but, at the same time, each pair of opposites forms a unity between themselves. Thus, Heraclitus concluded, hot and cold, wet and dry, high and low, good and evil, were all differing manifestations of the same thing. This entity that encompassed all pairs of opposites and unified them was the Ultimate. Heraclitus called this Ultimate Logos.

Heraclitus was vigorously opposed by his contemporaries, particularly by Parmenides and his pupil Zeno. These two belonged to the Eleatic school of philosophy, which championed the idea of a single Divine Principle that stood above everything and directed the universe. This Divine Principle, said Parmenides, was eternal and unchanging. Therefore, he argued, reality is in a constant and unalterable state of "Being", and all of the apparent changes which we observe are in fact unreal and illusory.

The conflict between the "Being" of Parmenides and the "Becoming" of Heraclitus raged for decades before the so-called "Atomists" attempted to reconcile the two. Democritus, the most important of the Atomists, attempted to unify the two outlooks by postulating that there existed some eternal and unchanging substance (the "Being") which produced change by interacting with itself in various ways (the "Becoming"). "Cosmic substance," Democritus wrote, "is made up of an infinite number of elements or particles, physically invisible, indestructible and infinite, which vary in size and shape, and are in eternal motion." These eternal and indestructible things were "atoms", the smallest unit of matter.

By thus dividing the Being and the Becoming into two separate processes, the Atomists created the rift between emotion and reason, religion and science, soul and body, spirit and matter, that has yet to be resolved in the West. After reality was divided into the realms of matter (the atom) and spirit (the laws which governed the motions of atoms), the Greeks went on to emphasize the study of the spiritual side of reality, and began detailed inquiries into the fields of ethics, religion and philosophy.

The philosopher Pythagorus concentrated on the study of mathematics and concluded that all matter was guided by mathematical principles. "All things," he declared, "are numbers."

Plato, after a detailed consideration of geometry, concluded that the physical world was composed of nothing but perfect geometrical shapes, and believed that the study of geometry was the study of reality. Plato later expanded his idea into the outlook known as "objective idealism". All parts of the universe, he wrote, are simply the physical manifestation of some perfect underlying Form or Ideal, and these Ideals were the metaphysical "foundation" for all reality. A horse, for example, was nothing more than the physical incarnation of the Ideal "Horseness", while a circle was the manifestation of "Roundness". These Forms were in turn unified and directed by the Divine Principle, which Plato termed The Good. Thus, Plato argued, the things we see in the world are not real, but are merely transitory images of the underlying Forms. Plato held that the study of the eternal and unchanging Forms was more important than the study of the actual material world.

This basic attitude did not change for over a thousand years. Throughout the Middle Ages, the Church supported the view that the study of the Divine Principle was more important than that of the physical world. The Church, of course, concluded that the Divine Principle was God, and held that all things were as they were through the intervention of God. St. Thomas Aquinas, one of the chief proponents of this view, wrote, "There is a certain Eternal Law, to wit, Reason, existing in the mind of God and governing the whole Universe." When the Apostle Paul introduced Christianity to the Greeks, knowing that they were familiar with the works of Heraclitus, he declared, "In the beginning was Logos , and Logos was with God, and Logos was God." (This has been widely mis-translated as "The Word", but, in the original context, Paul was referring to the Logos of Heraclitus.) Thus, Paul argued to the Greeks, not only was the Christian God a part of the all-encompassing Logos, but God actually *was* Logos . Since the Church, at that time, played a considerable role in maintaining the established social order, these ideas had far reaching political and economic ramifications. The feudal order was characterized by the political doctrine of Divine Right, which held that the King was King because God wanted him to be King, and the world was the way it was because God wanted it to be that way. Therefore, the Church declared, the serf was a serf because God desired it, and to rebel against one's condition of serfdom was not only a political crime but a sin against God. By remaining content with one's inevitable lot in life, the Church concluded, one could avoid sinning and thus find happiness in Heaven after death.

It was not until the decay of feudalism (along with the decay of the Church which supported it) that the physical world first came under serious scrutiny. The rising merchant class turned to the material sciences as an ideological weapon against the feudal doctrine of Divine Right, and also had an interest in using an understanding of the natural world in order to extract raw materials and produce commodities for exchange. This ideological and economic struggle produced the Enlightenment, a flowering of European scientific thought.

Galileo was one of the first to observe the natural process directly and to attempt to explain it materially, without reference to God or Divine Intervention. The Church, recognizing that Galileo's outlook was a mortal threat to the established social order, promptly excommunicated him and forced him to recant his ideas.

A short time later, Rene Descartes further separated the material world into two entities—matter (*extensa*) and mind (*cogitans*), and pronounced the famous formula, "I think, therefore I am." By thus separating the observer from that which is being observed, Descartes formed the scientific attitude, which holds that matter can be observed impartially and objectively, with no consideration for the position or attitude of the observer.

Expanding on the ideas of Descartes, Isaac Newton developed the postulate that matter was subjected to a never-ending chain of cause and effect, and that the study of this process was the way to discover the nature of reality. Newton and the other "mechanistic materialists" held that the universe was governed by universal "natural laws", which operated regardless of time, space or the position of the observer. The universe was in effect a giant machine, which ran on inexorably in accordance with eternal and unchanging laws.

This effort was carried to its conclusion by LaPlace, who expanded the Newtonian laws of motion and used them to explain in great detail the motions of all the known heavenly bodies. Napoleon is said to have jokingly remarked that LaPlace had described the workings of the universe without once having mentioned its Creator. "I had no need of that hypothesis," the French scientist replied.

A short time later, Charles Darwin began an intensive study of biology, and uncovered a set of "laws" that determined the development of biological diversity. Darwin called this process "natural selection" or "evolution". By the 19th century, attention was being turned from the natural sciences of physics and biology to the "social sciences" of economics and political science. The new wave of scientists hoped to discover the "universal laws of nature" which guided the development of social processes, just as Newton had discovered the laws of mechanics and Darwin had discovered the laws of biology. It was during this search that Marxism came into being.

Marx began his philosophical inquiry as a student of the late German philosopher Georg Hegel. Hegel's outlook was one of the first to regard history, not as a mere collection of names and dates, but as a process leading to definite ends. Hegelian philosophy enjoyed considerable influence in the first half of the 19th century and had a profound impact on the development of Marxism.

Hegel's philosophy was based on the dialectic. Simply stated, the dialectic holds that reality is fluid and flowing, in a constant state of change produced by the simultaneous interaction of opposing entities. This interaction changes these entities until they become something entirely new. These new entities in turn interact dialectically to continue the process.

Hegel was of the Idealist school of philosophy, which, like Plato, holds that the ultimate source of reality is ideal or spiritual, and that all material reality is a mere reflection or incarnation of these unchanging Ideals. In describing these ideals, Hegel remarked. "To these powers, individuals are related as accidents are to substance, and it is in the individuals that these powers are represented, have the shape of appearance, and become actualized." The totality of these Ideals was the Absolute Spirit.

By applying the dialectic outlook to these Ideals, Hegel concluded, it could be shown that History is a process that is constantly moving towards the actualization of Ideals and the Absolute Spirit. This process takes place dialectically.

The dialectic opposites of thesis and anti-thesis, Hegel pointed out, are fluid and dynamic. "Each thing is a combination of contraries," he wrote, "because it is made up of elements which, although linked together, at the same time eliminate one another." Hegel thus saw history as a flow of ideas merging with other ideas to produce new ideas, all the while moving towards the actualization of the unchanging Absolute Spirit.

Hegel further asserted that these Ideals were the basis for human social reality, and that human society changed as the actualization of these ideals changed. "History," Hegel wrote, "is mind clothing itself with the form of events or the immediate actuality of nature."

Finally, Hegel concluded, the ultimate and most complete manifestation of the Absolute Spirit was to be found in the political state. "The state," he asserted, "is the actuality of the ethical idea." As such, it was perfect in its form and could not be changed by human action without a corresponding change in the governing Ideals. Thus

Hegel, who was himself an official of the Prussian state, bitterly opposed the revolutionary movements of the 1840's and defended the Prussian government. "The state is the divine will, in the sense that it is mind present on earth, unfolding itself to be the actual shape and organization of the world," he wrote. "It is in the organization of the state that the Divine enters into the real."

Thus Hegel, who had condemned the dogmatism of the Church, nevertheless continued to hold the same social viewpoint as the medieval Church. Society was the way it was, he said, because it was intended to be that way, and rather than attempt to rebel against conditions, one ought to simply accept and bear them.

Soon, however, Hegel's philosophy came under increasing attack from the more liberal of his students, the so-called "Young Hegelians". While most of the Young Hegelians busied themselves with obscure doctrinal or metaphysical interpretations, the most radical of Hegel's disciples, Marx, sought to apply the Hegelian dialectic to social reality. While Hegel's dialectical viewpoint was correct, Marx concluded, his entire metaphysical line of reasoning was "standing on its head". "It must be turned right side up again," Marx wrote, "if you would discover the rational kernel within the mystical shell."

Marx soon rejected Hegel's Idealism as being divorced from reality. He scoffed at the Idealists, saying, "Hitherto, men have constantly made up for themselves false conceptions about themselves, about what they are and what they ought to be. . . . The phantoms of their brains have gotten out of their hands." Marx declared that reality could not be found in philosophy, in what humans declared themselves to be, but in what they were empirically determined to be. "All social life," he wrote, "is essentially practical. All mysteries which lead to mysticism find their rational solution in human practice and in the comprehension of this practice."

When his rejection of Idealism led him to begin the study of philosophical Materialism, Marx turned to the writings of the German mechanistic materialist Ludwig Feuerbach, who was himself a student of Hegel. Marx found himself quickly disappointed. While Idealism emphasized the action of human ideas on the social environment, Materialism tended to place humans in a deterministic chain of cause and effect, and therefore in a social situation about which humans could do little. Man strongly disagreed with this viewpoint:

"The chief defect of all materialism up to now (including Feuerbach's) is that the object, reality, what we apprehend through our senses, is understood only in the form of the object of contemplation, but not as sensuous human activity, as practice; not subjectively. Hence in opposition to Materialism the active side was developed abstractly by Idealism—which of course does not know real sensuous activity as such."

Feuerbach's notion of blind, deterministic materialism, said Marx, failed to account for the ability of human beings to exercise influence over their surroundings through conscious actions. Thus Marx was led to reject both Hegelian Idealism and Feuerbachian Materialism. Neither, he concluded, was capable of explaining the action of human societies.

Marx found the answer to his puzzle in a combination of Materialism and Idealism into the system now known as philosophical Naturalism. Naturalism as a philosophy holds that reality is composed of neither pure matter nor pure idea, but by the interactions of both. Materialism and Idealism, according to this point of view, are merely different sides of the same process.

By combining Hegel's dialectical idealism with Feuerbach's mechanistic materialism, Marx formed the philosophical outlook now known as "dialectical materialism", or, more correctly, dialectical naturalism. "Here we can see," Marx writes, "how consistent naturalism or humanism is distinct from both Idealism and Materialism, and constitutes at the same time the unifying truth of both. We can also see how only naturalism is capable of comprehending the action of world history."

Marx continues: "My dialectic method is not only different from the Hegelian, but is its direct opposite. To Hegel, the life processes of the human brain. i.e , the process of thinking, which, under the name 'The Idea', he even transforms into an independent subject, is the demiurgos of the real world, and the real world is only the external, phenomenal form of the 'Idea'. With me, on the contrary, the ideal is nothing else than the material world reflected by the human mind and translated into forms of thought."

Hegel had begun his analysis by studying the Ideas which, he thought, directed the process of history. Marx, on the other hand, began by examining the material conditions of society which, he concluded, formed the basis for these ideas: "The first premise of human history is, of course, the existence of living human individuals.

Thus the first fact to be established is the physical organization of these individuals and their consequent relation to the rest of nature."

Since the task of any human population, stated in its simplest terms, is to stay alive, Marx asserted that the primary factor influencing the organization of any group of human beings was the manner in which they obtained food, constructed shelters and produced their living, and also in the manner in which these necessities were distributed among the members of the group. These factors were the major focus of the science of economics, and therefore, Marx concluded that the cause of human social behavior was largely economic in nature. Engels writes:

"The materialist conception of history starts from the proposition that the production of the means to support human life and, next to production, the exchange of things produced is the basis of all social structure; that in every society that has appeared in history, the manner in which wealth is distributed and society divided into classes or orders is dependent upon what is produced, how it is produced, and how the products are exchanged.

"From this point of view the final causes of all social changes and revolutions are to be sought, not in men's brains, not in men's better insights into eternal truth and justice, but in the modes of production and exchange. They are to be sought not in the philosophy but in the economics of each particular epoch.

Marx, therefore, began a period of intensive study in the field of economics, and was particularly influenced by the British economists Adam Smith and David Ricardo. During this time, Marx began to work closely with Friederich Engels, who had earlier attracted Marx's attention with his book *The Condition of the Working Class in England*.

Through his study of political economy, Marx came to conclude that the basic structure of any human society was made up of the various institutions and relationships that were necessary for the production of the means of life and for the replication of social relationships:

"The mode of production must not be considered solely as being the reproduction of the physical existence of individuals. Rather, it is a definite form of activity on their part. As individuals express their life, so they are. What they are therefore coincides with their production, both with what they produce and with how they produce. The nature of individuals thus depends on the material conditions determining their production."

The social and political relationships which made up this mode of living were themselves based on the need to regulate and protect the economic process:

"The fact is, therefore, that definite individuals who are productively active in a definite way enter into these definite social and political relations. Empirical observation must in each separate instance bring out empirically, and without any mystification and speculation, the connection of the social and political structure with production. The social structure and the state are continually evolving out of the life-processes of definite individuals, but of individuals not as they appear in their own or other people's imaginations, but as they really are, i.e., as they operate, produce materially and hence as they work under definite material limits, presuppositions and conditions independent of their will."

In addition, Marx noted, the division of labor within the economic system, combined with the relationships produced by the social and political structures, leads to the formation of groups of individuals who perform similar social and economic functions. Marx called these socio-politico-economic groupings "classes". Every society, Marx concluded, was composed of different classes, whether these be slave and master, serf and feudal lord, or worker and owner.

The interests of these classes were always at odds, and a constant struggle took place between them. To Marx, these "class struggles" were crucial. "The history of all hitherto society," he wrote, "is the history of class struggles." In these struggles, Marx concluded, were to be found the concrete process of the Hegelian dialectic.

In any society, no matter how many classes there might be, one class is able to assume a dominant position over the others by virtue of its control over the means of production and the social apparatus. This ruling class would then take its living at the expense of the lower classes, who were powerless to prevent the exploitation. Thus, the feudal lords made their living by exploiting the labor of their serfs and appropriating a portion of the serfs' produce.

Modern capitalist society, Marx pointed out, is composed of four classes: the capitalists or bourgeoisie, made up of large property owners and stockholders; the "middle class" or petty bourgeoisie, made up of professionals and salaried managers; the proletariat or working class, made up of wage-earning workers; and the lumpenproletariat, made up of the unemployed and the unemployable. The primary struggle in capitalism, Marx concluded, is between the bourgeoisie and the proletariat, with the other classes gradually being forced to support one side or the other.

In each phase of human history, moreover, the social and political structures were controlled and dominated by the same class that had control of the economy. The social conventions of law, government, philosophy and religion now served not only to support and safeguard the economic structures which produced the means of life, but also served as instruments whereby the ruling class protected its own privileged positions within these structures.

In this manner, the feudal lords used the ethics of loyalty and chivalry and the religious doctrine of Divine Right to keep the serfs under control, while the modern capitalists use the "work ethic" and a maze of property laws to keep the workers under control. As Marx noted, "The ruling ideas of each age have always been the ideas of its ruling class."

Marx pointed out that the class struggle was constantly raging on all fronts — economic, political, religious and philosophical. Each class produced ideas and actions which influenced human society to a greater or lesser extent, but the ideas of the ruling class, backed by the coercive power of the state, always remained supreme. Nevertheless, each of these ideological conflicts finds its place in the economic and social struggles.

Though the exploited classes were in an inferior position, Marx concluded that the necessity of adapting human social constructions to existing material circumstances would one day produce a crisis in the old order, as it outgrew its applicability to its surroundings. At this point, a new class would remove the old social order and replace it with a new one, one that was better suited to material conditions. In this manner, the French bourgeoisie had risen and overthrown the feudal monarchy in 1789, and had proceeded to re-mold society in accordance with its own needs and desires.

Here, Marx concluded, was the Hegelian dialectic at work. The thesis, in this case the feudal aristocracy, was faced with its anti-thesis, the rising bourgeois merchant class. The two combine, in the French Revolution, to transcend each other and produce a new social order, the capitalist republic. But, Marx concluded, this synthesis had now become a new thesis, to be in turn confronted with a new anti-thesis: the industrial working class. Inevitably, writes Marx, a new synthesis will be formed to replace the capitalist order, the socialist mode of production.

In his giant work *Capital*, Marx describes in great detail the process of the transition from the bourgeois capitalist order to the proletarian socialist one. He examines the process of capitalist production and details its development and contradictions, based on the labor theory of value and the fetishism of commodities. Marx points out several contradictions which limit the ability of capitalism to adapt to its surroundings, and will eventually lead to its downfall.

In his examination of capitalism, Marx makes great use of the Hegelian concept of "alienation". Hegel asserted that humans are separated or alienated from the Absolute Ideals, and that the process of human history was the struggle to re-unify humans with their "absolute essences". Marx modified this concept to fit his own view of human development and social relationships. To Marx, the term "alienation" came to signify a division which attempted to separate two things which were in fact inextricably united.

In the Marxian world-view, things are seen in their totality as a series of interpenetrating dialectical relationships. Since people must carry on certain activities in order to live and reproduce, humans and their activities are inseparably linked to each other. Since humans exist in a social setting, individual humans depend for their survival on their social and economic links to each other. And, since people must constantly interact with their natural surroundings in order to extract and produce their means of life, humans as a social unit must maintain an inseparable link with nature and the natural process.

Under capitalism, each of these fundamental unities has been breeched by the unique social institutions of the capitalist order. In capitalist society, human interaction with nature takes place largely through the process of industrial extraction and production. The vast majority of society, however, which owns no capital, has no control over this process or over the ends to which it is put. The relationship between human activity and natural surroundings, therefore, does not exist for the majority of human society. The industrialists who do interact with nature view it as a mere economic commodity, a mere source of wealth to be "utilized" and "exploited". Humans are thus separated or "alienated" from their natural surroundings, and nature confronts them, not as an inseparable extension of social life, but as an alien and hostile power.

Similarly, the social and class antagonisms engendered by capitalism place severe restrictions and limits on the cooperation and interaction necessary for social existence, thus alienating or separating humans from each other and presenting the illusion that each individual is a separate and independent unit. The capitalist myth of "rugged individualism" ignores the fact that humans cannot exist in isolation, and that they are dependent for their existence on the activities of their fellow humans. The farmer may be able to produce his own food, but he cannot produce the lumber with which to build his home, or the steel to fabricate his plow, or the cloth which makes his clothing, or the gasoline which fuels his machinery. Similarly, the lumber worker, the steelworker, the tailor and the oil worker are dependent on each other for these things, as well as on the farmer for their food.

The capitalist division of labor forces humans to interact cooperatively to produce the means of life. However, rather than allowing social individuals to work together cooperatively for the common good, capitalism uses the myth of "individualism" to force a large part of the population to labor for the benefit of a small group which does not labor at all. Individuals in capitalist society confront each other as hostile "competitors", not as social beings who are fundamentally interrelated.

Finally, capitalist society alienates humans from their own individual activities, since individuals under capitalism have no control over the use of their labor or the disposition of the products of their labor, and thus have little control over their own individual life-activities. As Marx puts it: "The exercise of labor-power, labor, is the worker's own life-activity, the manifestation of his life. And this life-activity he sells to another person in order to secure the necessary means of subsistence."

Rather than being a method of allowing human society to fully understand and produce its needs, labor under capitalism is an alienating and unnatural activity. The worker in capitalist society becomes dehumanized, regarded by the capitalists as simply another piece of equipment which is necessary for the production of profit, merely another expense which the capitalist must pay. The workers become less than human. They have no time to enjoy their lives through education or culture, since they are forced by capitalist social organization to sell one-third of their lives in order to "make a living". Workers are so busy procuring the means of life (and at the same time enriching the capitalists) that they have no time left to live their lives. As Marx puts it, the worker becomes "a mere appendage of flesh on a machine of iron."

Marx may sound like an idealistic moralizer, but this is not his intention. Marx never characterized communism as "good" and capitalism as "bad". Capitalism, he noted, was "inhuman" because it alienated human individuals from their surroundings, but, he noted, so too did every other social system hitherto in existence. The inhumanity, he pointed out, lay not in the system, but in the alienation which had produced it. "What is the kernel of evil?" Marx asks. "That the individual locks himself in his empirical nature against his eternal nature."

In order for this alienation to end, Marx reasoned, it would be necessary to insure that the labor of each individual was of benefit to the entire group, that the economic interests of any individual were no different from those of the social group as a whole, and that all social relationships were based on direct face-to-face links between social individuals. This, in turn, meant that the control of the means of production and of social relationships could no longer be in the hands of any particular social class, but in the hands of the social group as a whole. In short, it meant the end of private ownership over capital.

Marx realized that this ideology already existed, in the form of French socialism and communism. In the early 1800's, the social ideas of the French radicals Comte, Blanc, Babeuf and Proudhon had enjoyed considerable influence and had played a large role in the revolutionary movements of 1848. Each of these idealists preached a series of social reforms based on the common ownership of property. Marx, however, saw communism not so much as a social reform program or an ideology, but as a necessary consequence of and prerequisite for the transcendence of human alienation. This transcendence, he pointed out, was only possible within the framework of the abolition of private property and the wage system:

"The positive transcendence of private property as the appropriation of human life is, therefore, the positive transcendence of all alienation—that is to say, the return of man from religion, family, state, etc., to his human, i.e., social, mode of existence."

Thus, Marx saw communism as a return of human society to its social roots, free from alienation and class exploitation. This transcendence, Marx concluded, could only take place after a long historical process had brought about the necessary preconditions for it.

In formulating this concept of "historical preconditions" for communism, Marx broke sharply with the so-called "Utopian socialists" of the 1800's. The Utopians, led by Fourier, St. Simon and Owen, held that communism was the "ideal" social system, one that embodied the ideals of perfect Justice and Freedom. Communism, the Utopians argued, had only to be believed in, embraced and constructed in order to remove all of the ills from the human condition.

Marx bitterly attacked this notion, pointing out that communism was not simply an ideology but also a process of historical development. The theories of the communists, he pointed out, were dependent on the dialectical development of material conditions for their actualization, just as the historical process itself was being influenced by these ideas and theories. What we think about our surroundings is a part of those surroundings, but at the same time, the thoughts that we have are developed from our surroundings. "Thinking and being," Marx pointed out, "are thus certainly distinct, but at the same time they are in unity with each other."

The basis of private property in an economic and social system, Marx concluded, is the fact that, in an economy which is unable to produce abundant material goods for all of its members, some method must be found to channel things to certain people and deny them to others. Of course, in each social system of organization, those who controlled the production and distribution of goods were able to channel the lion's share of products to themselves.

Under feudalism, for instance, where food production was unable to keep pace with population and famine was common, the feudal aristocrats used taxes and the feudal *corvee* system to insure that they received enough food, even at the expense of others. In modern capitalism, where the economy is unable to provide enough TV sets, houses, or other material things for everybody, the price system determines who will get these goods and who will not, thus insuring that the capitalists, who have all the money and who thus can pay higher prices, get whatever they want, even at the expense of everyone else.

If private property is to be done away with, the economy must be capable of producing abundance for everybody, thus eliminating the need for a property-owning class which appropriates scarce resources for itself. Neither the slave-holding economy nor the feudal economy were able to reach this level of economic organization and productivity. Thus, when each system reached the limits of its economic productive ability, it was forced to give way to a new system that was able to take the existing economic structures and modify them in such a way as to expand production.

This process reached its highest point in capitalism, which has assembled productive powers and abilities on a scale which far exceeds anything created before. The economic productive capacity assembled by capitalism, therefore, makes the abolition of private property at last a feasible undertaking for human society.

In the Marxian conception, then, communism is not an ideal social system which can be constructed any time that humans choose to do so. Rather, it is the result of a long process of historical and economic development. "The theoretical conclusions of the Communists," Marx wrote, "are in no way based on ideas or principles which have been invented or discovered by this or that would-be universal reformer. They merely express, in general terms, actual relations springing from the existing class struggle, from a historical movement going on under our very eyes."

Thus, the Marxian outlook can best be summarized as a relational view of totality, in which all things interact with each other, producing changes which lead to newer forms of interaction. That humans are, on the whole, unable to see this process of mutual interaction is due to the aims and goals of their social organizations, which are based upon mutually antagonistic classes. In each system of social organization, the needs of the dominant class run roughshod over the needs of human society, and social organizations benefit the ruling class at the expense of human society.

The ruling class does this through a process of alienation, by constructing a system of artificial human relationships which then come to be seen and accepted as "real", replacing the natural relationships of dialectical interpenetration. For instance, the capitalist social order uses its artificial economic structures to portray human relationships as atomistic and independent, as individualist actions which are controlled by an "eternal and natural system" of "economic laws". Under this scheme, the rich stay rich because they are the lucky victors in the "laws of the marketplace" run by an impartial "invisible hand"—not because they dominate all social relationships and use social powers to maintain their position of privilege.

Most people are conditioned by their social existence to accept these artificial abstractions as real, and are thus unable to see the unifying human relationships which these restrictions cut off and alienate. In order to understand the process of totality, it is necessary to go beyond the accepted categories and alienations created by human social construction, and to look at the relationships which produce and propagate these structures. These continuously changing interrelationships are the basis for the dialectical view of history.

After Marx's death, his thought was adopted and codified by a group of German socialists who formed a new international organization to propagate them, the Second International. The theorists of the Second International in turn modified the dialectical nature of Marxism, and began to refer to it as a "science", which could explain and predict the motions of human society as Darwin explained and predicted the development of biological species and Newton explained and predicted the motion of physical objects. Under the Second International, Marxism was transformed into a series of natural "laws" which, theorists claimed, made the introduction of socialism a historical inevitability, regardless of human intentions or actions.

The Marxist-Leninists, in their Third International, took this process of codification even further. The Leninists asserted that (1) Marxism described the natural laws which govern the development of human society, (2) trained Marxist-Leninists are able to interpret these laws and thus to predict the future development of human society, and (3) the party of trained Marxist-Leninists should therefore be allowed to rule over society to insure that it is guided, according to these "natural laws", down the inevitable path to socialism.

The "science" of Marxism had been born.

Marxism was based on the direct observation of the phenomenon being examined, in this case, human social development. Marx rooted his inquiry in the direct observation of the social process. He kept up a steady stream of criticism at the Hegelian idealists, pointing out that their high-sounding ideals and abstractions had no connection to reality:

"The most recent of them have found the correct expression for their activity when they declare that they are only fighting against 'phrases'. They forget, however, that to these phrases they themselves are only opposing other phrases, and that they are in no way combating the real world when they are merely combating the phrases of the world."

"It has not occurred to any one of these philosophers to inquire into the connection of German philosophy with German reality, the relation of their criticism to their material surroundings."

To Marx, the Ideals of the philosophers were merely illusions, intellectual abstractions from reality:

"For philosophers, one of the most difficult tasks is to descend from the world of thought to the actual world. Language is the immediate actuality of thought; just as philosophers have given thought an independent existence, so they had to make language into an independent realm. This is the secret of philosophical language, in which thoughts in the form of words have their own content. The problem of descending from the world of thoughts to the actual world is turned into the problem of descending from language to life. . . . The philosophers would only have to dissolve their language into the ordinary language, from which it is abstracted, to recognize it as the distorted language of the actual world, and to realize that neither thoughts nor language in themselves form a realm of their own, that they are only manifestations of actual life."

The solution, said Marx, was to abandon the illusions of the Idealists and to begin the direct observation of concrete reality:

"One has to 'leave philosophy aside', one has to leap out of it and devote oneself like an ordinary man to the study of actuality. . . Philosophy and the study of the actual world have the same relationship to one another as masturbation and sexual intercourse."

"When we conceive things thus, as they really are and happened, every profound philosophical problem is resolved . . . quite simply into an empirical fact."

Engels echos that the Marxian method is based on scientific empirical observation rather than on philosophical or intellectual speculation:

"If we reduce the world schematism not from our minds, but only through our minds from the real world, deducing the basic principles of being from what is, what we need for this purpose is not philosophy but positive knowledgle of the world and what goes on in it, and the result of this deduction is not philosophy either, but positive science."

"The materialistic outlook on nature," Engels concluded, "means nothing more than the simple conception of nature just as it is, without alien addition."

Marx thus asserted that theory and reality are in fact interconnected, and that, while theory was a part of reality, it was itself derived from the study of reality. This naturalistic attitude conflicted with the Cartesian scientific attitude of objectivity, but

Marx was not the only prominent scientist to realize that all intellectual hypotheses are mere abstractions from existing reality. Decades after Marx's death, Einstein echoed: "In practice the world of phenomena uniquely determines the theoretical system, in spite of the fact that there is no theoretical bridge between phenomena and their theoretical principles."

Marx also concluded that metaphysical prattle and pointless talk about impractical or unknowable things were mere wastes of time. He scoffed at those philosophers who seriously argued over whether the world was real, as well as religious scholars who carried on long discussions about the number of angels who could sit on the head of a pin or whether angels had navels. Such nonsense, Marx wrote, was pointless; "The dispute over the reality or nonreality of thinking that is isolated from practice is purely a scholastic question." As author David Caute points out, Marxism is above all practical and to the point: "Asked whether he can be sure the food on his plate is real, and not simply a figment of his imagination, the Marxist materialist answers; eat it and see."

Marx's contemporaries, the Young Hegelians, viewed history as a process that unfolded with definite pre-determined aims, towards the final goal of the actualization of the Absolute Spirit. Under this point of view, for instance, the "purpose" of the American Revolution in 1776 was to spark the French Revolution of 1789. Marx scoffed at this idea, saying that the Hegelian personification of "History" was an absurd abstraction:

"History does nothing; it 'possesses no wealth', it 'wages no battles'. It is man, real man, that does all that, that possesses and fights; 'history' is not a person apart, using man as a means for its own particular aims; history is nothing other than the activity of man pursuing his aims."

Engels, in his work *The Dialectics of Nature*, points out that all idealist abstractions are necessarily based on the interaction of material entities. "Time and space," he wrote, were "forms of the existence of matter". They were "nothing without matter, empty concepts, abstractions which exist only in our minds".

The interdependence of all things is seen clearly in Marx's naturalist philosophy. Marx rejected the Idealist notion that spirit or idea is the basis for reality, and also rejected the Materialist postulate that reality is based upon matter. Matter and Idea, Marx argued, were merely different sides of the same coin. Both were intimately and unalterably interconnected. Marx held that the body and the mind were not separate entities, with one "controlling" the other. Rather, he said, both constituted different facets of natural existence.

Marx further asserted that everything in the natural process is interconnected, and that what appears to be the object of a certain subject is at the same tame the subject of that object. "The sun," Marx writes, "is the object of the plant—an indispensable object to it confirming its life—just as the plant is the object of the sun, being an expression of the life-awakening power of the sun, of the sun's objective essential power."

Human social processes are also interconnected in the Marxian view. In his analysis and writings, Marx viewed capitalist society as a "mutual interaction" which "takes place between the various elements", and declared that these elements were themselves simply "different sides of one unit". On another occasion, he describes capitalist society as resulting from the "reciprocal actions of these various sides on one another."

Marx also noted that, not only are human economic and social actions a product of the interlocking relationships of capitalism, but the nature of physical and material objects is likewise a function of the social relationships within which they are found. A hammer as a physical object may always be a hammer, but its nature and role changes drastically according to the social situation within which it is examined. A hammer used by a tribal craftsman, for instance, is merely a tool to enable the craftsman to perform his work. The same hammer in the hands of a wage worker in a capitalist economy, however, is a means of enabling the capitalist to extract surplus value from the worker. A hammer used by a tribalist craftsman is not capital, for it produces no surplus value; a hammer used by a wage worker, however, *is* capital, and performs a definite social role within the capitalist system.

Marx thus saw reality as a vast intermingling web of relations, each influencing the others and each in turn being influenced by others. To study this web of interconnections in any scientific or empirical way demands that its component parts be "separated" and examined in isolation. This, however, poses an awkward problem; it is impossible to tell just where one element begins and another element ends, since each is an interpenetrating part of the other. As Marxist scholar Bertell Ollman points out, "What emerges from this interpretation is that the problem Marx faces in his exposition is not how to link separate parts, but how to individuate instrumental units in a social whole which finds expression everywhere."

If Marx is to attempt to communicate his insights about these interpenetrating units, he must use words and language which are understandable to everyone else, but which are at the same time unsuited to expressing these concepts. For this reason, Marx's writings are often imprecise and ambiguous, not because he was unsure about what he wished to communicate, but because there is no verbal manner in which he could communicate it precisely. As a result, one writer has noted, Marx's words are somewhat like bats; one can see in them something of a mouse and something of a bird.

Engels, in an introduction to one of Marx's major works, acknowledges the problems associated with attempting to isolate and define the elements of an interpenetrating system, saying that it is "self-evident that a theory which views modern capitalist production as a mere passing stage in the economic history of mankind must make use of terms different from those habitual to writers who look upon that form of production as imperishable and final." Engels also noted that, as these dialectical relationships were altered and changed, the concepts and definitions which were used to describe them must change as well, and thus a definition which was valid there and then may not be so here and now: "Where things and their interrelationship are conceived, not as fixed, but as changing, their mental images, the ideas, are likewise subject to change and transformation, and they are not encapsulated in rigid definitions, but are developed in their historical or logical process of formulation."

Marxian definitions and concepts thus mean different things when they are used to examine different aspects of any given social relationship. The word "ideology", for example, is used by Marx at various times to mean nonscientific or nonempirical abstractions such as religion and philosophy, at other times to mean the non-material spiritual side of reality, and at still other times simply the ideological justification which is used by the ruling class to maintain its domination of social relationships. The Marxian concept of "mode of production" is at various times and places defined as "the economic structure of society", "the economic foundation", and "social existence". Similar variations can be found in the Marxian concepts of "class" and "alienation". Since the meaning of these words varied according to the specific relationship under study, Engels points out, there are no "fixed, cut-to-measure, once and for all applicable definitions in Marx's works." Marx himself adds, "It is not a question here of a definition which things must be made to fit. We are dealing here with definite functions which must be expressed in definite categories."

Marxian definitions are also interpenetrating and relative, reflecting the dialectical relationships which they are meant to define. In the Marxian scheme, "Labor" can only be defined in terms of its relationship to "Capital", and vice versa. Neither has an independent existence or definition, for both can exist only by virtue of their relationship with each other; there can be no Wage Worker without a Capitalist. The same is true of all the other elements of capitalist society. As Bertell Ollman writes, "Capital, labor, value, commodity, etc., are all grasped as relations, containing in themselves, as integral elements of what they are, those parts with which we tend to see them externally tied."

Marx's problems of description are further complicated by the fact that he is attempting to present a system of thinking which is opposed to the accepted paradigm of capitalist society, yet he is forced to use capitalist conceptions and outlooks in order to describe it. As Marx points out, human knowledge of reality is mediated and filtered by the categories and concepts which our minds have been conditioned to accept as a part of our social reality: "In the study of economic categories, as in the case of every historical and social science, it must be borne in mind that as in reality so in our mind the subject, in this case modern bourgeois society, is given and that the categories are therefore but forms of expression, manifestations of existence, and frequently but one-sided aspects of this subject, this definite society." These categories, Marx says, "serve as the expression of its conditions and the comprehension of its own organization."

In order to rationally examine this interpenetrating whole, it is necessary to intellectually divide that reality into sub-elements which may fall outside of the traditional paradigm, in ways which fall under different categorical assumptions. Capitalist society, for instance, is conditioned by its social relationships to view the economy as a separate and independent part of reality which operates according to its own independent "economic laws". Marx, however, declared this conception to be artificial and false, and asserted that the economy was interdependent with the political, social, legal, ethical and other spheres of society. This new categorization allowed Marx to see and understand new relationships which were invisible to those who refused to give up the accepted "common sense" paradigm.

And, since all of these intellectual divisions and categories were artificial, Marx was free to "carve up" capitalist society in any way he wished, in order to emphasize or understand any particular aspect of this interpenetrating whole. He was also free to redefine his categories and sub-units as he changed the problems and relationships which he sought to explain with them. Since social reality was a seamless interpenetrating whole, it made no difference how one divided it up in order to understand it, so long as one recognized that one's point of view was completely arbitrary and could be changed and varied at will to emphasize different aspects of the relational totality.

Marx also pointed out that humanity itself, like any other part of the natural process, is not a separate entity, but is linked to everything else by the unifying process of Nature:

"Physically, man lives only on those products of nature, whether they appear in the form of food, heating, clothing, a dwelling, etc. The universality of man appears in practice precisely in the universality which makes all nature his inorganic body — both inasmuch as nature is (1) his direct means of life, and (2) the material, the object, and the instrument of his life activity. Nature is man's inorganic body — nature, that is, insofar as it is not itself human body. Man lives in nature — this means that nature is his body, within which he must remain in continuous intercourse if he is not to die. That man's physical and spiritual life is linked to nature means simply that nature is linked to itself, for man is a part of nature."

To Marx, the intercourse between nature and humanity takes the practical form of industry and economic activity, and the intellectual form of the sciences and their application to industry:

"The celebrated 'unity of man with nature' has always existed in industry and has existed in various forms in every epoch, according to the greater or lesser development of industry, just like the 'struggle' of man with nature, right up to the development of productive powers, on a corresponding basis."

Thus, Marx concluded, the natural sciences as well as the so-called "social sciences" were intrinsically related to each other, with each scientific discipline concerning itself with one aspect of the total process of nature. In the end, concluded Marx, all of these facets will unite into the simple study of nature and of humanity's role in it — "there will be one Science".

This basic interdependence of the sciences was later confirmed by social scientists. When the psychologist Maslov determined that the primary motivation for human behavior was to obtain the "necessities of life", i.e., food, clothing and shelter, and that no other psychological needs could be met until these basic needs had been fulfilled, he confirmed Marx's conclusion that economic needs were primary and that no other social needs could be met unless the economic requirements of society were fulfilled. Similarly, social scientists now concede that the spheres of political science, economics, psychology and sociology are largely interconnected, and can best be understood in terms of the others. The sciences, therefore, are like the blind men examining the elephant; each is able to describe a part, but none is able to obtain an overview of the whole.

Marx also declared that the arbitrary division of humans into national groups was pointless, and consistently argued in favor of internationalism, in which human interests rather than national interests were dominant. And Marx condemned the arbitrary position of domination by men over women, and was among the first to call for full equality between the sexes, including the right of women to vote and hold property. Marx further asserted that communism would make possible a human society without class or social distinctions, in which human society developed as an organic whole.

Marx never explicitly states that his theories of class structure and class struggle are also intellectual concepts with no validity in and of themselves. But it is apparent that, though Marx's description of the class struggle may help us to understand social reality, it itself is not reality.

The realisation that all things are a part of one interrelating whole destroys the Cartesian idea of "objective observation". Since the observer and the thing being observed are in fact parts of the same process, there can be no such thing as the separation of the observer from the observed, no view of the universe "from the outside", and thus no "objective" view of reality. Einstein showed that even the fundamental idea of time has no objective existence; it is completely dependent upon the circumstances of the observer. In addition, as Fritjof Capra points out, all scientists are a part of the natural system which they are observing, whether they realize it or not:

"The patterns scientists observe in nature are intimately connected with the patterns of their minds — with their concepts, thoughts and values. Hence, the scientific results they obtain and the technological applications they investigate will be conditioned by their frame of mind. Although much of their detailed research will not depend explicitly on their value system, the larger framework within which this research is pursued will never be value-free."

The impossibility of objectivity is seen most clearly in the social sciences, where human beings are studying human processes of which they themselves are a part. Social scientists show at least a measure of subjectivity in their choice of subjects for study and, in many cases, in the framework within which their data is interpreted. Even Marx, who is repeatedly claimed to be an impartial scientific observer of capitalist development, was nevertheless unable to prevent a subjective involvement with his subject. Marx openly declared that his sentiments lay strongly with the oppressed proletariat, and that it was not his purpose to interpret or to explain the social system, but to change it.

Marx's sentiments, therefore, were not based on "scientific objectivity" or "value-free study". Marx recognized that there are no "objective" observers, since every observer was a part of an existing social network, one which has, through its social relationships, conditioned, predisposed and limited the things that any observer can think and feel. Ethics and value judgments, Marx held, are a part of the social and economic framework within which they operate, and thus are not eternal or unchanging. Modern observers hold slavery to be morally objectionable, for instance, but in the time of slave-holding economies, slavery was accepted as a normal "natural" part of the social order. Similarly, people in capitalist society view wage labor as a natural accepted part of life, but an observer looking back from some future society will not view it in this way.

Any attempt to apply universal moral or value judgments would simply be an attempt to extend the outlooks of the prevailing social order, to universalize them and project them onto other societies. To declare that slavery is wrong while wage labor is right, for instance, is merely to project bourgeois values onto other times and places, where these outlooks have no validity.

There can therefore be no "objectively verifiable" criteria for determining "right" and "wrong", since these definitions are dependent upon the social circumstances in which they are considered. Marx, for instance, condemns capitalism as an inhuman and repressive social system, but he does not hold this to be true throughout its history. Rather, in the beginning of the bourgeois social order, when it overthrew feudalism and expanded economic productive capacity, Marx praised capitalism as a revolutionary progressive epoch. It was only when capitalism began to outlive the circumstances which had produced it that Marx deemed it "un-progressive".

Marx therefore avoided producing moral judgments based upon some non-existent "objective standard". For Marx, the social and economic position of the working class produced in it values and ethics suited to these conditions, and, in a dialectical interrelationship, these values and ethics in turn spur the proletariat to change those conditions. What we think about the world is a part of that world, but what we think comes from the circumstances we see around us. In this way, Marx writes, values and theories can themselves become a "material force" which changes reality.

Marx, in his writings, also attacked the concept of "causality". Marx criticized the materialists for asserting that matter was the "cause" of all actions, and likewise attacked the idealists for claiming that ideas produced all human actions. To the Hegelians, who asserted that History and the Absolute Ideals were the causes of human actions, Marx replied that "History" was an abstraction that was incapable of "doing" or "causing" anything. While social reality was influenced by the ideas of humanity, Marx pointed out, those ideas were themselves the products of existing social reality. Thus, he countered, humans produced their social reality to as great an extent as the existing social reality produced humans. Neither was the "cause" of the other; rather, they were both parts of the same dialectical process.

The descriptions and definitions which Marx gives for this interpenetrating process are difficult to understand in a social framework which views things linearly in a one-to-one causal relationship. Therefore, after Marx's death, those socialists who were unable to grasp the Marxian concept of dialectical totality took it upon themselves to modify, simplify and re-define Marxism. This new conception has been called "dialectical materialism", "historical materialism" or "economic determinism"; all terms which Marx himself never used.

These socialists, first of the Second International and later the Marxist-Leninist Third International, reduced all of Marx's profound insights into the simple formula, "Material economic conditions determine consciousness." In other words, these theorists concluded,

Marxism was a positive science which described and analyzed the objective laws of human development just as Newton had studied physics and Darwin had studied biology. According to these positivists, Marxism asserted that prevailing economic conditions directly determined all of the rest of societal organization, including the religious, political, legal and ethical spheres, and these spheres could not be changed to any significant degree by human actions unless the underlying economic conditions were first altered.

Thus, according to the economic determinist view, human development is determined by the action of economics, and this motion is determined by regular and predictable natural laws which humans are powerless to avoid or escape. The economic base directly determines and controls the social superstructure which is built upon it.

It can be seen that this "scientific Marxism" is nothing more than a return to the Feuerbachian materialism which Marx himself had studied and rejected. Marx never asserted that material conditions are the sole determinant of human thoughts and actions; rather, he asserted that human thoughts and existing material conditions were united in a dialectical interplay, with each influencing the development of the other. The materialist economic determinist conception of the "base/superstructure" is based on the notion of linear causality, which Marxism rejects in favor of relational dialectical totality.

The economic sphere cannot "cause" the structures of the non-economic superstructure, since the relationships of the superstructure are themselves large factors in constructing economic relationships. The economic determinist, for example, asserts that legal property regulations are a "reflection" which is determined by existing capitalist economic relationships, but ignores the fact that these economic relationships are themselves conditioned in large part by legal property laws; these non-economic structures are in fact an integral part of the economic structures they supposedly "reflect". Marx concluded that the relationship between the economic and the non-economic is co-determining and dialectical, and does not form a one-to-one cause and effect relationship.

A large part of the blame for the later distortion of their thought must be borne by Marx and Engels themselves. Engels had at one time, it is true, explicitly stated that "economics", narrowly understood according to its definition in bourgeois society, did not determine social structures, and that he and Marx had never said that they did:

"According to the materialist conception of history, the determining moment of history is ultimately the production and reproduction of real life. More than this neither Marx nor I have ever asserted. If therefore somebody twists this into the statement that the economic moment is the only determining one, he transforms it into a meaningless, abstract and absurd phrase."

Engels pointed out that he and Marx were forced to overjustify the role of economic structures in society because so many others, including philosophers and theorists, tended to underestimate it or give it no role at all. Marx also, unfortunately, continued to use the word "materialism" to describe his outlook, in order to distinguish it clearly from Hegel's idealist viewpoint—even though Marx's outlook was a rejection of Feuerbachian mechanistic materialism and asserted a dialectical and naturalist view of reality.

Marx recognized that capitalist society was not simply a political and legal superstructure erected upon an economic base, but was a complex interpenetrating totality in which all of the various parts influenced and determined each other. "I shall therefore publish," he declared, "the critique of law, ethics, politics, etc., in a series of distinct, independent pamphlets, and afterwards try in a special work to present them again as a connected whole showing the interrelationship of the separate parts."

Unfortunately, Marx did not live long enough to finish his projected series. Similarly, Marx was unable to begin any works on the various non-economic relationships of oppression in capitalist society---sexism, racism, nationalism, heterosexism, authoritarianism—and how these relationships influenced and were influenced by the economic and social structures of capitalism. Because of this, Marxism has come under justified criticism from partisans of these struggles for ignoring the roles of these relationships in economic class struggles. Fortunately, a new generation of Marxists is making headway in integrating these struggles into a theory of unified opposition to bourgeois social constructions.

Thus, it is completely alien to Marx's viewpoint to assert that the economic struggle is the "cause" of social development, or that the struggle between economic classes is the sole determinant of the other social struggles. Rather, Marx asserted, all of these relationships are dialectical, interpenetrating and co-determining, and must be understood as parts of a totality if they are to be understood at all.

Marx saw reality as being in a state of constant change, with everything in a constant process of becoming something else. Engels points out, "Motion is the mode of existence of matter. Never anywhere has there been matter without motion, nor can there be."

Adopting the Hegelian dialectic, Marx held that the driving force behind this motion was the cyclical interplay of opposites, which together produced a synthesis. As Engels notes. "The two poles of an antithesis, like positive and negative, are just as inseparable from each other as they are opposed, and despite all their opposition they mutually penetrate each other."

By recognizing this "unity of opposites", Marx was able to conclude that all pairs of opposites are unified within the framework of totality: "We see how subjectivism and objectivism, spiritualism and materialism, activity and suffering, only lose their antithetical character, and thus their existence as such antitheses, within the framework of society." Both of the parties in the class struggle, he points out, are parts of the same social process, and are thus inseparable:

"As such they form a whole. They are both formations of the world of private property. What concerns us here is to define the particular position they take within the opposition. It is not enough to say that they are two sides of a whole. Private property, as private property, as wealth, is forced to maintain its own existence and thereby the existence of its opposite, the proletariat. It is the positive side of the opposition, private property satisfied in itself. The proletariat, on the other hand, is forced, as proletariat, to abolish itself, and with this, its antithesis, the condition which makes it a proletariat-private property. It is the negative side of the contradiction, its principle of unrest, private property dissolved and in the process of its dissolution."

Engels points out that the contradiction between these two poles is the result of the dialectical relationship between them;

"So long as we consider things as static and lifeless, each one by itself, alongside of and after each other, it is true that we do not run up against any contradictions in them. . . . But the position is quite different as soon as we consider things in their motion, their change, their life, their reciprocal influences on one another. Then we immediately become involved in contradictions."

In his writings, Marx also referred to the "alienation" of humans from their natural essence. Humans, wrote Marx, are by their very circumstances of existence social creatures, or, as he puts it, a "species-being". The innate nature of Homo sapiens is to form gregarious social groups which work together for the survival of the colony. Social conventions in the economic and social spheres, however, brought about by antagonistic class interests, have largely separated humans from this natural essence, dividing human society into groups and classes. In capitalist society, this trend has reached an extreme, so that a large portion of the population is forced to labor for the benefit of a small clique of property owners, who do not labor at all.

Human labor, instead of performing its natural role of producing the means for the group to live, now serves only to enrich the capitalist class, while the laborers themselves live in misery and depravation. The labor of the workers, instead of producing things which will benefit their lives, instead produces things which are then turned over to the capitalists for sale; meanwhile, the workers who have produced these things cannot afford to buy them and will never use them. Thus, writes Marx, "Labor is external to the worker, i.e., it does not belong to his essential being":

"In his work, therefore, he does not affirm himself, but denies himself, does not feel content but unhappy, does not develop freely his mental and physical energy but mortifies his body and ruins his mind."

Marx concluded that private property and capitalism are simply the latest developments of the artificial contrivances which alienate humans from their natural beings: "Private property is thus the product, the result, the necessary consequence of alienated labor, or of the external relation of the worker to nature and to himself."

This alienation of humans from their labor is now so great that it is not at all uncommon for workers to deny that their jobs are actually part of their lives. Labor is not a natural part of living; it is rather something that we put up with in order to "make a living". It has become a source of tensions and anxieties—a producer, not of things which will give the worker a better life, but of ulcers, headaches and nervous breakdowns.

The conflict between social production and private distribution can be solved only by removing the artificial constructions which have brought it about. Thus, the power of human labor must be returned to its natural role, in which human labor is of benefit to the whole social group rather than solely to private property owners. This, of course, means a system of social production and social distribution, which in turn means the abolition of private property.

This abolition could not take place until human society possessed the means of producing economic abundance for all, and this possibility did not exist until the development of mechanization and productivity under capitalism. The proletarian revolution, Marx concludes, is thus dependent upon several historical and economic trends, but its driving force is much more basic. The working class, says Marx, is, in the final analysis, driven to revolt because of the "contradiction between its humanity and its situation, which is an open, clear, and absolute negation of its humanity."

One of the strongest artificial creations which contributes to human alienation, Marx notes, is that of organized religion. Marx had a humanist and naturalist point of view, in which human spiritual life, as well as physical life, is tied to the natural process. He bitterly attacked the organized church, charging it with being a manipulative tool of the ruling class. He likewise criticized the worship of a so-called "supernatural being", saying that nothing existed that was outside of nature or the natural process. Marx compared the tales of God, Satan and Hell to the beliefs of a person who carves an idol out of wood and then bows to it, worshipping his own creation. Humans were not created by God, Marx said; rather, God was created from the imaginations of humans and in the image of humans.

Under an alienated society, the natural role of man's spiritual life has been twisted and perverted. Religion, instead of serving as a means to recognize and fulfill one's role in the natural process, has become distorted into a simple escape from a dreadful and unbearable social reality:

"Religious misery is in one way the expression of real misery, and in another a protest against real misery. Religion is the sigh of the afflicted creature, the soul of a heartless world, as it is also the spirit of spiritless conditions. It is the opium of the people."

Religion, Marx concluded, was a feeble, half-hearted attempt by humans to recognize and embrace once again their natural essence by giving this essence an external existence. So long as humans refused to recognize their humanistic essence, the artificial substitutes created by the church would remain: "Religion is only the illusory sun that revolves around man so long as he does not revolve around himself."

To rectify the situation and remove the artificial restraints imposed by religion, radical changes must be made. However, Marx notes, "To be radical is to grasp things by the root. But for man, the root is Man himself." Therefore, he concluded, the only true "religion" for humans is that of humanism or naturalism, which simply involves renouncing all of the artificial constructions of an alienated religion and realizing the place of humans in the scheme of nature.

Human energies, Marx wrote, should be spent on improving life here and now, and not wasted by worrying about some imaginary "life after death". Thus, Marx declares, "The criticism of religion ends with the doctrine that Man is the highest being for man. "

Sadly, however, Marxism has fallen victim to the very idealization and rigid structuring that it has tried to dispel. "Communists" in the USSR and elsewhere reduced Marx's profound historical world view to a mere cry for "worldwide revolution", and turned it into a tool of their own nationalist desires. Others have chosen to see Marxism simply as an ideological system of social reform, and reduce Marx's profound insights to a mere program of nationalized industries and collective farms.

Marx asserts that reality is not something which is brought into existence by some "Divine Being". The source of reality, both conclude, is intrinsic to reality itself.

To the natural or social scientists, the source of reality manifests itself in the form of "natural laws" which direct the motion of things. Discovering and interpreting these laws is the primary aim of science. However, as physicist Fritjof Capra notes, there are problems with this "intellectual" approach to reality:

"Abstraction is a crucial feature of this knowledge, because in order to compare and to classify the immense variety of shapes, structures and phenomena around us we cannot take all of their features into account, but have to select a few significant ones. Thus we construct an intellectual map of reality in which things are reduced to their general outlines."

But, Capra notes:

"The natural world, on the other hand, is one of infinite varieties and complexities, a multi-dimensional world which contains no straight lines or completely regular shapes, where things do not happen in sequences, but all together; a world where—as modern physics tells us—even empty space is curved."

Thus, writes Capra;

"In thinking about the world we are faced with the same kind of problem as the cartographer who tries to cover the curved face of the earth with a sequence of plane maps. We can only expect an approximate representation of reality from such a procedure, and all rational knowledge is therefore necessarily limited."

Einstein had precisely these limits in mind when he said: "As far as the laws of mathematics refer to reality, they are not certain; and as far as they are certain, they do not refer to reality."

The task of scientific thought is, therefore, to produce generalizations and simplifications which loosely describe reality so that we can grasp it more easily. These generalizations, however, can never be more than approximations of reality, not reality itself. No description of reality can be substituted for the direct experience of reality.

This criticism is particularly applicable to those "economic determinists" who assert that Marx has discovered the "natural laws" which govern the development of human society. According to this viewpoint, the development and actions of human society are directly determined by the development of their economic structures, which produce inescapable reactions in the political, ethical and social spheres. In this manner, human societies change in regular and predictable ways, as these "natural laws" alter the fundamental economic structures. Although Marx often referred to the "laws of the dialectic" and the "laws of capitalist motion", it is apparent that these took on, in the Marxian conception, a definition which is very different from those given them by the Leninists and other "scientific Marxists". Marx, as we have seen, viewed the development of the capitalist social system as being the result of the mutual interactions of many various elements, and found it impossible to explain how capitalism (or any other human society) works unless each of these elements are described and understood.

But, Marx realized, what these elements *are* is at the same time dependent upon what they *were*. Therefore, it is also necessary to understand how these various elements developed as they did through their mutual interactions, and how this process of development affects the possible directions they can take in the future. The chances of future development in any particular direction, therefore, are limited by the developmental process these elements have already undergone.

Marx referred to this process of dialectical limits as a "law of motion". This "law", he pointed out, is not an iron necessity, but rather a tendency — "Law is chance". Engels writes that it was not Marx's intention to say that the human social development he describes was "inevitable" or "necessary":

"Marx does not dream of attempting to prove by this that the process was historically necessary. On the contrary, after he has proven from history that in fact the process has already partially occurred, and partially must occur in the future, he then also characterizes it as a process which develops in accordance with a definite dialectical law. That is all."

Thus, Marxian "laws" were not intended to be deterministic inevitabilities; they are merely tendencies which result from the prior development of human society through co-determining entities. The dialectic is a way of looking at and examining the process of social change after it has already occurred, not a predictive method of determining the future direction of social change. As Marx points out, the process of social change is undertaken by the actions of free living humans, who can alter dramatically the direction of these tendencies:

"Reality is only a product of the preceding intercourse of individuals themselves. Thus the Communists in practice treat the conditions created up to now by production and intercourse as inorganic conditions, without, however, imagining that it was the plan or the destiny of previous individuals to give them that material, and without believing that these conditions were inorganic for the individuals creating them."

Marx pointed out that "history" and "natural laws" are simply abstractions from actual human practice, and that history is produced by the free actions of humans, not the other way around. "Men make their own history," Marx wrote. "History is nothing other than man engaged in social practice."

Those who assert that human actions are "determined" by "natural laws" have merely substituted one alienating illusion for another. The dialectical materialists, having rejected the notion that God or Absolute Ideas are the moving forces of reality, instead assert that "Natural Law" and the "Dialectic" are, and have simply substituted the abstraction of "Natural Law" for that of "Divine Law".

Marx rejected this notion, and asserted that humans, acting within the limits imposed upon them by their circumstances, produced their own history. None of it was "predetermined" or "inevitable", and none of it was produced by any "laws". To scientifically know something, Engels wrote, was not to attempt to formulate a deterministic set of laws about it, but rather to "allocate to each its place in the interconnections of nature", where there are no laws and no process of cause and effect.

As Marxist scholar Bertell Ollman points out, "Those who cannot view reality dialectically require hooks on which to hang the dialectic. Unfortunately, once installed, these hooks, which may render some initial service, are almost impossible to remove."

Since Marx's death in 1883, his thought has undergone a continuous process of modification and re-definition. Marxism began its life as a method of examining the continuous development of human society. In this process of development, Marx realized, humans play an active role, and revolutionize their surroundings in the process of extracting their means of life from them. Thus, Marx declared, the essence of human activity is to change their surroundings through social praxis, and all intellectual thought that was separated from this process of praxis was scholastic and irrelevant. "The philosophers have only interpreted the world in various ways," Marx wrote. "The point is to change it."

This emphasis on human praxis led to Marx's consideration of the role of the working class, which, he saw, was driven by the circumstances of its existence to revolutionize its surroundings and produce a new social order, that of communism. Thus, not only was the Marxian outlook a method for the working class to view its surroundings and understand them, it was also a method whereby the working class could change those surroundings through revolutionary action.

Marx realized that revolutionary change was not automatic or self-fulfilling. If any social revolution was to take place, the working class had to take practical action to bring it about. During the time of the 1848 revolutions, practical revolutionary movements developed hand in hand with revolutionary outlooks and theories, and each was reinforced and developed by the other.

In the period preceding the First World War, however, revolutionary action died out, the working class movement became weak and scattered, and no practical actions were taken towards revolutionizing social surroundings. As a result, revolutionary theory was cut off from its practical base, and those who continued to hope for a revolutionary change were forced to modify the basic Marxian outlook. Instead of stressing the need for revolutionary ideology to develop in accordance with a practical revolutionary movement, the socialists of the Second International opined that the impersonal "scientific laws" of dialectical materialism would bring about socialism regardless of human desires or actions. It was, they comforted themselves by saying, a "historical inevitability".

In 1917, the Bolsheviks resurrected the Marxian emphasis on direct revolutionary action and seized power. But the Leninists, too, found their material circumstances unsuited for their ideological goals, and fell upon a new interpretation of Marxism in order to justify their own dictatorial government. Now, the Leninists asserted, human revolutionary action must take place within the "impersonal laws" of dialectical materialism, and, since the Leninist party is the only force capable of understanding and interpreting these laws, it alone should have the power to lead society down the inevitable path to socialism. All of the Marxist-Leninist's actions are justified by pointing to the needs of the "historical process".

As we have seen, the Marxian outlook is not "scientific" in the sense usually accepted for that term—that is, it is not a formulation of objective natural laws which are valid in all times and places and which operate independently of human will or agency. Instead, Marx recognized, social reality is determined by the conscious actions of humans, who act according to the needs brought on by their surroundings. Thus, the development of human society is not a linear process of cause and effect, but a constant process of mutual interpenetration which, in large part, determines itself through mutual interaction.

Marxism is "scientific" only in the sense that its methods and concepts are based on the empirical observation of reality, rather than on some utopian or idealist yearning. In this sense, Marx differed sharply from the "Utopian socialism" of Owen or St Simon. For Marx, "science" was simply the process of examining the empirical world and determining the interactions and unity which defines and forms them. Sensory perception reveals the external appearances of things, he said, but it takes a closer look to see the underlying connections and unity. As Ollman writes:

"For Marx, man's senses only bring him into contact with appearances; the essence of the thing, the major relations out of which it is composed, can only be learned through lengthy investigation and study. Here, controlled experiments (where possible), reductionism, imaginative reconstruction of broken links and the like make use of the results of immediate perception to uncover the "hidden substratum"."

In his work *Socialism; Utopian and Scientific*, Engels describes this process of examination:

"When we consider and reflect upon Nature at large or the history of mankind or our own intellectual activity, at first we see the picture of an endless entanglement of relations and reactions, permutations and combinations, in which nothing remains what, where and as it is, but everything moves, changes, comes into being and passes away. We see, therefore, at first the picture as a whole, with its individual parts still more or less kept into the background; we observe the movements, transitions, connections, rather than the things which move, combine and connect. This primitive, naive but intrinsically correct conception of the world is that of ancient Greek philosophy, and was first clearly formulated by Heraclitus; everything is and is not, for everything is fluid, constantly changing, constantly coming into being and passing away."

"This conception, correctly as it expresses the general character of the picture of appearances as a whole, does not suffice to explain the details that make up this picture, and so long as we do not understand these, we do not have a clear idea of the whole picture."

Engels continues:

"In order to understand these details we must detach them from their natural and historical connection and examine each one separately, its nature, special causes, effects, etc. This is, primarily, the task of natural science and historical research."

"But this method of work has left us as a legacy the habit of observing natural objects and processes in isolation, apart from their connection with the vast whole; of observing them in repose, not as variables; in their death, not in their life."

Furthermore, Engels adds:

"We find upon closer examination that the two poles of thesis and anti-thesis, positive and negative, e.g., are as inseparable as they are opposed, and that despite all their opposition, they mutually interpenetrate. And we find, in like manner, that cause and effect are only conceptions which hold good in their application to individual cases; but as soon as we consider the individual, cases in their general connection to the universe as a whole, they run into each other, and they become confounded when we contemplate that universal action and reaction in which cause and effect are eternally changing places, so that what is effect here and now will be cause there and then, and vice versa."

Engels concludes:

"An exact representation of the universe, its evolution, the development of mankind, and the reflection of this evolution in the minds of men, can therefore only be obtained by the methods of dialectics with its constant regard to the innumerable actions and reactions of life and death, or progressive and retrogressive changes."

Like the ancient sages, Marx was able to describe the innate unity and interdependence of all things, the unified interplay of cyclical opposites, the flowing circular nature of reality, the unsuitability of words and definitions to convey these concepts, and the artificial alienations which separate humans from the understanding of this unity.

Those who see Marxism as simply an ideology or a socio-economic system are missing the point. As Marx himself writes:

"Communism is not for us a state of affairs which is to be established, an ideal to which reality will have to adjust itself. We call Communism the real movement which abolishes the present state of things. The conditions of this movement result from the premises now in existence."

Thus, the Marxist is not interested in changing reality to suit a particular ideology or conception of how the world "ought to be". Rather, Marxism is concerned with the limits on human actions, which are placed upon them by their surroundings, and how these surroundings themselves result from prior human actions. Humans are free to act as they will, but only within the limits placed upon them by their circumstances. "Freedom does not consist in the dream of independence of natural laws," says Engels, "but in the knowledge of these laws and in the possibility thus afforded of making them work systematically towards definite ends. . . . Freedom of the will means nothing but the capacity to make decisions with real knowledge."

GLOSSARY

ALIENATION; In Marxism, a term that means the artificial separation of two entities that are in fact inalterably united and interpenetrating. Marx concluded that the social structures and relationships imposed upon human society by its class structures come to be viewed as "real", and thus replace the dialectical interpenetration of humans with each other, of humans with their labor, and of humans with their natural surroundings. Communism, in the Marxian view, is a means of eliminating these artificial alienations, and thus to return human society to its natural role.

CLASS: In Marxism, a socio-politico-economic unit that makes up the basic structure of any human society, made up of groups of people who perform similar social roles. In capitalist society, for instance, some people are wage workers while others are business owners, and this social stratification is the basis for the proletarian class and the bourgeoisie. Marx viewed human society as being made up of classes, and changes in this society were brought about by and through the hostile interactions of these classes.

DIALECTICS : In Marxism, the viewpoint that holds all reality to be fluid and ever-changing, in a constant process of creation and destruction. In the Marxian view, everything that exists is in a state of both being what it is and of becoming something else, and this process is the dialectic. Dialectical change is brought about by the diverse elements of a system, which mutually interpenetrate and co-determine each other. This constant interaction produces the dialectical process of change.

IDEALISM: In Marxism, the philosophical tradition that holds mind or spirit to be the ultimate reality and the source of all human or social actions. Religion is an idealist philosophy, since it holds that reality is determined by a non-material god, and that human actions are the result of insights gained into the will of this god. In philosophy, idealism holds that thought and idea are an independent realm of reality, which influence the development of material reality through their interpretation by humans. From this viewpoint, Justice and Truth are seen as independently existing realities, which become progressively more perfectly manifested on earth as human insights expand. Human consciousness therefore determines social and material reality.

MATERIALISM; In Marxism, the philosophical tradition that holds matter or objective reality to be the ultimate source of all human and social actions. Science is a materialist outlook, since it postulates that the motion of the universe is caused by the operation of independent and eternal "natural laws", which operate independently of human ideas or outlooks. Materialism holds that there is no independent realm of thought or spirit, and that all human thoughts are simply reflections of their material surroundings. Truth and Justice, for instance, are merely practical outlooks which develop from the surroundings of humans. In this view, social and material reality determine human consciousness.

NATURALISM; In Marxism, the philosophical tradition that holds that neither idea nor matter are the determinants of reality, but that both are different ways of looking at the same thing. Marxism is a naturalist outlook, since it holds that matter and idea interpenetrate dialectically to form the existing universe. Naturalism holds that there are no independent realms of thought or matter, and that one cannot exist without the other. Justice and Truth are ideological necessities brought about by existing material conditions, but at the same time they are themselves a part of material conditions, and act to change these surroundings. In this view, human social and material surroundings determine consciousness, but at the same time, consciousness determines those social and material surroundings.

Economic and Philosophic Manuscripts of 1844

Preface

I have already given notice in the *Deutsch-Franzsische Jahrbücher*, the critique of jurisprudence and political science in the form of a critique of the Hegelian Philosophy of Right. In the course of elaboration for publication, the intermingling of criticism directed only against speculation with criticism of the various subjects themselves proved utterly unsuitable, hampering the development of the argument and rendering comprehension difficult. Moreover the wealth and diversity of the subjects to be treated, could have been compressed into one work only in a purely aphoristic style; while an aphoristic presentation of this kind, for its part, would have given the impression of arbitrary systemizing. I shall therefore issue the critique of law, ethics, politics, etc., in a series of distinct, independent pamphlets, and at the end try in a special work to present them again as a connected whole showing the interrelationship of the separate parts, and finally, shall make a critique of the speculative elaboration of that material. For this reason it will be found that the interconnection between political economy and the state, law, ethics, civil life, etc., is touched on in the present work only to the extent to which political economy itself *ex professo* touches on these subjects.

It is hardly necessary to assure the reader conversant with political economy that my results have been won by means of a wholly empirical analysis based on a conscientious critical study of political economy.

Whereas the uninformed reviewer who tries to hide his complete ignorance and intellectual poverty by hurling the "utopian phrase" at the positive critic's head, or again such phrases as "pure, resolute, utterly critical criticism," the "not merely legal but social—utterly social—society," the "compact, massy mass," the "oratorical orators of the massy mass," this reviewer has yet to furnish the first proof that besides his theological family-affairs he has anything to contribute to a discussion of worldly matters.

It goes without saying that besides the French and English Socialists I have made use of German Socialist works as well. The only original German works of substance in this science, however— other than Weitling's writings—are the essays by Hess published in *Einundzwanzig Bogen*, and Engels's *Umrisse zu einer Kritik der NationalÃkonomie* in the *Deutsch-FranzÃsische Jahrbücher*, where, likewise, I indicated in a very general way the basic elements of this work.

Besides being indebted to these authors who have given critical attention to political economy, positive criticism as a whole—and therefore also German positive criticism of political economy—owes its true foundation to the discoveries of Feuerbach, against whose *Philosophie der Zukunft* and *Thesen zur Reform der Philosophie* in the *Anecdotis*, despite the tacit use that is made of them, the petty envy of some and the veritable wrath of others seem to have instigated a regular conspiracy of silence.

It is only with Feuerbach that positive, humanistic and naturalistic criticism begins. The less noise they make, the more certain, profound, widespread and enduring is the effect of Feuerbach's writings, the only writings since Hegel's *Phanomenologie* and *Logik* to contain a real theoretical revolution.

In contrast to the critical theologians of our day, I have deemed the concluding chapter of the present work—the settling of accounts with Hegelian dialectic and Hegelian philosophy as a whole—to be absolutely necessary, a task not yet performed. This lack of thoroughness is not accidental, since even the critical theologian remains a theologian. Hence, either he had to start from certain presuppositions of philosophy accepted as authoritative; or if in the process of criticism and as a result of other people's discoveries doubts about these philosophical presuppositions have arisen in him, he abandons them without vindication and in a cowardly fashion, abstracts from them showing his servile dependence merely in a negative, unconscious and sophistical manner.

In this connection the critical theologian is either forever repeating assurances about the purity of his own criticism, or tries to make it seem as though all that was let for criticism to deal with now was some other immature form of criticism outside itself — say eighteenth-century criticism — and the backwardness of the masses, in order to divert the observer's attention as well as his own from the necessary task of settling accounts between criticism and its point of origin — Hegelian dialectic and German philosophy as a whole — from this necessary raising of modern criticism above its own limitation and crudity. Eventually, however, whenever discoveries (such as Feuerbach's) are made about the nature of his own philosophic presuppositions, the critical theologian partly makes it appear as if he were the one who had accomplished this, producing that appearance by taking the results of these discoveries and, without being able to develop them, hurling them in the form of catch-phrases at writers still caught in the confines of philosophy; partly he even manages to acquire a sense of his own superiority to such discoveries by covertly asserting in a veiled, malicious and skeptical fashion elements of the Hegelian dialectic which he still finds lacking in the criticism of that dialectic (which have not yet been critically served up to him for his use) against such criticism — not having tried to bring such elements into their proper relation or having been capable of doing so, asserting, say, the category of mediating proof against the category of positive, self-originating truth, etc., in a way peculiar to Hegelian dialectic. For to the theological critic it seems quite natural that everything has to be done by philosophy, so that he can chatter away about purity, resoluteness, and utterly critical criticism; and he fancies himself the true conqueror of philosophy whenever he happens to feel some "moment" in Hegel to be lacking in Feuerbach — for however much he practices the spiritual idolatry of "self-consciousness" and "mind" the theological critic does not get beyond feeling to consciousness.

On close inspection theological criticism — genuinely progressive though is was at the inception of the movement — is seen in the final analysis to be nothing but the culmination and consequence of the old philosophical, and especially the Hegelian, transcendentalism, twisted into a theological caricature. This interesting example of the justice in history, which now assigns to theology, ever philosophy's spot of infection, the further role of portraying in itself the negative dissolution of philosophy—i.e., the process of its decay—this historical nemesis I shall demonstrate on another occasion.

How far, on the other hand, Feuerbach's discoveries about the nature of philosophy required still, for their proof at least, a critical settling of accounts with philosophical dialectic will be seen from my exposition itself.

First Manuscript
Wages Of Labor

Wages are determined by the fierce struggle between capitalist and worker. The capitalist inevitably wins. The capitalist can live longer without the worker than the worker can live without him. Combination among capitalists is habitual and effective, while combination among the workers is forbidden and has painful consequences for them. In addition to that, the landowner and the capitalist can increase their revenues with the profits of industry, while the worker can supplement his income from industry with neither ground rent nor interest on capital. This is the reason for the intensity of competition among the workers. It is, therefore, only for the worker that the separation of capital, landed property, and labor, is a necessary, essential, and pernicious separation. Capital and landed property need not remain constant in this abstraction, as must the labor of the workers.

So, for the worker, the separation of capital, ground rent, and labor, is fatal.

For wages, the lowest and the only necessary rate is that required for the subsistence of the worker during work and enough extra to support a family and prevent the race of workers from dying out. According to Adam Smith, the normal wage is the lowest which is compatible with common humanity—i.e., with a bestial existence.

The demand for men necessarily regulates the production of men, as of every other commodity. If the supply greatly exceeds the demand, then one section of the workers sinks into beggary or starvation. The existence of the worker is, therefore, reduced to the same condition as the existence of every other commodity. The worker has become a commodity, and he is lucky if he can find a buyer. And the demand on which the worker's life depends is regulated by the whims of the wealthy and the capitalists. If supply exceeds demand, one of the elements which go to make up the price — profit, ground rent, wages — will be paid below its price. A part of these elements is, therefore, withdrawn from this application, with the result that the market price gravitates towards the natural price as the central point. But 1. it is very difficult for the worker to direct his labor elsewhere where there is a marked division of labor; and 2. because of his subordinate relationship to the capitalist, he is the first to suffer.

So the worker is sure to lose and to lose most from the gravitation of the market price towards the natural price. And it is precisely the ability of the capitalist to direct his capital elsewhere which either drives the worker, who is restricted to one particular branch of employment, into starvation or forces him to submit to all the capitalist's demands.

The sudden chance fluctuations in market price hit ground rent less than that part of the price which constitutes profit and wages, but they hit profit less than wages. For every wage which rises, there is generally one which remains stationary and another which falls.

The worker does not necessarily gain when the capitalist gains, but he necessarily loses with him. For example, the worker does not gain if the capitalist keeps the market price above the natural price by means of a manufacturing or trade secret, a monopoly or a favorably placed property.

Moreover, the prices of labor are much more constant than the prices of provisions. They are often in inverse proportion. In a dear year, wages drop because of a drop in demand and rise because of an increase in the price of provisions. They, therefore, balance. In any case, some workers are left without bread. In cheap years, wages rise on account of the rise in demand, and fall on account of the fall in the price of provisions. So they balance.

Another disadvantage for the worker:

The price of the labor of different kinds of workers varies much more than the profits of the various branches in which capital is put to use. In the case of labor, all the natural, spiritual, and social variations in individual activity are manifested and variously rewarded, were as dead capital behaves in a uniform way and is indifferent to real individual activity.

In general, we should note that where worker and capitalist both suffer, the worker suffers in his very existence while the capitalist suffers in the profit on his dead mammon.

The worker has not only to struggle for his physical means of subsistence; he must also struggle for work—i.e., for the possibility and the means of realizing his activity. Let us consider the three main conditions which can occur in society and their effect on the worker.

(1) If the wealth of society is decreasing, the worker suffers most, although the working class cannot gain as much as the property owners when society is prospering, none suffers more cruelly from its decline than the working class.

(2) Let us now consider a society in which wealth is increasing. This condition is the only one favorable to the worker. Here, competition takes place among the capitalists. The demand for workers outstrips supply. But:

In the first place, the rise of wages leads to overwork among the workers. The more they want to earn the more they must sacrifice their time and freedom and work like slaves in the service of avarice. In doing so, they shorten their lives. But this is all to the good of the working class as a whole, since it creates a renewed demand. This class must always sacrifice a part of itself if it is to avoid total destruction.

Furthermore, when is a society in a condition of increasing prosperity? When the capitals and revenues of a country are growing. But this is only possible

(a) as a result of the accumulation of a large quantity of labor, for capital is accumulated labor; that is to say, when more and more of the workers' products are being taken from him, when his own labor increasingly confronts him as alien property and the means of his existence and of his activity are increasingly concentrated in the hands of the capitalist.

(b) The accumulation of capital increases the division of labor, and the division of labor increases the number of workers; conversely, the growth in the number of workers increases the division of labor, just as the growth in the division of labor increases the accumulation of capital. As a consequence of this division of labor, on the one hand, and the accumulation of capitals, on the other, the worker becomes more and more uniformly dependent on labor, and on a particular, very one-sided and machine-like type of labor. Just as he is depressed, therefore, both intellectually and physically to the level of a machine, and from being a man becomes an abstract activity and a stomach, so he also becomes more and more dependent on every fluctuation in the market price, in the investment of capital and in the whims of the wealthy. Equally, the increase in that class of men who do nothing but work increases the competition among the workers and therefore lowers their price. In the factory system, conditions such as these reach their climax.

(c) In a society which is becoming increasingly prosperous, only the very richest can continue to live from the interest on money. All the rest must run a business with their capital, or put it on the market. As a result, the competition among the capitalists increases, there is a growing concentration of capital, the big capitalists ruin the small ones, and a section of the former capitalists sinks into the class of the workers — which, because of this increase in numbers, suffers a further depression of wages and becomes even more dependent on the handful of big capitalists. Because the number of capitalists has fallen, competition for workers has increased, the competition among them has become all the more considerable, unnatural and violent. Hence, a section of the working class is reduced to beggary or starvation with the same necessity as a section of the middle capitalists ends up in the working class.

So, even in the state of society most favorable to him, the inevitable consequence for the worker is an early death, reduction to a machine, enslavement to capital which piles up in threatening opposition to him, fresh competition and starvation or beggary for a section of the workers.

An increase in wages arouses in the worker the same desire to get rich as in the capitalist, but he can only satisfy this desire by sacrificing his mind and body. An increase in wages presupposes, and brings about, the accumulation of capital, and thus opposes the product of labor to the worker as something increasingly alien to him. Similarly, the division of labor makes him more and more one-sided and dependent, introducing competition from machines as well as from men. Since the worker has been reduced to a machine, the machine can confront him as a competitor. Finally, just as the accumulation of capital increases the quantity of industry and, therefore, the number of workers, so it enables the same quantity of industry to produce a greater quantity of products. This leads to overproduction and ends up either by putting a large number of workers out of work or by reducing their wages to a pittance.

Such are the consequences of a condition of society which is most favorable to the worker — i.e., a condition of growing wealth.

But, in the long run, the time will come when this state of growth reaches a peak. What is the situation of the worker then?

(3) "In a country which had acquired that full complement of riches... both the wages of labor and the profits of stock would probably be very low... the competition for employment would necessarily be so great as to reduce the wages of labor to what was barely sufficient to keep up the number of laborers, and, the country being already fully peopled, that number could never be augmented." (Smith I, p. 84)

The surplus population would have to die.

So, in a declining state of society, we have the increasing misery of the worker; in an advancing state, complicated misery; and in the terminal state, static misery.

Smith tells us that a society of which the greater part suffers is not happy. But, since even the most prosperous state of society leads to suffering for the majority, and since the economic system, which is a society based on private interests, brings about such a state of prosperity, it follows that society's distress is the goal of the economic system.

We should further note in connection with the relationship between worker and capitalist that the latter is more than compensated for wage rises by a reduction in the amount of labor time, and that wage rises and increases in the interest on capital act on commodity prices like simple and compound interest respectively.

Let us now look at things from the point of view of the political economist and compare what he has to say about the theoretical and practical claims of the worker.

He tells us that, originally, and in theory, the whole produce of labor belongs to the worker. (Smith I, p. 57) But, at the same time, he tells us that what the worker actually receives is the smallest part of the product, the absolute minimum necessary; just enough for him to exist not as a human being but as a worker and for him to propagate not humanity but the slave class of the workers.

The political economist tells us that everything is bought with labor and that capital is nothing but accumulated labor, but then goes on to say that the worker, far from being in a position to buy everything, must sell himself and his humanity.

While the ground rent of the indolent landowner generally amounts to a third of the product of the soil, and the profit of the busy capitalist to as much as twice the rate of interest, the surplus which the worker earns amounts at best to the equivalent of death through starvation for two of his four children. (Smith I, p. 60))

According to the political economist, labor is the only means whereby man can enhance the value of natural products, and labor is the active property of man. But, according to this same political economy, the landowner and the capitalist, who as such are merely privileged and idle gods, are everywhere superior to the worker and dictate the law to him.

According to the political economist, labor is the only constant price of things. But nothing is more subject to chance than the price of labor, nothing exposed to greater fluctuations.

While the division of labor increases to the productive power of labor and the wealth and refinement of society, it impoverishes the worker and reduces him to a machine. While labor gives rise to the accumulation of capital, and so brings about the growing prosperity of society, it makes the worker increasingly dependent on the capitalist, exposes him to greater competition and drives him into the frenzied world of overproduction, with its subsequent slump.

According to the political economist, the interest of the worker is never opposed to the interest of society. But, society is invariably and inevitably opposed to the interest of the worker.

According to the political economist, the interest of the worker is never opposed to that of society: (1) because the rise in wages is more than made up for by the reduction in the amount of labor time, with the other consequences explained above, and (2) because in relation to society the entire gross product is net product, and only in relation to the individual does the net product have any significance.

But it follows from the analyses made by the political economists, even though they themselves are unaware of the fact, that labor itself — not only under present conditions, but in general, insofar as its goal is restricted to the increase of wealth — is harmful and destructive.

In theory, ground rent and profit on capital are deductions made from wages. But, in reality, wages are a deduction which land and capital grant the worker, an allowance made from the product of labor to the worker, to labor.

The worker suffers most when society is in a state of decline. He owes the particular severity of his distress to his position as a worker, but the distress as such is a result of the situation of society.

But, when society is in a state of progress, the decline and impoverishment of the worker is the product of his labor and the wealth produced by him. This misery, therefore, proceeds from the very essence of present-day labor.

A society at the peak of prosperity—an ideal, but one which is substantially achieved, and which is at least the goal of the economic system and of civil society—is static misery for the worker.

It goes without saying that political economy regards the proletarian—i.e., he who lives without capital and ground rent, from labor alone, and from one-sided, abstract labor at that—as nothing more than a worker. It can, therefore, advance the thesis that, like a horse, he must receive enough to enable him to work. It does not consider him, during the time when he is not working, as a human being. It leaves this to criminal law, doctors, religion, statistical tables, politics, and the beadle.

Let us now rise above the level of political economy and examine the ideas developed above, taken almost word for word from the political economists, for the answers to these two questions:

(1) What is the meaning, in the development of mankind, of this reduction of the greater part of mankind to abstract labor?

(2) What mistakes are made by the piecemeal reformers, who either want to raise wages and thereby improve the situation of the working class, or—like Proudhon—see equality of wages as the goal of social revolution?

In political economy, labor appears only in the form of wage-earning activity.

"It can be argued that those occupations which demand specific abilities or longer training have on the whole become more lucrative; while the commensurate wage for mechanically uniform activity, in which everyone can be quickly and easily trained, has fallen, and inevitably so, as a result of growing competition. And it is precisely this kind of labor which, under the present system of labor organization, is by far the most common.

"So, if a worker in the first category now earns seven times as much as he did 50 years ago, while another in the second category continues to earn the same as he did then, then on average they earn four times as much.

"But if in a given country there are only a thousand workers in the first category and a million in the second, then 999,000 are no better off than 50 years ago, and they are worse off if the prices of staple goods have risen.

"And yet people are trying to deceive themselves about the most numerous class of the population with superficial average calculations of this sort.

"Moreover, the size of wages is only one factor in evaluating a worker's income: it is also essential to take into account the length of time for which such wages are guaranteed, and there is no question of guarantees in the anarchy of so-called free competition with its continual fluctuations and stagnation. Finally, we must bear in mind the hours of work which were usual earlier and those which are usual now. And for the English cotton workers, the working day has been increased, as a result of the employers' greed, from 12 to 16 hours during the past 25 years or so—i.e., since labor-saving machines were introduced. This increase in one country and in one branch of industry inevitably carried over to a greater or lesser degree into other areas, for the rights of the wealthy to subject the poor to boundless exploitation are still universally acknowledged." (Wilhelm Schulz, *Die Bewegung der Produktion, eine geschichtlichstatistiscke Abhandlung*. Zurich and Winterthur, 1843, p. 65)

"But even even this were as true as it is false, that the average income of all classes of society has grown, the differences and relative intervals between incomes can still have grown bigger, so that the contrast between wealth and poverty becomes sharper. For it is precisely because total production rises that needs, desires, and claims also increase, and they increase in the same measure as production rises; relative poverty can therefore grow while absolute poverty diminishes. The Samoyed is not poor with his blubber and rancid fish, for in his self-contained society, everyone has the same needs. But, in a state which is making rapid headway, which, in the course of a decade, increases its total production in relation to the population by a third, the worker who earns the same at the end of the 10 years as he did at the beginning has not maintained his standard of living, he has grown poorer by a third." (Wilhelm Schulz, pp. 65-6)

But political economy knows the worker only as a beast of burden, as an animal reduced to the minimum bodily needs.

"If a people is to increase its spiritual freedom, it can no longer remain in thrall to its bodily needs, it can no longer be the servant of the flesh. Above all, it needs time for intellectual exercise and recreation. This time is won through new developments in the organization of labor.

"Nowadays, a single worker in the cotton mills, as a result of new ways of producing power and new machinery, can often do work that previously needed 100 or even 250-300 workers. All branches of industry have witnessed similar consequences, since external natural forces are increasingly being brought to bear on human labor. If the amount of time and human energy needed earlier to satisfy a given quantity of material needs was later reduced by half, then, without any forfeiture of material comfort, the margin for intellectual creation and recreation will have increased by half.

"But, even the sharing of the spoils which we win from old Chronos on his very own territory still depends on blind and unjust chance.

"In France, it has been estimated that, at the present stage of production, an average working day of five hours from each person capable of work would be sufficient to satisfy all society's material needs.... In spite of the time saved through improvements in machinery, the time spent in slave labor in the factories has increased for many people." (Wilhelm Schulz, pp. 67-8)

"The transition from complicated handicrafts presupposes a breaking down of such work into the simple operations of which it consists. To begin with, however, only a part of the uniformly recurring operations falls to the machines, while another part falls to men. Permanently uniform activity of this kind is by its very nature harmful to both soul and body — a fact which is also confirmed by experience; and so, when machinery is combined in this way, with the mere division of labor among a larger number of men, all the shortcomings of the latter inevitably make their appearance. These shortcomings include the greater mortality of factory workers....

"No attention has been paid to the essential distinction between how far men work through machines and how far they work as machines." (Wilhelm Schulz, pp. 69)

"In the future life of the nations, however, the mindless forces of nature operating in machines will be our slaves and servants." (Wilhelm Schulz, pp. 74)

"In the English spinning mills, only 158,818 men are employed, compared with 196,818 women. For every 100 men workers in the Lancashire cotton mills, there are 103 women workers, in Scotland, the figure is as high as 209. In the English flax mills in Leeds, there are 147 women for every 100 men workers; in Dundee, and on the east coast of Scotland, this figure is as high as 280. In the English silk-factories, there are many women workers; in the wool factories, where greater strength is needed, there are more men. As for the North American cotton mills, in 1833 there were no fewer than 38,927 women alongside 18,593 men.

"So, as a result of changes in the organization of labor, a wider area of employment opportunities has been opened up to members of the female sex... more economic independence for women... both sexes brought closer together in their social relations." (Wilhelm Schulz, pp. 71-2)

"Employed in the English spinning mills operated by steam and water in the year 1835 were: 20,558 children between 8 and 12 years of age; 35,867 between 12 and 13; and, finally, 108,208 between 13 and 18....

"True, the advances in mechanization, which remove more and more of the monotonous tasks from human hands, are gradually eliminating these ills. But, standing in the way of these more rapid advances is the fact that the capitalists are in a position to make use of the energies of the lower classes, right down to children, very easily and very cheaply, and to use them instead of machinery." (Wilhelm Schulz, pp. 70-1)

"Lord Brougham's appeal to the workers: 'Become capitalists!'...

"The evil that million are only able to eke out a living through exhausting, physically destructive, and morally and intellectually crippling, labor; that they are even forced to regard the misfortune of finding such work as fortunate." (Wilhelm Schulz, pp. 60)

"So, in order to live, the non-owners are forced to place themselves directly or indirectly at the service of owners—i.e., become dependent upon them." (C. Pecqueur, *Theorie nouvelle d'economie sociale et politique, ou etudes sur l'organisation des societes*, Paris, 1842, p. 409)

"Servants-pay; workers-wages; clerks-salaries or emoluments.... "hire out one's labor", "lend out one's labor at interest", "work in another's place", "hire out the materials of labor", "lend the materials of labor at interest", "make another work in one's place". (C. Pecqueur, p. 409-10, 411)

"This economic constitution condemns men to such abject employments, such desolate and bitter degradation, that by comparison savagery appears like a royal condition." "Prostitution of the non-owning class in all its forms." Rag-and-bone men. (C. Pecqueur, p. 417-18, 421)

Charles Loudon, in his work *Solution du probleme de la population*, gives the number of prostitutes in England as 60-70,000. The number of women of "doubtful virtue" is roughly the same.

"The average life span of these unfortunate creatures on the streets, after they have embarked on their career of vice, is about six or seven years. This means that, if the number of 60-70,000 prostitutes is to be maintained, there must be in the three kingdoms at least 8-9,000 women a year who take up this infamous trade—i.e., roughly 24 victims a day, which is an average of one an hour. So, if the same proportion is true for the whole surface of the planet, then at all times there must be one-and-a-half million of these unhappy creatures." (Charles Loudon, *Solution du probleme de la population et de la subsistence, soumise a un medecin dans une serie du lettres*, Paris, 1842, p. 229)

"The population of the poor grows with their poverty, and it is at the most extreme limit of need that human beings crowd together in the greatest numbers in order to fight among themselves for the right to suffer....

"In 1821, the population of Ireland was 6,801,827. By 1831, it had risen to 7,764,010; that is, a 14 per cent increase in 10 years. In Leinster, the most prosperous of the provinces, the population only grew by 8 per cent, while in Connaught, the poorest of the provinces, the increase was as high as 21 per cent. (Extract from Inquiries Published in England on Ireland, Vienna, 1840.) (Eugene Buret, *De la misere des classes laborieuses en Angleterre et en France*, 2 vols., Paris, 1840, Vol. I, pp. 36-7)

Political economy regards labor abstractly, as a thing; labor is a commodity; if the price is high, the commodity is much in demand; if it is low, then it is much in supply; "the price of labor as a commodity must fall lower and lower". (ibid., p. 43) This is brought about partly by the competition among the workers themselves.

"... the working population, seller of labor, is forced to accept the smallest part of the product... Is the theory of labor as a commodity anything other than a disguised theory of slavery?"

"Why then was labor regarded as nothing more than an exchange value?" (Eugene Buret, p. 43)

The big workshops prefer to buy the labor of women and children, because it costs less than that of men.

"Vis-a-vis his employer, the worker is not at all in the position of a free seller.... The capitalist is always free to employ labor, and the worker is always forced to sell it. The value of labor is completely destroyed if it is not sold at every instant. Unlike genuine commodities, labor can be neither accumulated nor saved.

"Labor is life, and if life is not exchanged every day for food, it suffers and soon perishes. If human life is to be regarded as a commodity, we are forced to admit slavery." (Eugene Buret, p. 49-50)

So, if labor is a commodity, it is a commodity with the most unfortunate characteristics. But, even according to economic principles, it is not one, for it is not the "free product of a free market". (ibid., p. 50) The present economic regime "reduces at the same time both the price and the remuneration of labor; it perfects the worker and degrades the man." (ibid., p. 52-3) "Industry has become a war, commerce a game." (ibid., p. 62)

"The machines for spinning cotton (in England) alone represent 84,000,000 handworkers." (Eugene Buret, p. 193)

Up to now, industry has been in the situation of a war of conquest: "it has squandered the lives of the men who composed its army with as much indifference as the great conquerors. Its goal was the possession of riches, and not human happiness." "These interests (i.e., economic interests), left to their own free development, ... cannot help coming into conflict; war is their only arbiter, and the decisions of war assign defeat and death to some and victory to others.... It is in the conflict of opposing forces that science looks for order and equilibrium; perpetual was, in the view of science, is the only means of achieving peace; this war is called competition." (Eugene Buret, pp. 20,23)

"The industrial war, if it is to be waged successfully, needs large armies which it can concentrate at one point and decimate at will. And neither devotion nor duty moves the soldiers of this army to bear the burden placed upon them; what moves them is the need to escape the harshness of starvation. They feel neither affection nor gratitude for their bosses, who are not bound in their subordinates by any feeling of goodwill and who regard them not as human beings but as instruments of production which bring in as much and cost as little as possible. These groups of workers, who are more and more crowded together, cannot even be sure they will always be employed; the industry which has summoned them together allows them to live only because it needs them; as soon as it can get rid of them, it abandons them without the slightest hesitation; and the workers are forced to offer their persons and their labor for whatever is the going price. The longer, more distressing and loathsome the work which is given them, the less they are paid; one can see workers who toil their way non-stop through a 16-hour day and who scarcely manage to buy the right not to die." (Eugene Buret, pp. 68-9)

"We are convinced... as are the commissioners appointed to look into the conditions of the handloom weavers, that the large industrial towns would quickly lose their population of workers if they did not all the time receive a continual stream of healthy people and fresh blood from the surrounding country areas." (Eugene Buret, pp. 362)

Profit Of Capital

1. Capital

(1) What is the basis of capital—i.e., of private property in the products of another's labor?

"Even if capital cannot be reduced to simple theft or fraud, it still needs the assistance of legislation to sanctify inheritance." (Jean-Baptiste Say, *Traie d'economie politique*, third edition, 2 volumes, Paris, 1817, I, p. 136, footnote)

How does one become an owner of productive stock? How does on become owner of the products created by means of this stock? Through positive law. (Say, II, p. 4)

What does one acquire with capital, with the inheritance of a large fortune, for example?

"The person who acquires, or succeeds to a great fortune, does not necessarily acquire or succeed to any political power.... The power which that possession immediately and directly conveys to him, is the power of purchasing; a certain command over all the labor, or over all the produce of labor, which is then in the market." (Smith, Wealth of Nations, I, pp. 26-7)

Capital is, therefore, the power to command labor, and its products. The capitalist possesses this power not on account of his personal or human properties but insofar as he is an owner of capital. His power is the purchasing power of his capital, which nothing can withstand.

Later, we shall see how the capitalist, by means of capital, exercises his power to command labor; but we shall then go on to see how capital, in its turn, is able to rule the capitalist himself.

What is capital?

"A certain quantity of labor stocked and stored up. .." (Smith, p. 295)

Capital is stored-up labor.

(2) Bonds, or stock, is any accumulation of the products of the soil or of manufacture. Stock is only called capital when it yields its owner a revenue or profit.

2. The Profit of Capital

The profit or gain of capital is altogether different from the wages of labor. This difference manifests itself in two ways: firstly, the profits of capital are regulated altogether by the value of the stock employed, although the labor of inspection and direction for different capitals may be the same. Furthermore, in many large factories, the whole labor of this kind is committed to some principal clerk, whose wages never bear any regular proportion to the capital of which he oversees the management. And the owner of this capital, though he is thus discharged of almost all labor, still expects that his profits should bear a regular proportion to his capital. (Smith, p. 43)

Why does the capitalist demand this proportion between profit and capital?

He could have no interest in employing these workers, unless he expected from the sale of their work something more than was sufficient to replace the stock advanced by him as wages; and he could have no interest to employ a great stock rather than a small one, unless his profits were to bear some proportion to the extent of his stock. (Smith, p. 42)

So the capitalist makes a profit first on the wages and secondly on the raw materials advanced by him.

What relation, then, does profit have to capital?

It is not easy to ascertain what are the average wages of labor even in a particular place and at a particular time, and it is even more difficult to determine the profit on capital. Variations of price in commodities which the capitalist deals in, the good or bad fortune both of his rivals and of his customers, a thousand other accidents to which his goods are liable in transit and in warehouses, all produce a daily, almost hourly, variation in profits. (Smith, pp. 78-9) But although it may be impossible to determine, with any degree of precision, the average profits of capital, some notion may be formed of them from the interest of money. Wherever a great deal can be made by the use of money, a great deal will be given for the use of it; wherever little can be made, little will be given. (Smith, p. 79)

"The proportion which the usual market rate of interest ought to bear to the ordinary rate of clear profit, necessarily varies as profit rises or falls. Double interest is in Great Britain reckoned what the merchants call a good, moderate, reasonable profit, terms which... mean no more than a common and usual profit." (Smith, p. 87)

What is the lowest rate of profit? And what is the highest?

The lowest rate of ordinary profit on capitals must always be something more than what is sufficient to compensate the occasional losses to which every employment of capital is exposed. It is this surplus value only which is the neat or clear profit. The same holds for the lowest rate of interest. (Smith, p. 86)

The highest rate to which ordinary profits can rise may be such as, in the price of the greater part of commodities, eats up the whole of the rent of the land and reduces the wages of labor expended in preparing the commodity and bringing it to market to the lowest rate, the bare subsistence of the laborer. The workman must always have been fed in some way or other while he was about the work; but the rent of land can disappear entirely. Examples: the servants of the East India Company in Bengal. (Smith, pp. 86-7)

Besides all the advantages of limited competition which the capitalist can exploit in such a case, he can keep the market price above the natural price, by quite honorable means.

Firstly, by secrets in trade, where the market is at a great distance from the residence of those who supply it; that is, by concealing a change in price, an increase above the natural level. The effect of this concealment is that other capitalists do not invest their capital in this branch of industry.

Secondly, by secrets in manufacture, which enable the capitalist to cut production costs and sell his goods at the same price, or even at a lower price than his competitors, while making a bigger profit. (Deceit by concealment is not immoral? Dealings on the Stock Exchange.) Furthermore, where production is confined to a particular locality (as in the case of select wines) and the effective demand can never be satisfied. Finally, through monopolies granted to individuals or companies. The price of monopoly is the highest which can be got. (Smith, pp. 53-4)

Other chance causes which can raise the profit on capital:

The acquisition of new territory, or of new branches of trade, may sometimes rise the profits of stock even in a wealthy country, because part of the capital is withdrawn from the old branches of trade, competition comes to be less than before, and the market is less fully supplied with commodities, the prices of which then rise: those who deal in these commodities can then afford to borrow at a higher interest. (Smith, p. 83) As any particular commodity comes to be more manufactured, that part of the price which resolves itself into wages and profit comes to be greater in proportion to that which resolves itself into rent. In the progress of the manufacture of commodity, not only the number of the profits increase, but every subsequent profit is greater than the preceding one; because the capital from which it is derived must always be greater. The capital which employs the weavers, for example, must be greater than that which employs the spinners; because it not only replaces that capital with its profits, but pays besides, the wages of the weavers; and the profits must always bear some proportion to the capital. (Smith, p. 45)

So, the growing role played by human labor in fashioning the natural product increases not the wages of labor but partly the number of profitable capitals and partly the size of each capital in proportion to those that precede it.

More later about the profit which the capitalist derives from the division of labor.

He profits in two ways: firstly, from the division of labor and secondly, and more generally, from the growing role played by human labor in fashioning the natural product. The larger the human share in a commodity, the larger the profit of dead capital.

In one and the same society, the average rates of profit on capital are more nearly upon a level than are the wages of different kinds of labor. (Smith, p. 45) In the different employments of capital, the ordinary rate of profit varies more or less with the certainty or uncertainty of the returns;

"... the ordinary profit of stock, though it rises with the risk, does not always seem to rise in proportion to it." (Smith, pp. 99-100)

Needless to say, profits also rise if the means of circulation (e.g., paper money) improve or become less expensive.

3. The Rule of Capital over Labor and the Motives of the Capitalist

"The consideration of his own private profit is the sole motive which determines the owner of any capital to employ it either in agriculture, in manufactures, or in some particular branch of the wholesale or retail trade. The different quantities of productive labor which may put it into motion, and the different values which it may add to the annual produce of the land and labor of the society, according as it is employed in one or other of those different ways, never enter into his thoughts." (Smith, p. 355)

"The most useful employment of capital for the capitalist is that which, with the same degree of security, yields him the largest profit; but this employment is not always the most useful for society... the most useful is that which... stimulates the productive power of its land and labor." (Say, II, pp. 130-31)

"The plans and projects of the employers of stock regulate and direct all the most important operations of labor, and profit is the end proposed by all those plans and projects. But the rate of profit does not, like rent and wages, rise with the prosperity and fall with the declension of the society. On the contrary, it is naturally low in rich and high in poor countries, and it is always highest in countries which are going fastest to ruin. The interest of this third order (those who live by profit), therefore, has not the same connection with the general interest of the society as that of the other two.... The interest of the dealer, however, in any particular branch of trade or manufactures, is always in some respects different from, and even opposite to, that of the public. To widen the market and to narrow the competition, is always the interest of the dealers... and order of men whose interest is never exactly the same as that of the public, who have generally an interest to decisive and even to oppress the public..." (Smith I, pp. 231-2)

4. The Accumulation of Capitals and the Competition among the Capitalists

The increase of capitals, which raises wages, tends to lower profits, as a result of the competition among capitalists. (Smith, p. 78)

If, for example, the capital which is necessary for the grocery trade of a particular town "is divided between two different grocers, their competition will tend to make both of them sell cheaper than if it were in the hands of one only; and if it were divided among 20, their competition would be just so much the greater, and the chance of their combining together, in order to raise the price, just so much the less." (Smith I, p. 322)

Since we already know that monopoly prices are as high as possible, since the interest of the capitalists, even from a straight-forwardly economic point of view, is opposed to the interest of society, and since the growth of profits acts on the price of the commodity like compound interest (Smith, pp. 87-8), it follows that the sole defense against the capitalists is competition, which in the view of political economy has the beneficial effect both of raising wages and cheapening commodities to the advantage of the consuming public.

But, competition is possible only if capitals multiply and are held by many different people. It is only possible to generate a large number of capitals as a result of multilateral accumulation, since capital in general stems from accumulation. But, multilateral accumulation inevitably turns into unilateral accumulation. Competition among capitalists increases accumulation of capitals. Accumulation—which, under the rule of private property, means concentration of capital in few hands—inevitably ensues if capitals are allowed to follow their own natural course. It is only through competition that this natural proclivity of capital begins to take shape.

We have already seen that the profit on capital is in proportion to its size. If we ignore deliberate competition for the moment, a large capital accumulates more rapidly, in proportion to its size, than does a small capital.

This means that, quite apart from competition, the accumulation of large capital takes place at a much faster rate than that of small capital. But, let us follow this process further.

As capitals multiply, the profits on capital diminish, as a result of competition. So, the first to suffer is the small capitalist.

"In a country which had acquired its full complement of riches ... as the ordinary rate of clear profit would be very small, so the usual market rate of interest which could be afforded out of it would be so low as to render it impossible for any but the very wealthiest of people to live upon the interest of their money. All people of small or middling fortunes would be obliged to super-intend themselves the employment of their own stocks. It would be necessary that almost every man should be a man of business, or engage in some sort of trade." (Smith I, p. 86)

This is the situation most dear to the heart of political economy.

"The proportion between capital and revenue, therefore, seems everywhere to regulate the proportion between industry and idleness. Wherever capital predominates, industry prevails: wherever revenue, idleness." (Smith, p. 301)

But, what about the employment of capital in this increased competition?

"As the quantity of stock to be lent at interest increases, the interest, or the price which must be paid for the use of that stock, necessarily diminishes, not only from those general causes, which make the market price of things commonly diminish as their quantity increases, but from other causes which are peculiar to this particular case.

"As capitals increase in any country, the profits which can be made by employing them necessarily diminish. It becomes gradually more and more difficult to find within the country a profitable method of employing any new capital. There arises, in consequence, a competition between different capitals, the owner of one endeavoring to get possession of that employment which is occupied by another.

"But, on most occasions he can hope to jostle that other out of this employment by no other means but by dealing upon more reasonable terms. He must not only sell what he deals in somewhat cheaper, but, in order to get it to sell, he must sometimes, too, buy it dearer.

"The demand for productive labor, by the increase of the funds which are destined for maintaining it, grows every day greater and greater. Laborers easily find employment, but the owners of capitals find it difficult to get laborers to employ. Their competition raises the wages of labor and sinks the profits of stock." (Smith p. 316)

The small capitalist, therefore, has two choices: he can either consume his capital, since he can no longer live on the interest—i.e., cease to be a capitalist; or, he can himself set up a business, sell his goods at a lower price, and buy them at a dearer price than the richer capitalist, and pay higher wages, which means that he would go bankrupt—since the market price is already very low as a result of the intense competition we presupposed. If, on the other hand, the big capitalist wants to squeeze out the smaller one, he has all the same advantages over him as the capitalist has over the worker. He is compensated for the smaller profits by the larger size of his capital, and he can even put up with short-term losses until the smaller capitalist is ruined and he is freed of this competition. In this way, he accumulates the profits of the small capitalist.

Furthermore: the big capitalist always buys more cheaply than the small capitalist, because he buys in larger quantities. He can, therefore, afford to sell at a lower price.

But, if a fall in the rate of interest turns the middle capitalists from rentiers into businessmen, conversely the increase in business capitals and the resulting lower rate of profit produce a fall in the rate of interest.

"But, when the profits which can be made by use of a capital are diminished... the price which can be paid for the use of it... must necessarily be diminished with them." (Smith p. 316)

"As riches, improvement, and population, have increased, interest has declined", and consequently the profits of stock; "...after these are diminished, stock may not only continue to increase, but to increase much faster than before.... A great stock, though with small profits, generally increases faster than a small stock with great profits. Money, says the proverb, makes money." (Smith p. 83)

So, if this large capital is opposed by small capitals with small profits, as in the case under the conditions of intense competition which we have presupposed, it crushes them completely.

The inevitable consequence of this competition is the deterioration in the quality of goods, adulteration, spurious production, and universal pollution to be found in large towns.

Another important factor in the competition between big and small capitals is the relationship between fixed capital and circulating capital.

Circulating capital is capital "employed in raising, manufacturing, or purchasing goods, and selling them again at a profit. The capital employed in this manner yields no revenue or profit to its employer, while it either remains in his possession or continues in the same shape.... His capital is continually going from him in one shape, and returning to him in another, and it is only by means of such circulation, or successive exchanges, that it can yield him any profit...."

Fixed capital is capital "employed in the improvement of land, in the purchase of useful machines and instruments, or in such like things....

"...Every saving in the expense of supporting the fixed capital of the undertaker of every work is necessarily divided between his fixed and his circulating capital. While his whole capital remains the same, the smaller the one part, the greater must necessarily be the other. It is the circulating capital which furnishes the materials and wages of labor, and puts industry into motion. Every saving, therefore, in the expense of maintaining the fixed capital, which does not diminish the productive powers of labor, must increase the fund which puts industry into motion...." (Smith, p. 257)

It is immediately clear that the relation between fixed capital and circulating capital is much more favorable to the big capitalist than it is to the smaller capitalist. The difference in volume between the amount of fixed capital needed by a very big banker and the amount needed by a very small one is insignificant. The only fixed capital they need is an office. The equipment needed by a big landowner does not increase in proportion to the extent of his land. Similarly, the amount of credit available to a big capitalist, compared with a smaller one, represents a bigger saving in fixed capital—namely, in the amount of money which he must have available at all times. Finally, it goes without saying that where industrial labor is highly developed—i.e., where almost all manual crafts have become factory labor—the entire capital of the small capitalist is not enough to procure for him even the necessary fixed capital. It is well known that large-scale (agricultural) cultivation generally requires only a small number of hands.

The accumulation of large capitals is generally accompanied by a concentration and simplification of fixed capital, as compared with the smaller capitalists. The big capitalist establishes for himself some kind of organization of the instruments of labor.

"Similarly, in the sphere of industry every factory and every workshop is a more comprehensive combination of a larger material property with numerous and varied intellectual abilities and technical skills which have as their shared aim the development of production.... Where legislation preserves the unity of large landed properties, the surplus quantity of a growing population crowds together into industry, and it is therefore mainly in industry that the proletariat gathers in large numbers, as in Great Britain. But, where legislation allows the continuous division of the land, as in France, the number of small, debt-ridden proprietors increases and many of them are forced into the class of the needy and the discontented. Should this division and indebtedness go far enough, in the same way as big industry destroys small industry; and since larger landholding complexes once more come into being, many propertyless workers no longer needed on the land are, in this case too, forced into industry." (Schulz, pp. 58-9)

"The character of commodities of the same sort changes as a result of changes in the nature of production, and in particular as a result of mechanization. Only by eliminating human labor has it become possible to spin from a pound of cotton worth 3s. 8d., 350 hanks worth 25 guineas and 167 miles in length." (Schulz, p. 62)

"On average, the prices of cotton goods have fallen by 11/12ths over the past 45 years, and according to Marshall's calculations a quantity of manufacture costing 16s. in 1814 now cost 1s. 10d. The drop in prices of industrial products has meant both a rise in home consumption and an increase in the foreign market; as a result, the number of cotton workers in Great Britain not only did not fall after the introduction of machinery, but rose from 40,000 to 1.5 million. As for the earnings of industrial employers and workers, the growing competition among factory owners has inevitably resulted in a drop in profits in proportion to the quantity of products. Between 1820 and 1833, the gross profit made by Manchester manufacturers on a piece of calico fell from 4s. 1.5d. to 1s. 9d. But, to make up for this loss, the rate of production has been correspondingly increased. The consequence is that there have been instances of overproduction in some branches of industry; that there are frequent bankruptcies, which create fluctuations of property within the class of capitalists and masters of labor, and force a number of those who have been ruined economically into the ranks of the proletariat; and that frequent and sudden restriction in employment among the class of wage-earners." (Schulz, p. 63)

"To hire out one's labor is to begin one's enslavement; to hire out the materials of labor is to achieve one's freedom.... Labor is man, while matter contains nothing human." (Pecqueur, pp. 411-12)

"The element of matter, which can do nothing to create wealth without the element of labor, acquires the magical property of being fruitful for them (that is, for the property owners), as if they themselves had provided this indispensable element." (Pecqueur, p. 412)

"If we assume that a worker can earn an average of 400 francs a year from his daily labor, and that this sum is sufficient for one adult to eke out a living, then anyone who receives 2,000 francs in interest or rent is indirectly forcing 5 men to work for him; an income of 100,000 francs represents the labor of 250 men; and 1,000,000 francs the labor of 2,500 (300 million — Louis Philippe — therefore represents the labor of 750,000 workers)." (Pecqueur, pp. 412-13)

"The property owners have received from human law the right to use and abuse the materials of all labor — i.e., to do as they wish with them.... There is no law which obliges them punctually and at all time to provide work for those who do not own property or to pay them a wage which is at all times adequate, etc." (Pecqueur, p. 413)

"Complete freedom as to the nature, the quantity, the quality, and the appropriateness of production, the use and consumption of wealth and the disposal of the materials of all labor. Everyone is free to exchange his possessions as he chooses, without any other consideration than his own interest as an individual." (Pecqueur, p. 413)

"Competition is simply an expression of free exchange, which is itself the immediate and logical consequence of the right of any individual to use and abuse all instruments of production. These three economic moments, which are in reality only one — the right to use and abuse, freedom of exchange and unrestricted competition — have the following consequences: each produces what he wants, how he wants, when he wants, where he wants; he produces well or he produces badly, too much or not enough, too late or too early, too dear or too cheap; no one knows whether he will sell, to whom he will sell, how he will sell, when he will sell, where he will sell; the same goes for buying. The producer is acquainted with neither the needs nor the resources, neither the demand nor the supply. He sells when he wants, then he can, where he wants, to whom he wants and at the price he wants. The same goes for buying. In all this he is at all times the plaything of chance, the slave of the law of the strongest, of the least pressed, of the richest.... While at one point there is a shortage of wealth, at another there is a surfeit and squandering of the same. While one producer sells a great deal, or at high prices and with an enormous profit, another sells nothing or sells at a loss.... Supply is ignorant of demand, and demand is ignorant of supply. You produce on the basis of a preference or a fashion prevalent among the consuming public; but by the time you are preparing to put your commodity on the market, the mood has passed and some other kind of product has come into fashion.... The inevitable consequences are continual and spreading bankruptcies, miscalculations, sudden collapses, and unexpected fortunes; trade crises, unemployment, periodic surfeits and shortages; instability and decline of wages and profits; the loss or enormous waste of wealth, of time, and of effort in the arena of fierce competition." (Pecqueur, p. 414-16)

Ricardo in his book (*On the Principles of Political Economy et al*) (rent of land): Nations are merely workshops for production, and man is a machine for consuming and producing. Human life is a piece of capital. Economic laws rule the world blindly. For Ricardo, men are nothing, the product everything. In Chapter 26, of the French translation, we read: "To an individual with a capital of 20,000 pounds, whose profits were 2,000 per annum, it would be a matter quite indifferent whether his capital would employ a hundred or a thousand men... is not the real interest of the nation similar? Provided its net real income, its rents and profits, be the same, it is of no importance whether the nation consists of 10 or 12 million inhabitants." (Ricardo, pp. 234-5)

"In truth," says M. de Sismondi, "it remains only to desire that the king, who has been left quite alone on the island, should, by continuously cranking up a number of automatons, get all England's work done." (J. C. L. Simonde de Sismondi, *Nouveaux principes d'economic politique*, 2 volumes, Paris, 1819, II, p. 331)

"The master who buys a worker's labor at a price so low that it is barely enough to meet his most pressing needs is responsible neither for the low wages nor the long hours of work: he himself is subject to the law which he imposes.... Misery is the product not so much of men as of the power of things." (Buret, I, p. 82)

"The inhabitants of many different parts of Great Britain have not capital sufficient to improve and cultivate all their lands. The wool of the southern counties of Scotland is, a great part of it, after a long land carriage through very bad roads, manufactured in Yorkshire, for want of capital to manufacture it at home. There are many little manufacturing towns in Great Britain, of which the inhabitants have not capital sufficient to transport the produce of their own industry to those distant markets where there is demand and consumption for it. If there are any merchants among them, they are properly only the agents of wealthier merchants who reside in some of the greater commercial cities." (Smith, I, pp. 326-7)

"The annual produce of the land and labor of any nation can be increased in its value by no other means but by increasing either the number of its productive laborers, or the productive powers of those laborers who had before been employed.... In either case, an additional capital is almost always required." (Smith, I, pp. 306-7)

"As the accumulation of stock must, in the nature of things, previous to the division of labor, so labor can be more and more subdivided in proportion only as stock is previously more and more accumulated. The quantity of materials which the same number of people can work up, increases in a great proportion as labor comes to be more and more subdivided; and as the operations of each workman are gradually reduced to a greater degree of simplicity, a variety of new machines come to be invented for facilitating and abridging these operations. As the division of labor advances, therefore, in order to give constant employment to an equal number of workmen, an equal stock of provisions, and a greater stock of materials and tools than what would have been necessary in a ruder state of things, must be accumulated beforehand. But the number of workmen in every branch of business generally increases with the division of labor in that branch, or rather it is the increase of their number which enables them to class and subdivide themselves in this manner." (Smith, I, pp. 241-2)

"As the accumulation of stock is previously necessary for carrying on this great improvement in the productive powers of labor, so that accumulation naturally leads to this improvement. The person who employs his stock in maintaining labor, necessarily wishes to employ it in such a manner as to produce as great a quantity of work as possible. He endeavors, therefore, both to make among his workmen the most proper distribution of employment, and to furnish them with the best machines which he can either invent or afford to purchase. His abilities in both these respects are generally in proportion to the extent of his stock, or to the number of people it can employ. The quantity of industry, therefore, not only increases in every country with the increase of the stock which employs it, but, in consequence of that increase, the same quantity of industry produces a much greater quantity of work." (Smith, I, p. 242)

Hence overproduction.

"More extensive combinations of productive forces... in trade and industry through the unification of more numerous and more varied human and natural forces for undertakings on a larger scale. Also, there are already a number of cases of closer links among the main branches of production themselves. Thus, large manufacturers will try to acquire large estates in order to avoid depending on others for at least a part of the raw materials they need for their industry; or they will set up a trading concern linked to their industrial enterprises and not only sell their own products but buy up and retail other sorts of goods to their workers. In England, where there are some factory owners who employ between 10- and 12,000 workers... similar combinations of different branches of production under the control of one man, small states or provinces within a state, are not uncommon. For example, the mine-owners near Birmingham recently took over the entire process of iron production, which was previously in the hands of several different entrepreneurs and owners. (See '*Der bergannische Distrikt bei Birmingham*', *Deutsche Vierteljahrsschrift*, no.3, 1838.) Finally, in the larger joint-stock companies, which have become so numerous, we find extensive combinations of the financial resources of many shareholders with the scientific and technical knowledge and skills of others to whom the execution of the work is entrusted. In this way, it is possible for many capitalists to apply their savings in a more diversified way and even invest them simultaneously in agricultural, industrial, and commercial production; as a result, their interests also become more diversified and the conflict between agricultural, industrial, and commercial interests begins to fade away. But the greater ease with which capital can be employed fruitfully in the most varied fields inevitably increases the conflict between the propertied and the propertyless classes." (Schulz, pp. 241-2)

The enormous profit which the landlords make out of misery. The greater the misery caused by industry, the higher the rent.

It is the same with the rate of interest on the vices of the proletariat. (Prostitution, drinking, the pawnbroker.)

The accumulation of capitals increases and the competition between them diminishes, as capital and landed property are united together in one hand and capital is enabled, because of its size, to combine different branches of production.

Indifference towards men. Smith's 20 lottery tickets. (Smith, I, p. 94)

Say's net and gross revenue.

Rent Of Land

The right of the landowners can be traced back to robbery. (Say, I, p. 136, n.2) Landowners, like all other men, love to reap where they never sowed, and demand a rent even for the natural produce of the land. (Smith, I, p. 44)

"The rent of land, it may be thought, is frequently no more than a reasonable profit or interest for the stock laid out by the landlord upon its improvement. This, no doubt, may be partly the case upon some occasions.... The landlord demands a rent even for unimproved land, and the supposed interest or profit upon the expense of improvement is generally an addition to this original rent. Those improvements, besides, are not always made by the stock of the landlord, but sometimes by that of the tenant. When the lease comes to be renewed, however, the landlord commonly demands the same augmentation of rent as if they had been all made by his own.

"He sometimes demands rents for what is altogether incapable of human improvements." (Smith, I, p. 131)

Smith gives as an example of this last case, kelp, a species of seaweed which, when burnt, yields an alkaline salt useful for making glass, soap, etc. It grows in several parts of Great Britain, especially in Scotland, but only upon such rocks as lie within the high water mark, which are twice every day covered with the sea and of which the produce, therefore, was never augmented by human industry. The landlord, however, whose estate is bounded by a kelp shore of this kind, demands a rent for it as much as for his corn fields. The sea in the neighborhood of the islands of Shetland is more than commonly abundant in fish, which make a great part of the subsistence of their inhabitants. But in order to profit by the produce of the water, they must have a habitation on the neighboring land. The rent of the landlord is in proportion, not to what the farmer can make by the land, but by what he can make both by the land and by the water.

"This rent may be considered as the produce of those power, the use of which the landlord lends to the farmer. It is greater or smaller according to the supposed extent of those powers, or in other words, according to the supposed natural of improved fertility of the land. It is the work of nature which remains after deducting or compensation everything which can be regarded as the work of man." (Smith, I, pp. 324-5)

"The rent of land, therefore, considered as the price paid for the use of land, is naturally a monopoly price. It is not at all proportioned to what the landlord may have laid out upon the improvement of the land, or to what he can afford to take; but to what the farmer can afford to give." (Smith, I, p. 131)

"They (landlords) are the only ones of the three orders whose revenue costs them neither labor nor care, but comes to them, as it were, of its own accord, and independent of any plan or project of their own. (Smith, I, p. 230)

We have already seen how the volume of rent depends upon the degree of fertility of the land.

"The rent of land not only varies with its fertility, whatever be its produce, but with its situation, whatever be its fertility." (Smith, I, p. 133)

"The produce of lands, mines, and fisheries, when their natural fertility is equal, is in proportion to the extent and proper application of the capitals employed about them. When the capitals are equal and equally well applied, it is in proportion to their natural fertility." (Smith, I, p. 249)

These proportions of Smith are important, because they reduce the rent land, where costs of production and size are equal, to the degree of fertility of the soil. This clearly demonstrates the perversion of concepts in political economy, which turns the fertility of the soil into an attribute of the landlord.

But let us now examine the relation between landlord and tenant.

"In adjusting the terms of the lease, the landlord endeavors to leave him no greater share of the product than what is sufficient to keep up the stock from which he furnishes the seed, pays the labor, and purchases and maintains the cattle and other instruments of husbandry, together with the ordinary profits of farming stock in the neighborhood. This is evidently the smallest share with which the tenant can content himself without being a loser, and the landlord seldom means to leave him any more. Whatever part of the produce, or, what is the same thing, whatever part of the price is over and above this share, he naturally intends to reserve himself as the rent of his land, which is evidently the highest the tenant can afford to pay in the actual circumstances of the land.... This portion... may still be considered as the natural rent of land, or the rent for which it is actually meant that land should for the most part be let." (Smith, I, p. 130-31)

"The landlords," says Say, "operate a certain kind of monopoly against the tenants. The demands for their commodity, which is land, is capable of an infinite expansion; but the supply can only increase up to a certain point.... The agreement reached between landlord and tenant is always as advantageous as possible to the former.... Apart from the advantage which he derives from the nature of the case, he derives a further one from his position, his larger fortune, his credit and his standing; but the first of these advantages is in itself enough to enable him at all times to profit from the favorable circumstances of the land. The opening of a canal or road and a growth in population and prosperity in a canton always raise the price of the rent.... What is more, even if the tenant makes improvement on his plot of land at his own expense, he can only benefit from this capital for the duration of his lease; when his lease runs out, this capital remains in the hands of the landlord. From this moment on, it is the latter who reaps the interest, even though it was not he who made the original outlay; for now the rent is raised proportionately." (Say, II, pp. 142-3)

"Rent, considered as the price paid for the use of land, is naturally the highest which the tenant can afford to pay in the actual circumstances of the land." (Smith, I, p. 130)

"The rent of an estate above ground commonly mounts to what is supposed to be a third of the gross produce; and it is generally a rent certain and independent of the occasional variations in the crop." (Smith, I, p. 153)

Rent "is seldom less than a fourth, and frequently more than a third of the whole produce." (Smith, I, p. 325)

Ground rent cannot be paid in the case of all commodities. For example, in many districts no rent is paid for stones.

"Such parts only of the produce of land can commonly be brought to market of which the ordinary price is sufficient to replace the stock which must be employed in bringing them thither, together with its ordinary profits. If the ordinary price is more than this, the surplus part of it will naturally go to the rent of the land. If it is not more, though the commodity may be brought to market, it can afford no rent to the landlord. Whether the price is or is not more depends upon the demand." (Smith, I, p. 132)

"Rent, it is to be observed, therefore, enters into the composition of the price of commodities in a different way from wages and profit. High or low wages and profit are the causes of high or low prices; high or low rent is the effect of it." (Smith, I, p. 132)

Among the products which always yield a rent is food.

"As men, like all other animals, naturally multiply in proportion the means of subsistence, food is always, more or less, in demand. It can always purchase or command a greater or smaller quantity of labor, and somebody can always be found who is willing to do something in order to obtain it. The quantity of labor, indeed, which it can purchase is not always equal to what it could maintain, if managed in the most economical manner, on account of the high wages which are sometimes given to labor. But it can always purchase such a quantity of labor as it can maintain, according to the rate at which that sort of labor is commonly maintained in the neighborhood.

"But land, in almost any situation, produces a greater quantity of food than what is sufficient to maintain all the labor necessary for bringing it to market in the most liberal way in which that labor is ever maintained. The surplus, too, is always more than sufficient to replace the stock which employed that labor, together with its profits. Something, therefore, always remains for a rent to the landlord." (Smith, I, p. 132-3)

"Food is, in this manner, not only the original source of rent, but every other part of the produce of land which afterwards affords rent derives that part of its value from the improvement of the powers of labor in producing food by means of the improvement and cultivation of land." (Smith, I, p. 150)

"Human food seems to be the only produce of land which always and necessarily affords a rent to the landlord." (Smith, I, p. 147)

"Countries are populous not in proportion to the number of people whom their produce can clothe and lodge, but in proportion to that of those whom it can feed." (Smith, I, p. 149)

"After food, clothing, and lodging, are the two great wants of mankind." (Smith, I, p. 147) They generally yield a rent, but not necessarily.

Let us now see how the landlord exploits everything which is to the benefit of society.

(1) The rent of land increases with population.

(2) We have already learnt from Say how ground rent rises with railways, etc., and with the improvement, security, and multiplication of the means of communication.

(3) "... every improvement in the circumstances of the society tends either directly or indirectly to raise the real rent of land, to increase the real wealth of the landlord, his power of purchasing the labor, or the produce of the labor of other people.

"The extension of improvement and cultivation tends to raise it directly. The landlord's share of the produce necessarily increases with an increase of the produce.

"That rise in the real price of those parts of the rude produce of land... the rise in the price of cattle, for example, tends too to raise the rent of land directly, and in a still greater proportion. The real value of the landlord's share, his real command of the labor of other people, not only rises with the real value of the produce, but the proportion of his share to the whole produce rises with it. That produce, after the rise in its real price, requires no more labor to collect it than before. A smaller proportion of it will, therefore, be sufficient to replace, with the ordinary profit, the stock which employs that labor. A greater proportion of it must, consequently, belong to the landlord." (Smith, I, pp. 228-29)

The greater the demand for raw products and the consequent rise in their value may partly be a result of the increase in population and the growth of their needs. But every new invention and every new application in manufacture of a raw material which was previously not used at all or only used rarely, makes for an increase in the ground rent. For example, the rent of coal-mines rose enormously when railways, steamships, etc., were introduced.

Besides this advantage which the landlord derives from manufacture, discoveries, and labor, there is another that we shall see presently.

(4) "All those improvements in the productive powers of labor, which tend directly to reduce the real price of manufactures, tend indirectly to raise the real rent of land. The landlord exchanges that part of his rude produce, which is over and above his own consumption, or what comes to the same thing, the price of that part of it, for manufactured produce. Whatever reduces the real price of the latter, raises that of the former. An equal opportunity of the former becomes thereby equivalent to a greater quantity of the latter; and the landlord is enabled to purchase a greater quantity of the

conveniences, ornaments, or luxuries, which he has occasion for." (Smith, I, pp. 228-29)

But it is foolish to conclude, as Smith does, that since the landlord exploits everything which is of benefit to society, the interest of the landlord is always identical with that of society. In the economic system, under which the rule of private property, the interest which any individual has in society is in inverse proportion to the interest which society has in him, just as the interest of the moneylender in the spendthrift is not at all identical with the interest of the spendthrift.

We mention only in passing the landlord's obsession with monopoly against the landed property of foreign countries, which is the reason, for example, for the corn laws. We shall similarly pass over mediaeval serfdom, slavery in the colonies and the distress of the rural population—the day-laborers—in Great Britain. Let us confine ourselves to the propositions of political economy itself.

(1) The landlord's interest in the well-being of society means, according to the principles of political economy, that he is interested in the growth of its population and its production and the increase of its needs, in a word, in the increase of wealth; and the increase of wealth is, if our previous observations are correct, identical with the growth of misery and slavery. The relationship of rising rents and rising misery is one example of the landlord's interest in society, for a rise in house rent also means a rise in ground rent—the interest on the land on which the house stands.

(2) According to the political economists themselves, the interest of the landlord is fiercely opposed to that of the tenant, and therefore of a considerable section of society.

(3) The landlord is in a position to demand more rent from the tenant the less wages the tenant pays out, and the more rent the landlord demands the further the tenant pushes down the wages. For this reason, the landlord's interest is just as opposed to that of the farm laborer as the manufacturer's is to that of the workers. It likewise pushes wages down to a minimum.

(4) Since a real reduction in the price of manufactured products puts up the rent of land, the landowner has a direct interest in depressing the wages of the factory worker, in competition among the capitalists, in overproduction and in all the misery occasioned by industry.

(5) So the interest of the landowner, far from being identical with the interest of society, is fiercely opposed to the interests of the

tenants, the farm laborers, the factory workers, and the capitalists. But, as a result of competition, the interest of one landowner is not even identical with that of another. We shall now take a look at competition.

Generally speaking, large landed property and small landed property are in the same relation to one another as large and small capital. In addition, however, there are special circumstances which lead, without fail, to the accumulation of large landed property and the swallowing up of small properties.

(1) Nowhere does the number of workers and the amount of equipment decline so greatly in proportion to the size of the stock as in landed property. Similarly, nowhere does the possibility of many-sided exploitation, the saving of proportion costs and the judicious division of labor increase more in proportion to that stock than in this sphere. Whatever the size of the plot, there is a certain minimum of tools required — a plough, a saw, etc. — below which it is impossible to go, whereas there is no such lowermost limit to the size of the property.

(2) Large landed property accumulated for itself the interest on the capital which the tenant has invested in the improvement of the land. Small landed property must employ its own capital. The entire profit on this capital is lost to the investor.

(3) While every social improvement benefits the large landed property, it harms the small one, since it makes an increasingly large amount of ready money necessary.

(4) There are two further important laws of this competition to be considered:

(a) "... the rent of the cultivated land, of which the produce is human food, regulates the rent of the greater part of the other cultivated land." (Smith, I, p. 144)

In the long run, only the large estate can produce sources of food such as cattle, etc. It is, therefore, in a position to regulate the rent of other land and force it down to a minimum.

The small landowner who works on his own account is, therefore, in the same relation to the big landowner as the craftsman who owns his own tools is to the factory owner. The small estate has become a mere tool. Ground rent disappears entirely for the small landowner; at the most, there remains to him the interest on his capital and the wages of his labor, for ground rent can be forced so low by competition that it becomes nothing more than the interest on capital not invested by the owner himself.

(b) Furthermore, we have already seen that given equal fertility and equally effective exploitation of lands, mines, and fisheries, the produce is in proportion to the extent of capital employed. Hence, the victory of the large landowner. Similarly, where equal amounts of capital are invested, the produce is in proportion to the degree of fertility. That is to say, where capitals are equal, victory goes to the owner of the more fertile land.

(c) "A mine of any kind may be said to be either fertile or barren, according as the quantity of mineral which can be brought from it by a certain quantity of labor is greater or less than what can be brought by an equal quantity from the greater part of other mines of the same kind." (Smith, I, p. 151)

"The most fertile coal-mine, too, regulates the price of coals at all the other mines in its neighborhood. Both the proprietor and the undertaker of the work find, the one that he can get a greater rent, the other that he can get a greater profit by somewhat underselling all their neighbors. Their neighbors are soon obliged to sell at the same price, though they cannot so well afford it, and though it always diminishes, and sometimes takes away altogether both their rent and their profit. Some works are abandoned altogether; others can afford no rent, and can be wrought only by the proprietor." (Smith, I, pp. 152-3)

"After the discover of the mines of Peru, the silver-mines of Europe were, the greater part of them, abandoned.... This was the case, too, with the ancient mines of Peru, after the discovery of those of Potosi." (Smith, I, p. 154)

What Smith says here of mines is more-or-less true of landed property in general.

(d) "The ordinary market price of land, it is to be observed, depends everywhere upon the ordinary market rate of interest... if the rent of land should fall short of the interest of money by a greater difference, nobody would buy the land, which would soon reduce its ordinary price. On the contrary, if the advantages should much more than compensate the difference, everybody would buy the land, which would soon raise its ordinary price." (Smith, I, p. 320)

If follows from this relation between ground rent and interest on money that ground rent must continue to fall until eventually only the richest people can afford to live from it. This means an increase in competition between those landowners who do not lease out their land. Some of them are ruined. There is once again an accumulation of large landed property.

This competition has the further consequence that a large part of landed property falls into the hands of the capitalists; thus, the capitalist becomes landowners, just as the smaller landowners are, in general, nothing more than capitalists. In this way, a part of large landed property becomes industrial.

So, the final consequence of the abolition of the distinction between capitalist and landowner — which means that, in general, there remain only two classes in the population: the working class and the capitalist class. This selling off of landed property, and transformation of such property into a commodity, marks the final collapse of the old aristocracy and the final victory of the aristocracy of money.

(1) We refuse to join in the sentimental tears which romanticism sheds on this account. Romanticism always confuses the infamy of selling off the land with the entirely reasonable and, within the system of private property, inevitable and desirable consequence of the selling off of private property in land. In the first place, feudal landed property is already in essence land which has been sold off, land which has been estranged from man and now confronts him in the shape of a handful of great lords.

In feudal landownership, we already find the domination of the earth as of an alien power over men. The serf is an appurtenance of the land. Similarly, the heir through primogeniture, the firstborn son, belongs to the land. It inherits him. The rule of private property begins with property in land, which is its basis. But in the system of feudal landownership, the lord at least appears to be king of the land. In the same way, there is still the appearance of a relationship between owner and land which is based on something more intimate than mere material wealth. The land is individualized with its lord, it acquires his status, it is baronial or ducal with him, has his privileges, his jurisdiction, his political position, etc. It appears as the inorganic body of its lord. Hence the proverb, *nulle terre sans maitre* ("No land without its master"), which expresses the blending of nobility and landed property. In the same way, the rule of landed property does not appear directly as the rule of mere capital. Its relationship to those dependent upon it is more like that of a fatherland. It is a sort of narrow personality.

In the same way, feudal landed property gives its name to its lord, as does a kingdom to its king. His family history, the history of his house, etc. — all this individualizes his estate for him, and formally turns it into his house, into a person. Similarly, the workers on the estate are not in the position of day-laborers; rather, they are partly the property of the landowner, as are serfs, and they are partly linked to him through a relationship based on respect, submissiveness, and duty. His relation to them is therefore directly political, and even has an agreeable aspect. Customs, character, etc., vary from one estate to another and appear to be one with their particular stretch of land; later, however, it is only a man's purse, and not his character or individuality, which ties him to the land. Finally, the feudal landowner makes no attempt to extract the maximum profit from his property. Rather, he consumes what is there and leaves the harvesting of it to his serfs and tenants. Such is the aristocratic condition of landownership, which sheds a romantic glory on its lords.

It is inevitable that this appearance should be abolished and that landed property, which is the root of private property, should be drawn entirely into the orbit of private property and become a commodity; that the rule of the property owner should appear as the naked rule of private property, of capital, divested of all political tincture; that the relationship between property owner and worker should be reduced to the economic relationship between the property owner and his property should come to an end, and that the property itself should become purely material wealth; that the marriage of interest with the land should take over from the marriage of honor, and that land, like man, should sink to the level of a venal object. It is inevitable that the root of landed property — sordid self-interest — should also manifest itself in its cynical form. It is inevitable that immovable monopoly should become mobile and restless monopoly, competition; and that the idle employment of the products of the sweat and blood of other people should become a brisk commerce in the same. Finally, it is inevitable under these conditions of competition that landed property, in the form of capital, should manifest its domination both over the working class and over the property owners themselves, inasmuch as the laws of the movement of capital are either ruining or raising them. In this way, the mediaeval saying *nulle terre sans seigneur* gives way to the modern saying *l'argent n'a pas de maitre* ("Money knows no master"), which is an expression of the complete domination of dead matter over men.

(2) The following observations can be made in connection with the controversy over whether or not to divide up landed property.

The division of landed property negates the large-scale monopoly of landed property, abolishes it, but only by generalizing it. It does not abolish the basis of monopoly, which is private property. It attacks the existence, but not the essence, of monopoly. The consequence is that it falls foul of the laws of private property. For to divide up landed property corresponds to the movement of competition in the industrial sphere. Apart from the economic disadvantages of this division of the instruments of labor and separation of labor (not to be confused with the division of labor; this is not a case of dividing up work among a number of individuals, but of each individual doing the same work; it is a multiplication of the same work), this division of the land, like competition in industry, inevitably leads to further accumulation.

So wherever landed property is divided up, monopoly will inevitably reappear in an even more repulsive form—unless, that is, the division of landed property itself is negated or abolished. This does not mean a return to feudal property, but the abolition (*Aufhebung*) of private property is land altogether. The first step in the abolition of monopoly is always to generalize and extend its existence. The abolition of monopoly, when it has reached its broadest and most comprehensive existence, is its complete destruction. Association, when applied to the land, retains the benefits of large landed property from an economic point of view and realizes for the first time the tendency inherent in the division of land, namely equality. At the same time, association restores man's intimate links to the land in a rational way, no longer mediated by serfdom, lordship, and an imbecile mystique of property. This is because the earth ceases to be an object of barter, and through free labor and free employment once again becomes authentic, personal property for man. One great advantage of the division of the land is that its masses, who are no longer prepared to tolerate servitude, are destroyed by property in a different way from those in industry.

As for large landed property, its apologists have always sophistically identified the economic advantages inherent in large-scale agriculture with large landed property, as if these advantages would not on the one hand attain their fullest degree of development and on the other hand become socially useful for the first time once property abolished. Similarly, they have attacked the trading spirit of the small landowners, as if large-scale landownership, even in its feudal form, did not already contain within it the elements of barter — not to mention the modern English form, in which the feudalism of the landowner is combined with the huckstering and the industry of the tenant farmer.

Just as large-scale landed property can return the reproach of monopoly made against it by the advocated of division of the land, for the division of the land is also based on the monopoly of private property, so can the advocates of division return the reproach of partition, for partition of the land also exists — though in a rigid, ossified form — on the large estates. Indeed, division is the universal basis of private property. Besides, as the division of landed property leads once more to large landed property in the form of capital wealth, feudal landed property inevitably advances towards division or at least falls into the hands of the capitalists, however much it might twist and turn.

For large-scale landed property, as in England, drives the overwhelming majority of the population into the arms of industry and reduces its own workers to total misery. In this way, it creates and increases the power of its enemy, capital and industry, by driving the poor and an entire range of activities over to the other side. It makes the majority of the country industrial, and hence antagonistic to landed property. Where industry has acquired great power, as in England, it gradually forces large landed property to give up its monopoly against foreign countries and obliges it to compete with foreign landed property. For under the rule of industry, landed property could maintain its feudal proportions only by means of a monopoly against foreign countries, so as to protect itself against the universal laws of trade which contradict its feudal nature. Once exposed to competition, it is forced to obey the laws of competition, just like any other commodity which is subject to them. It too begins to fluctuate, to increase and diminish, to fly from one hand into another, and no law is any longer capable of keeping it in a few predestined hands, or, at any event, surrender to the power of the industrial capitalists.

Finally, large landed property, which has been forcibly preserved in this way and which has given rise alongside itself to an extensive industry, leads more rapidly to a crisis than does the division of landed property, alongside which the power of industry invariably takes second place.

It is clear from the case of England that large landed property has cast off its feudal character and assumed an industrial character insofar as it wants to make as much money as possible. It yields the owner the biggest possible rent and the tenant the biggest possible profit on his capital. As a consequence, the agricultural workers have already been reduced to a minimum, and the class of tenant farmers already represents within landed property the might of industry and capital. As a result of foreign competition, ground rent more or less ceases to be an independent source of income. A large part of the landowners is forced to take over from the tenants, some of whom are consequently reduced to the proletariat. On the other hand, many tenants will take possession of landed property; for the big landowners, who have given themselves up for the most part to squandering their comfortable revenue and are generally not capable of large-scale agricultural management, in many cases have neither the capital nor the ability to exploit the land. Therefore, a section of the big landowners is also ruined. Eventually wages, which have already been reduced to a minimum, must be reduced even further in order to meet the new competition. This then leads necessarily to revolution.

Landed property had to develop in each of these two ways, in order to experience in both of them its necessary decline; just as industry had to ruin itself both in the form of monopoly and in the form of competition before it could believe in man.

Estranged Labor

We have started out from the premises of political economy. We have accepted its language and its laws. We presupposed private property; the separation of labor, capital, and land, and likewise of wages, profit, and capital; the division of labor; competition; the conception of exchange value, etc. From political economy itself, using its own words, we have shown that the worker sinks to the level of a commodity, and moreover the most wretched commodity of all; that the misery of the worker is in inverse proportion to the power and volume of his production; that the necessary consequence of competition is the accumulation of capital in a few hands and hence the restoration of monopoly in a more terrible form; and that, finally, the distinction between capitalist and landlord, between agricultural worker and industrial worker, disappears and the whole of society must split into the two classes of property owners and propertyless workers.

Political economy proceeds from the fact of private property. It does not explain it. It grasps the material process of private property, the process through which it actually passes, in general and abstract formulae which it then takes as laws. It does not comprehend these laws—i.e., it does not show how they arise from the nature of private property. Political economy fails to explain the reason for the division between labor and capital. For example, when it defines the relation of wages to profit, it takes the interests of the capitalists as the basis of its analysis—i.e., it assumes what it is supposed to explain. Similarly, competition is frequently brought into the argument and explained in terms of external circumstances. Political economy teaches us nothing about the extent to which these external and apparently accidental circumstances are only the expression of a necessary development. We have seen how exchange itself appears to political economy as an accidental fact. The only wheels which political economy sets in motion are greed, and the war of the avaricious—Competition.

Precisely because political economy fails to grasp the interconnections within the movement, it was possible to oppose, for example, the doctrine of competition to the doctrine of monopoly, the doctrine of craft freedom to the doctrine of the guild, and the doctrine of the division of landed property to the doctrine of the great estate; for competition, craft freedom, and division of landed property were developed and conceived only as accidental, deliberate, violent consequences of monopoly, of the guilds, and of feudal property, and not as their necessary, inevitable, and natural consequences.

We now have to grasp the essential connection between private property, greed, the separation of labor, capital and landed property, exchange and competition, value and the devaluation of man, monopoly, and competition, etc.—the connection between this entire system of estrangement and the money system.

We must avoid repeating the mistake of the political economist, who bases his explanations on some imaginary primordial condition. Such a primordial condition explains nothing. It simply pushes the question into the grey and nebulous distance. It assumes as facts and events what it is supposed to deduce—namely, the necessary relationships between two things, between, for example, the division of labor and exchange. Similarly, theology explains the origin of evil by the fall of Man—i.e., it assumes as a fact in the form of history what it should explain.

We shall start out from a present-day economic fact.

The worker becomes poorer the more wealth he produces, the more his production increases in power and extent. The worker becomes an ever cheaper commodity the more commodities he produces. The devaluation of the human world grows in direct proportion to the increase in value of the world of things. Labor not only produces commodities; it also produces itself and the workers as a commodity and it does so in the same proportion in which it produces commodities in general.

This fact simply means that the object that labor produces, it product, stands opposed to it as something alien, as a power independent of the producer. The product of labor is labor embodied and made material in an object, it is the objectification of labor. The realization of labor is its objectification. In the sphere of political economy, this realization of labor appears as a loss of reality for the worker, objectification as loss of and bondage to the object, and appropriation as estrangement, as alienation.

So much does the realization of labor appear as loss of reality that the worker loses his reality to the point of dying of starvation. So much does objectification appear as loss of the object that the worker is robbed of the objects he needs most not only for life but also for work. Work itself becomes an object which he can only obtain through an enormous effort and with spasmodic interruptions. So much does the appropriation of the object appear as estrangement that the more objects the worker produces the fewer can he possess and the more he falls under the domination of his product, of capital.

All these consequences are contained in this characteristic, that the workers is related to the product of labor as to an alien object. For it is clear that, according to this premise, the more the worker exerts himself in his work, the more powerful the alien, objective world becomes which he brings into being over against himself, the poorer he and his inner world become, and the less they belong to him. It is the same in religion. The more man puts into God, the less he retains within himself. The worker places his life in the object; but now it no longer belongs to him, but to the object. The greater his activity, therefore, the fewer objects the worker possesses. What the product of his labor is, he is not. Therefore, the greater this product, the less is he himself. The externalization of the worker in his product means not only that his labor becomes an object, an external existence, but that it exists outside him, independently of him and alien to him, and beings to confront him as an autonomous power; that the life which he has bestowed on the object confronts him as hostile and alien.

Let us not take a closer look at objectification, at the production of the worker, and the estrangement, the loss of the object, of his product, that this entails.

The workers can create nothing without nature, without the sensuous external world. It is the material in which his labor realizes itself, in which it is active and from which, and by means of which, it produces.

But just as nature provides labor with the means of life, in the sense of labor cannot live without objects on which to exercise itself, so also it provides the means of life in the narrower sense, namely the means of physical subsistence of the worker.

The more the worker appropriates the external world, sensuous nature, through his labor, the more he deprives himself of the means of life in two respects: firstly, the sensuous external world becomes less and less an object belonging to his labor, a means of life of his labor; and, secondly, it becomes less and less a means of life in the immediate sense, a means for the physical subsistence of the worker.

In these two respects, then, the worker becomes a slave of his object; firstly, in that he receives an object of labor, i.e., he receives work, and, secondly, in that he receives means of subsistence. Firstly, then, so that he can exists as a worker, and secondly as a physical subject. The culmination of this slavery is that it is only as a worker that he can maintain himself as a physical subject and only as a physical subject that he is a worker.

(The estrangement of the worker in his object is expressed according to the laws of political economy in the following way:

the more the worker produces, the less he has to consume;

the more value he creates, the more worthless he becomes;

the more his product is shaped, the more misshapen the worker;

the more civilized his object, the more barbarous the worker;

the more powerful the work, the more powerless the worker;

the more intelligent the work, the duller the worker and the more he becomes a slave of nature.)

Political economy conceals the estrangement in the nature of labor by ignoring the direct relationship between the worker (labor) and production. It is true that labor produces marvels for the rich, but it produces privation for the worker. It produces palaces, but hovels for the worker. It produces beauty, but deformity for the worker. It replaces labor by machines, but it casts some of the workers back into barbarous forms of labor and turns others into machines. It produces intelligence, but it produces idiocy and cretinism for the worker.

The direct relationship of labor to its products is the relationship of the worker to the objects of his production. The relationship of the rich man to the objects of production and to production itself is only a consequence of this first relationship, and confirms it. Later, we shall consider this second aspect. Therefore, when we ask what is the essential relationship of labor, we are asking about the relationship of the worker to production.

Up to now, we have considered the estrangement, the alienation of the worker, only from one aspect—i.e., his relationship to the products of his labor. But estrangement manifests itself not only in the result, but also in the act of production, within the activity of production itself. How could the product of the worker's activity confront him as something alien if it were not for the fact that in the act of production he was estranging himself from himself? After all, the product is simply the resume of the activity, of the production. So if the product of labor is alienation, production itself must be active alienation, the alienation of activity, the activity of alienation. The estrangement of the object of labor merely summarizes the estrangement, the alienation in the activity of labor itself.

What constitutes the alienation of labor?

Firstly, the fact that labor is external to the worker—i.e., does not belong to his essential being; that he, therefore, does not confirm himself in his work, but denies himself, feels miserable and not happy, does not develop free mental and physical energy, but mortifies his flesh and ruins his mind. Hence, the worker feels himself only when he is not working; when he is working, he does not feel himself. He is at home when he is not working, and not at home when he is working. His labor is, therefore, not voluntary but forced, it is forced labor. It is, therefore, not the satisfaction of a need but a mere means to satisfy needs outside itself. Its alien character is clearly demonstrated by the fact that as soon as no physical or other compulsion exists, it is shunned like the plague. External labor, labor in which man alienates himself, is a labor of self-sacrifice, of mortification. Finally, the external character of labor for the worker is demonstrated by the fact that it belongs not to him but to another, and that in it he belongs not to himself but to another. Just as in religion the spontaneous activity of the human imagination, the human brain, and the human heart, detaches itself from the individual and reappears as the alien activity of a god or of a devil, so the activity of the worker is not his own spontaneous activity. It belongs to another, it is a loss of his self.

The result is that man (the worker) feels that he is acting freely only in his animal functions — eating, drinking, and procreating, or at most in his dwelling and adornment — while in his human functions, he is nothing more than animal.

It is true that eating, drinking, and procreating, etc., are also genuine human functions. However, when abstracted from other aspects of human activity, and turned into final and exclusive ends, they are animal.

We have considered the act of estrangement of practical human activity, of labor, from two aspects: (1) the relationship of the worker to the product of labor as an alien object that has power over him. The relationship is, at the same time, the relationship to the sensuous external world, to natural objects, as an alien world confronting him, in hostile opposition. (2) The relationship of labor to the act of production within labor. This relationship is the relationship of the worker to his own activity as something which is alien and does not belong to him, activity as passivity, power as impotence, procreation as emasculation, the worker's own physical and mental energy, his personal life — for what is life but activity? — as an activity directed against himself, which is independent of him and does not belong to him. Self-estrangement, as compared with the estrangement of the object mentioned above.

We now have to derive a third feature of estranged labor from the two we have already examined.

Man is a species-being, not only because he practically and theoretically makes the species — both his own and those of other things — his object, but also — and this is simply another way of saying the same thing — because he looks upon himself as the present, living species, because he looks upon himself as a universal and therefore free being.

Species-life, both for man and for animals, consists physically in the fact that man, like animals, lives from inorganic nature; and because man is more universal than animals, so too is the area of inorganic nature from which he lives more universal. Just as plants, animals, stones, air, light, etc., theoretically form a part of human consciousness, partly as objects of science and partly as objects of art—his spiritual inorganic nature, his spiritual means of life, which he must first prepare before he can enjoy and digest them—so, too, in practice they form a part of human life and human activity. In a physical sense, man lives only from these natural products, whether in the form of nourishment, heating, clothing, shelter, etc. The universality of man manifests itself in practice in that universality which makes the whole of nature his inorganic body, (1) as a direct means of life and (2) as the matter, the object, and the tool of his life activity. Nature is man's inorganic body—that is to say, nature insofar as it is not the human body. Man lives from nature—i.e., nature is his body—and he must maintain a continuing dialogue with it is he is not to die. To say that man's physical and mental life is linked to nature simply means that nature is linked to itself, for man is a part of nature.

Estranged labor not only (1) estranges nature from man and (2) estranges man from himself, from his own function, from his vital activity; because of this, it also estranges man from his species. It turns his species-life into a means for his individual life. Firstly, it estranges species-life and individual life, and, secondly, it turns the latter, in its abstract form, into the purpose of the former, also in its abstract and estranged form.

For in the first place labor, life activity, productive life itself, appears to man only as a means for the satisfaction of a need, the need to preserve physical existence. But productive life is species-life. It is life-producing life. The whole character of a species, its species-character, resides in the nature of its life activity, and free conscious activity constitutes the species-character of man. Life appears only as a means of life.

The animal is immediately one with its life activity. It is not distinct from that activity; it is that activity. Man makes his life activity itself an object of his will and consciousness. He has conscious life activity. It is not a determination with which he directly merges. Conscious life activity directly distinguishes man from animal life activity. Only because of that is he a species-being. Or, rather, he is a conscious being—i.e., his own life is an object for him, only because he is a species-being. Only because of that is his activity free activity.

Estranged labor reverses the relationship so that man, just because he is a conscious being, makes his life activity, his being, a mere means for his existence.

The practical creation of an objective world, the fashioning of inorganic nature, is proof that man is a conscious species-being—i.e., a being which treats the species as its own essential being or itself as a species-being. It is true that animals also produce. They build nests and dwelling, like the bee, the beaver, the ant, etc. But they produce only their own immediate needs or those of their young; they produce only when immediate physical need compels them to do so, while man produces even when he is free from physical need and truly produces only in freedom from such need; they produce only themselves, while man reproduces the whole of nature; their products belong immediately to their physical bodies, while man freely confronts his own product. Animals produce only according to the standards and needs of the species to which they belong, while man is capable of producing according to the standards of every species and of applying to each object its inherent standard; hence, man also produces in accordance with the laws of beauty.

It is, therefore, in his fashioning of the objective that man really proves himself to be a species-being. Such production is his active species-life. Through it, nature appears as his work and his reality. The object of labor is, therefore, the objectification of the species-life of man: for man produces himself not only intellectually, in his consciousness, but actively and actually, and he can therefore contemplate himself in a world he himself has created. In tearing away the object of his production from man, estranged labor therefore tears away from him his species-life, his true species-objectivity, and transforms his advantage over animals into the disadvantage that his inorganic body, nature, is taken from him.

In the same way as estranged labor reduces spontaneous and free activity to a means, it makes man's species-life a means of his physical existence.

Consciousness, which man has from his species, is transformed through estrangement so that species-life becomes a means for him.

(3) Estranged labor, therefore, turns man's species-being—both nature and his intellectual species-power—into a being alien to him and a means of his individual existence. It estranges man from his own body, from nature as it exists outside him, from his spiritual essence, his human existence.

(4) An immediate consequence of man's estrangement from the product of his labor, his life activity, his species-being, is the estrangement of man from man. When man confronts himself, he also confronts other men. What is true of man's relationship to his labor, to the product of his labor, and to himself, is also true of his relationship to other men, and to the labor and the object of the labor of other men.

In general, the proposition that man is estranged from his species-being means that each man is estranged from the others and that all are estranged from man's essence.

Man's estrangement, like all relationships of man to himself, is realized and expressed only in man's relationship to other men.

In the relationship of estranged labor, each man therefore regards the other in accordance with the standard and the situation in which he as a worker finds himself.

We started out from an economic fact, the estrangement of the worker and of his production. We gave this fact conceptual form: estranged, alienated labor. We have analyzed this concept, and in so doing merely analyzed an economic fact.

Let us now go on to see how the concept of estranged, alienated labor must express and present itself in reality.

If the product of labor is alien to me, and confronts me as an alien power, to whom does it then belong?

To a being other than me.

Who is this being?

The gods? It is true that in early times most production — e.g., temple building, etc., in Egypt, India, and Mexico — was in the service of the gods, just as the product belonged to the gods. But the gods alone were never the masters of labor. The same is true of nature. And what a paradox it would be if the more man subjugates nature through his labor and the more divine miracles are made superfluous by the miracles of industry, the more he is forced to forgo the joy or production and the enjoyment of the product out of deference to these powers.

The alien being to whom labor and the product of labor belong, in whose service labor is performed, and for whose enjoyment the product of labor is created, can be none other than man himself.

If the product of labor does not belong to the worker, and if it confronts him as an alien power, this is only possible because it belongs to a man other than the worker. If his activity is a torment for him, it must provide pleasure and enjoyment for someone else. Not the gods, not nature, but only man himself can be this alien power over men.

Consider the above proposition that the relationship of man to himself becomes objective and real for him only through his relationship to other men. If, therefore, he regards the product of his labor, his objectified labor, as an alien, hostile, and powerful object which is independent of him, then his relationship to that object is such that another man—alien, hostile, powerful, and independent of him—is its master. If he relates to his own activity as unfree activity, then he relates to it as activity in the service, under the rule, coercion, and yoke of another man.

Every self-estrangement of man from himself and nature is manifested in the relationship he sets up between other men and himself and nature. Thus, religious self-estrangement is necessarily manifested in the relationship between layman and priest, or, since we are dealing here with the spiritual world, between layman and mediator, etc. In the practical, real world, self-estrangement can manifest itself only in the practical, real relationship to other men. The medium through which estrangement progresses is itself a practical one. So through estranged labor man not only produces his relationship to the object and to the act of production as to alien and hostile powers; he also produces the relationship in which other men stand to his production and product, and the relationship in which he stands to these other men. Just as he creates his own production as a loss of reality, a punishment, and his own product as a loss, a product which does not belong to him, so he creates the domination of the non-producer over production and its product. Just as he estranges from himself his own activity, so he confers upon the stranger and activity which does not belong to him.

Up to now, we have considered the relationship only from the side of the worker. Later on, we shall consider it from the side of the non-worker.

Thus, through estranged, alienated labor, the worker creates the relationship of another man, who is alien to labor and stands outside it, to that labor. The relation of the worker to labor creates the relation of the capitalist—or whatever other word one chooses for the master of labor—to that labor. Private property is therefore the product, result, and necessary consequence of alienated labor, of the external relation of the worker to nature and to himself.

Private property thus derives from an analysis of the concept of alienated labor—i.e., alienated man, estranged labor, estranged life, estranged man.

It is true that we took the concept of alienated labor (alienated life) from political economy as a result of the movement of private property. But it is clear from an analysis of this concept that, although private property appears as the basis and cause of alienated labor, it is in fact its consequence, just as the gods were originally not the cause but the effect of the confusion in men's minds. Later, however, this relationship becomes reciprocal.

It is only when the development of private property reaches its ultimate point of culmination that this, its secret, re-emerges; namely, that is (a) the product of alienated labor, and (b) the means through which labor is alienated, the realization of this alienation.

This development throws light upon a number of hitherto unresolved controversies.

(1) Political economy starts out from labor as the real soul of production and yet gives nothing to labor and everything to private property. Proudhon has dealt with this contradiction by deciding for labor and against private property (see his 1840 pamphlet, *Qu'est-ce que la propriete?*). But we have seen that this apparent contradiction is the contradiction of estranged labor with itself and that political economy has merely formulated laws of estranged labor.

It, therefore, follows for us that wages and private property are identical: for there the product, the object of labor, pays for the labor itself, wages are only a necessary consequence of the estrangement of labor; similarly, where wages are concerned, labor appears not as an end in itself but as the servant of wages. We intend to deal with this point in more detail later on: for the present we shall merely draw a few conclusions.

An enforced rise in wages (disregarding all other difficulties, including the fact that such an anomalous situation could only be prolonged by force) would therefore be nothing more than better pay for slaves and would not mean an increase in human significance or dignity for either the worker or the labor.

Even the equality of wages, which Proudhon demands, would merely transform the relation of the present-day worker to his work into the relation of all men to work. Society would then be conceived as an abstract capitalist.

Wages are an immediate consequence of estranged labor, and estranged labor is the immediate cause of private property. If the one falls, then the other must fall too.

(2) It further follows from the relation of estranged labor to private property that the emancipation of society from private property, etc., from servitude, is expressed in the political form of the emancipation of the workers. This is not because it is only a question of their emancipation, but because in their emancipation is contained universal human emancipation. The reason for this universality is that the whole of human servitude is involved in the relation of the worker to production, and all relations of servitude are nothing but modifications and consequences of this relation.

Just as we have arrived at the concept of private property through an analysis of the concept of estranged, alienated labor, so with the help of these two factors it is possible to evolve all economic categories, and in each of these categories—e.g., trade, competition, capital, money—we shall identify only a particular and developed expression of these basic constituents.

But, before we go on to consider this configuration, let us try to solve two further problems.

(1) We have to determine the general nature of private property, as it has arisen out of estranged labor, in its relation to truly human and social property.

(2) We have taken the estrangement of labor, its alienation, as a fact and we have analyzed that fact. How, we now ask, does man come to alienate his labor, to estrange it? How it this estrangement founded in the nature of human development? We have already gone a long way towards solving this problem by transforming the question of the origin of private property into the question of the relationship of alienated labor to the course of human development. For, in speaking of private property, one imagines that one is dealing with something external to man. In speaking of labor, one is dealing immediately with man himself. This new way of formulating the problem already contains its solution.

As to (1): The general nature of private property and its relationship to truly human property.

Alienated labor has resolved itself for us into two component parts, which mutually condition one another, or which are merely different expressions of one and the same relationship. Appropriation appears as estrangement, as alienation; and alienation appears as appropriation, estrangement as true admission to citizenship.

We have considered the one aspect, alienated labor in relation to the worker himself — i.e., the relation of alienated labor to itself. And as product, as necessary consequence of this relationship, we have found the property relation of the non-worker to the worker and to labor. Private property as the material, summarized expression of alienated labor embraces both relations — the relation of the worker to labor and to the product of his labor and the non-workers, and the relation of the non-worker to the worker and to the product of his labor.

We have already seen that, in relation to the worker who appropriates nature through his labor, appropriation appears as estrangement, self-activity as activity for another and of another, vitality as a sacrifice of life, production of an object as loss of that object to an alien power, to an alien man. Let us now consider the relation between this man, who is alien to labor and to the worker, and the worker, labor, and the object of labor.

The first thing to point out is that everything which appears for the worker as an activity of alienation, of estrangement, appears for the non-worker as a situation of alienation, of estrangement.

Secondly, the real, practical attitude of the worker in production and to the product (as a state of mind) appears for the non-worker who confronts him as a theoretical attitude.

Thirdly, the non-worker does everything against the worker which the worker does against himself, but he does not do against himself what he does against the worker.

Let us take a closer look at these three relationships.

(First Manuscript breaks off here.)

Second Manuscript
The Relationship Of Private Property
... forms the interest on his capital. The worker is the subjective manifestation of the fact that capital is man completely lost to himself, just as capital is the objective manifestation of the fact that labor is man lost to himself. But the worker has the misfortune to be a living capital, and, hence, a capital with needs, which forfeits its interest and hence its existence every moment it is not working. As capital, the value of the worker rises or falls in accordance with supply and demand, and even in a physical sense his existence, his life, was and is

treated as a supply of a commodity, like any other commodity. The worker produces capital and capital produces him, which means that he produces himself; man as a worker, as a commodity, is the product of this entire cycle. The human properties of man as a worker—man who is nothing more than a worker—exist only insofar as they exist for a capital which is alien to him. But, because each is alien to the other, and stands in an indifferent, external, and fortuitous relationship to it, this alien character inevitably appears as something real. So, soon as it occurs to capital—whether from necessity or choice—not to exist any longer for the worker, he no longer exists for himself; he has no work, and hence no wages, and since he exists not as a man but as a worker, he might just as well have buried himself, starve to death, etc. The worker exists as a worker only when he exists for himself as capital, and he exists as capital only when capital exists for him. The existence of capital is his existence, his life, for it determines the content of his life in a manner indifferent to him. Political economy, therefore, does not recognize the unoccupied worker, the working man insofar as he is outside this work relationship. The swindler, the cheat, the beggar, the unemployed, the starving, the destitute, and the criminal working man are figures which exist not for it, but only for other eyes—for the eyes of doctors, judges, grave-diggers, beadles, etc. Nebulous figures which do not belong within the province of political economy. Therefore, as far as political economy is concerned, the requirements of the worker can be narrowed down to one: the need to support him while he is working and prevent the race of workers from dying out. Wages, therefore, have exactly the same meaning as the maintenance and upkeep of any other productive instrument, or as the consumption of capital in general which is necessary if it is to reproduce itself with interest—e.g., the oil which is applied to wheels to keep them turning. Wages, therefore, belong to the necessary costs of capital and of the capitalist, and must not be in excess of this necessary amount. It was, therefore, quite logical for the English factory owners, before the Amendment Bill of 1834 (Poor Laws), to deduct from the worker's wages the public alms which he received from the Poor Rate, and to consider these aims as an integral part of those wages.

Production does not produce man only as a commodity, the human commodity, man in the form of a commodity; it also produces him as a mentally and physically dehumanized being... Immorality, malformation, stupidity of workers and capitalists... the human commodity... A great advance by Ricardo, Mill, etc., on Smith and Say, to declare the existence of the human being—the greater or lesser human productivity of the commodity—to be indifferent and even harmful. The real aim of production is not how many workers a particular sum of capital can support, but how much interest it brings in and how much it saves each year. Similarly, English political economy took a big step forward, and a logical one, when—while acknowledging labor as the sole principle of political economy—it showed with complete clarity that wages and interest on capital are inversely related and that, as a rule, the capitalist can push up his profits only by forcing down wages, and vice versa. Clearly, the normal relationship is not one in which the customer is cheated, but in which the capitalist and the worker cheat each other. The relation of private property contains latent within itself the relation of private property as labor, the relation of private property as capital, and the connection of these two. On the one hand, we have the production of human activity as labor—i.e., as an activity wholly alien to itself, to man, and to nature, and hence to consciousness and vital expression, the abstract existence of man as a mere workman who, therefore, tumbles day-after-day from his fulfilled nothingness into absolute nothingness, into his social and, hence, real non-existence; and, on the other, the production of the object of human labor as capital, in which all the natural and social individuality of the object is extinguished and private property has lost its natural and social quality (i.e., has lost all political and social appearances and is not even apparently tainted with any human relationships), in which the same capital stays the same in the most varied natural and social circumstance, totally indifferent to its real content. This contradiction, driven to its utmost limit, is necessarily the limit, the culmination and the decline of the whole system of private property.

It is, therefore, yet another great achievement of recent English political economy to have declared ground rent to be the difference between the interest on the worst and the best land under cultivation, to have confuted the romantic illusions of the land-owner—his alleged social importance and the identity of his interest with the interest of society, which Adam Smith continued to propound after the Physiocrats—and to have anticipated and prepared the changes in reality which will transform the land-owner into a quite ordinary and prosaic capitalist, thereby simplifying the contradiction, bringing it to a head and hastening its resolution. Land as land and ground rent as ground rent have thereby lost their distinction in rank and have become dumb capital and interest—or, rather, capital and interest which only talk hard cash. The distinction between capital and land, between profit and ground rent, and the distinction between both and wages, industry, agriculture, and immovable and movable private property, is not one which is grounded in the nature of things, it is a historical distinction, a fixed moment in the formation and development of the opposition between capital and labor. In industry, etc., as opposed to immovable landed property, only the manner in which industry first arose and the opposition to agriculture within which industry developed, are expressed. As a special kind of work, as an essential, important, and life-encompassing distinction, this distinction between industry and agriculture survives only as long as industry (town life) is developing in opposition to landed property (aristocratic feudal life) and continues to bear the feudal characteristics of its opposite in the form of monopoly, crafts, guilds, corporations, etc. Given these forms, labor continues to have an apparently social meaning, the meaning of genuine community, and has not yet reached the stage of indifference towards its content and of complete being-for-itself—i.e., of abstraction from all other being and, hence, of liberated capital.

But, the necessary development of labor is liberated industry constituted for itself as such, and liberated capital. The power of industry over its antagonist is, at once, manifested in the emergence of agriculture as an actual industry, whereas previously most of the work was left to the soil itself and to the slave of the soil, through whom the soil cultivated itself. With the transformation of the slave into a free worker—i.e., a hireling—the landowner himself is transformed into a master of industry, a capitalist. This transformation at first took place through the agency of the tenant farmer. But the tenant farmer is the representative, the revealed secret, of the landowner; only through him does the landowner have his economic existence, his existence as a property owner—for the ground rent of his land exists only because of the competition between the tenants. So, in the person of the tenant the landowner has already essentially become a common capitalist. And this must also be effected in reality; the capitalist engaged in agriculture—the tenant—must become a landlord, or vice-versa. The industrial trade of the tenant is the industrial trade of the landlord, for the existence of the former posits the existence of the latter.

But, remembering their conflicting origins and descent, the landowner sees the capitalist as his presumptuous, liberated, and enriched slave of yesterday, and himself as a capitalist who is threatened by him; the capitalist sees the landowner as the idle, cruel, and egotistical lord of yesterday; he knows that the landowner is harmful to him as a capitalist, and yet that he owes his entire present social position, his possessions and his pleasures, to industry; the capitalist sees in the landowner the antithesis of free industry and free capital, which is independent of all natural forces—this opposition is extremely bitter, and each side tells the truth about the other. One only need read the attacks launched by immovable on movable property, and vice-versa, in order to gain a clear picture of their respective worthlessness. The land-owner emphasizes the noble lineage of his property, the feudal reminiscences, the poetry of remembrance, his high-flown nature, his political importance, etc. When he is talking economics, he avows that agriculture alone is productive. At the same time, he depicts his opponent as a wily, huckstering, censorious, deceitful, greedy, mercenary, rebellious, heartless, and soulless racketeer who is estranged from his community and busily trades it away, a profiteering, pimping, servile, smooth, affected trickster, a desiccated sharper who breeds, nourishes, and encourages competition and pauperism, crime and the dissolution of all social ties, who is without honor, principles, poetry, substance, or anything else. (See, among others, the Physiocrat Bergasse, whom Camille Desmoulins has already flayed in his journal Revolutions de France et de Brabant; see also von Vincke, Lancizolle, Haller, Leo, Kosegarten, and Sismondi.)

(See also the pompous Old Hegelian theologian Funke, who, according to Herr Leo, told with tears in his eyes how a slave had refused, when serfdom was abolished, to cease being a noble possession. See also Justus Moser's Patriotische Phantasien, which are distinguished by the fact that they never for one moment leave the staunch, petty-bourgeois, "Home-baked", ordinary, narrow-minded horizon of the philistine, and, yet still, remain pure fantasy. It is this contradiction which has made them so plausible to the German mind.)

Movable property, for its part, points to the miracles of industry and change. It is the child, the legitimate, only-begotten son, of the modern age. It feels sorry for its opponent, whom it sees as a half-wit unenlightened as to his own nature (an assessment no one could disagree with) and eager to replace moral capital and free labor by brute, immoral force and serfdom. It paints him as a Don Quixote, who, under the veneer of directness, probity, the general interest, and stability, hides an inability and evil intent. It brands him as a cunning monopolist. It discountenances his reminiscences, his poetry, and his enthusiastic gushings, by a historical and sarcastic recital of the baseness, cruelty, degradation, prostitution, infamy, anarchy, and revolt forged in the workshops of his romantic castles.

Movable property, itself, claims to have won political freedom for the world, to have loosed the chains of civil society, to have linked together different worlds, to have given rise to trade, which encourages friendship between peoples and to have created a pure morality and a pleasing culture; to have given the people civilized instead of crude wants and the means with which it satisfy them. The landowner, on the other hand—this idle and vexatious speculator in grain—puts up the price of the people's basic provisions and thereby forces the capitalist to put up wages without being able to raise productivity, so making it difficult, and eventually impossible, to increase the annual income of the nation and to accumulate the capital which is necessary if work is to be provided for the people and wealth for the country. As a result, the landowner brings about a general decline. Moreover, he inordinately exploits all the advantages of modern civilization without doing the least thing in return, and without mitigating a single one of his feudal prejudices. Finally, the landlord—for whom the cultivation of the land and the soil itself exist only as a heaven-sent source of money—should take a look at the tenant farmer and say whether he himself is not a downright, fantastic, cunning scoundrel, who in his heart and in actual fact has for a long time been part of free industry and well-loved trade, however much he may resist them and prattle of historical memories and moral or political goals. All the arguments he can genuinely advance in his own favor are only true for the cultivator of the land (the capitalist and the laborers), of whom the landowner is rather the enemy; thus, he testifies against himself. Without capital, landed property is dead, worthless matter. The civilized victory of movable capital has precisely been to reveal and create human labor as the source of wealth in place of the dead thing. (See Paul-Louis Courier, Saint-Simon, Ganilh, Ricardo, Mill, MacCulloch, Destutt de Tracy, and Michael Chevalier.)

The real course of development (to be inserted here) leads necessarily to the victory of the capitalist—i.e., of developed private property—over undeveloped, immature private property—the landowner. In the same way, movement inevitably triumphs over immobility, open and self-conscious baseness over hidden and unconscious baseness, greed over self-indulgence, the avowedly restless and versatile self-interest of enlightenment over the parochial, worldly-wise, artless, lazy and deluded self-interest of superstition, just as money must triumph over the other forms of private property. Those states which have a foreboding of the danger of allowing the full development of free industry, pure morality, and that trade which encourages friendship among peoples, attempt—although quite in vain—to put a stop to the capitalization of landed property.

Landed property, as distinct from capital, is private property, capital, which is still afflicted with local and political prejudices, which has not yet entirely emerged from its involvement with the world and come into its own; it is capital which is not yet fully developed. In the course of its formation on a world scale, it must attain its abstract, i.e., pure, expression. The relation of private property is labor, capital, and the connection between these two. The movement through which these parts have to pass is:

First—Unmediate or mediated unity of the two. Capital and labor, at first, still united; later, separated and estranged, but reciprocally developing and furthering each other as positive conditions.

Second—Opposition of the two. They mutually exclude each other; the worker sees in the capitalist his own non-existence, and vice-versa; each tries to wrench from the other his existence.

Third—Opposition of each to itself. Capital = stored-up labor = labor. As such, it divides into itself (capital) and its interest; this latter divides into interest and profit. Complete sacrifice of the capitalist. He sinks into the working class, just as the worker—but only by way of exception—becomes a capitalist. Labor as a moment of capital, its costs. i.e., wages a sacrifice of capital.

Labor divides into labor itself and wages of labor. The workers himself a capital, a commodity.

Hostile reciprocal opposition.

Third Manuscript
Private Property And Labor

The subjective essence of private property, private property as activity for itself, as subject, as person, is labor. It, therefore, goes without saying that only that political economy which recognized labor as its principle (Adam Smith), and which therefore no longer regarded private property as nothing more than a condition external to man, can be regarded as both a product of the real energy and movement of private property (it is the independent movement of private property become conscious of itself, it is modern industry as self), a product of modern industry, and a factor which has accelerated and glorified the energy and development of this industry and transformed it into a power belonging to consciousness. Therefore, the supporters of the monetary and mercantile system, who look upon private property as a purely objective being for man, appear as fetish-worshippers, as Catholics, to this enlightened political economy, which has revealed — within the system of private property — the subjective essence of wealth. Engels was, therefore, right to call Adam Smith the Luther of political economy (in Engels 1843 Outlines of a Critique of Political Economy). Just as Luther recognized religion and faith as the essence of the external world and, in consequence, confronted Catholic paganism; just as he transcended religion external religiosity by making religiosity the inner essence of man; just as he negated the idea of priests as something separate and apart from the layman by transferring the priest into the heart of the layman; so wealth as something outside man, and independent of him — and, therefore, only to be acquired acquired and maintained externally — is abolished, i.e., its external and mindless objectivity is abolished inasmuch as private property is embodied in man himself and man himself is recognized as its essence — but this brings man himself into the province of religion. So, although political economy, whose principle is labor, appears to recognize man, it is, in fact, nothing more than the denial of man carried through to its logical conclusion: for man himself no longer stands in a relation of external tension to the external essence of private property — he himself has become the tense essence of private property. What was formerly being-external-to-oneself, man's material externalization, has now become the act of alienation — i.e., alienation through selling. This political economy, therefore, starts out by seeming to recognize man, his independence, his spontaneous activity, etc. Since it transfers private property into the very being of man, it can no longer be conditioned by local or national features of private property as something existing outside it. It (political economy) develops a cosmopolitan, universal energy which breaks through every limitation and bond and sets itself up as the only policy, the only universality, the only limitation, and the only bond. But then, as it continues to develop, it is forced to cast off its hypocrisy and step forth in all its cynicism. This it does, without troubling its head for one moment about all the apparent contradiction to which this doctrine leads, by developing in a more one-sided way, and, thus, more sharply and more logically, the idea of labor as the sole essence of wealth, by showing that the conclusions of this doctrine, unlike the original conception, are anti-human, and finally be delivering the death-blow to ground rent—that last individual and natural form of private property and source of wealth independent of the movement of labor, that expression of feudal property which has already become entirely economic and is therefore incapable of putting up any resistance to political economy. (The Ricardo School.) Not only does political economy become increasingly cynical from Smith through Say to Ricardo, Mill etc., inasmuch as the consequences of industry appeared more developed and more contradictory to the latter; the latter also became more estranged—consciously estranged—from man than their predecessors. But this is only because their science develops more logically and more truly. Since they make private property in its active form the subject, thereby making man as a non-being the essence, the contradiction in reality corresponds entirely to the contradictory essence which they have accepted as their principle. The discordant reality of industry, far from refusing their internally discordant principle, actually confirms it. Their principle is in fact the principle of this discordance.

The physiocratic doctrine of Dr Quesnay forms the transition from the mercantile system to Adam Smith. Physiocracy is, in a direct sense, the economic dissolution of feudal property, but it is therefore just as directly the economic transformation and restoration of that property. The only real difference is that its language is no longer feudal but economic. All wealth is resolved into land and agriculture. The land is not yet capital; it is still a particular mode of existence of capital whose value is supposed to lie in its natural particularity. But land is a universal natural element, whereas the mercantile system considered that wealth existed only in precious metals. The object of wealth, its matter, has therefore attained the greatest degree of universality possible within the limits of nature—insofar as it is directly objective wealth even as nature. And it is only through labor, through agriculture, that land exists for man. Consequently, the subjective essence of wealth is already transferred to labor. But, at the same time, agriculture is the only productive labor. Labor is, therefore, not yet grasped in its universal and abstract form, but is still tied to a particular element of nature as its matter and if for that reason recognized only in a particular mode of existence determined by nature. It is, therefore, still only a determinate, particular externalization of man — just as its product is conceived as a determinate form of wealth, due more to nature than to itself. Here, the land is still regarded as part of nature which is independent of man, and not yet as capital — i.e., as a moment of labor itself. Rather, labor appears as a moment of nature. But, since the fetishism of the old external wealth, which exists only as an object, has been reduced to a very simple element of nature, and since its essence has been recognized — even if only partially and in a particular way — in its subjective essence, the necessary advance has taken place in the sense that the universal nature of wealth has been recognized and labor has, therefore, been elevated in its absolute — i.e., abstract — form to that principle. It is possible to argue against the Physiocrats that agriculture is no different from an economic point of view — that is, from the only valid point of view — from any other industry, and that the essence of wealth is therefore not a particular form of labor tied to a particular element, a particular manifestation of labor, but labor in general.

Physiocracy denies particular, external, purely objective wealth by declaring labor to be its essence. But, for physiocracy, labor is in the first place merely the subjective essence of landed property — it starts out from the type of property which appears historically as the dominant and recognized type. It simple turns landed property into alienated man. It abolishes the feudal character of landed property by declaring industry (agriculture) to be its essence; but it sets its face against the world of industry and acknowledges the feudal system by declaring agriculture to be the only industry.

Clearly, once the subjective essence is grasped of industry constituting itself in opposition to landed property — i.e., as industry — this essence includes within it that opposition. For, just as industry absorbs annulled landed property, so the subjective essence of industry at the same time absorbs the subjective essence of landed property.

Just as landed property is the first form of private property, and industry at first confronts it historically as nothing more than a particular sort of private property—or, rather, as the liberated slave of landed property—so this process is repeated in the scientific comprehension of the subjective essence of private property, of labor; labor appears at first only as agricultural labor, but later assumes the form of labor in general.

All wealth has become industrial wealth, wealth of labor, and industry is fully developed labor, just as the factory system is the perfected essence of industry—i.e., of labor—and industrial capital the fully developed objective form of private property.

Thus, we see that it is only at this point that private property can perfect its rule over men and become, in its most universal form, a world-historical power.

Private Property And Communism

But the antithesis between propertylessness and property is still an indifferent antithesis, not grasped in its active connection, its inner relation, not yet grasped as contradiction, as long as it is not understood as the antithesis between labor and capital. In its initial form, this antithesis can manifest itself even without the advanced development of private property—as, for example, in ancient Rome, in Turkey, etc. In such cases, it does not yet appear as established by private property itself. But labor, the subjective essence of private property as exclusion of property, and capital, objective labor as exclusion of labor, constitute private property in its developed relation of contradiction: a vigorous relation, therefore, driving towards resolution.

ad ibidem.

The supersession of self-estrangement follows the same course self-estrangement. Private property is first considered only in its objective aspect, but still with labor as its essence. Its form of existence is therefore capital, which is to be abolished "as such" (Proudhon). Or the particular form of labor—leveled down, parceled, and, therefore, unfree—is taken as the source of the harmfulness of private property and its humanly estranged existence. For example, Fourier, like the Physiocrats, regarded agriculture as at least the best form of labor, while Saint-Simon, on the other hand, declared industrial labor as such to be the essence and consequently wants exclusive rule by the industrialists and the improvement of the condition of the workers. Finally, communism is the positive expression of the abolition of private property, and, at first, appears as universal private property. In grasping this relation in its universality, communism is

(1) in its initial form only a generalization and completion of that relation (of private property). As such, it appears in a dual form: on the one hand, the domination of material property bulks so large that it threatens to destroy everything which is not capable of being possessed by everyone as private property; it wants to abstract from talent, etc., by force. Physical, immediate possession is the only purpose of life and existence as far as this communism is concerned; the category of worker is not abolished but extended to all men; the relation of private property remains the relation of the community to the world of things; ultimately, this movement to oppose universal private property to private property is expressed in bestial form— marriage (which is admittedly a form of exclusive private property) is counterposed to the community of women, where women become communal and common property. One might say that this idea of a community of women is the revealed secret of this as yet wholly crude and unthinking communism. Just as women are to go from marriage into general prostitution, so the whole world of wealth—i.e., the objective essence of man—is to make the transition from the relation of exclusive marriage with the private owner to the relation of universal prostitution with the community. This communism, inasmuch as it negates the personality of man in every sphere, is simply the logical expression of the private property which is this negation. Universal envy constituting itself as a power is the hidden form in which greed reasserts itself and satisfies itself, but in another way. The thoughts of every piece of private property as such are at least turned against richer private property in the form of envy and the desire to level everything down; hence these feelings in fact constitute the essence of competition. The crude communist is merely the culmination of this envy and desire to level down on the basis of a preconceived minimum. It has a definite, limited measure. How little this abolition of private property is a true appropriation is shown by the abstract negation of the entire world of culture and civilization, and the return to the unnatural simplicity of the poor, unrefined man who has no needs and who has not yet even reached the stage of private property, let along gone beyond it.

(For crude communism) the community is simply a community of labor and equality of wages, which are paid out by the communal capital, the community as universal capitalist. Both sides of the relation are raised to an unimaginary universality—labor as the condition in which everyone is placed and capital as the acknowledged universality and power of the community.

In the relationship with woman, as the prey and handmaid of communal lust, is expressed the infinite degradation in which man exists for himself—for the secret of this relationship has its unambiguous, decisive, open and revealed expression in the relationship of man to woman and in the manner in which the direct, natural species- relationship is conceived. The immediate, natural, necessary relation of human being to human being is the relationship of man to woman. In this natural species-relationship, the relation of man to nature is immediately his relation to man, just as his relation to man is immediately his relation to nature, his own natural condition. Therefore, this relationship reveals in a sensuous form, reduced to an observable fact, the extent to which the human essence has become nature for man or nature has become the human essence for man. It is possible to judge from this relationship the entire level of development of mankind. It follows from the character of this relationship of this relationship how far man as a species-being, as man, has become himself and grasped himself; the relation of man to woman is the most natural relation of human being to human being. It therefore demonstrates the extent to which man's natural behavior has become human or the extent to which his human essence has become a natural essence for him, the extent to which his human nature has become nature for him. This relationship also demonstrates the extent to which man's needs have become human needs, hence the extent to which the other, as a human being, has become a need for him, the extent to which in his most individual existence he is at the same time a communal being.

The first positive abolition of private property—crude communism—is therefore only a manifestation of the vileness of private property trying to establish itself as the positive community.

(2) Communism

(a) still of a political nature, democratic or despotic;

(b) with the abolition of the state, but still essentially incomplete and influenced by private property—i.e., by the estrangement of man.

In both forms, communism already knows itself as the reintegration, or return, of man into himself, the supersession of man's self-estrangement; but since it has not yet comprehended the positive essence of private property, or understood the human nature of need, it is still held captive and contaminated by private property. True, it has understood its concept, but not yet in essence.

(3) Communism is the positive supersession of private property as human self-estrangement, and hence the true appropriation of the human essence through and for man; it is the complete restoration of man to himself as a social—i.e., human—being, a restoration which has become conscious and which takes place within the entire wealth of previous periods of development. This communism, as fully developed naturalism, equals humanism, and as fully developed humanism equals naturalism; it is the genuine resolution of the conflict between man and nature, and between man and man, the true resolution of the conflict between existence and being, between objectification and self-affirmation, between freedom and necessity, between individual and species. It is the solution of the riddle of history and knows itself to be the solution.

The entire movement of history is therefore both the actual act of creation of communism—the birth of its empirical existence—and, for its thinking consciousness, the comprehended and known movement of its becoming; whereas the other communism, which is not yet fully developed, seeks in isolated historical forms opposed to private property a historical proof for itself, a proof drawn from what already exists, by wrenching isolated moments from their proper places in the process of development (a hobbyhorse Cabet, Villegardelle, etc., particularly like to ride) and advancing them as proofs of its historical pedigree. But all it succeeds in showing is that be far the greater part of this development contradicts its assertions and that if it did not once exist, then the very fact that it existed in the past refutes its claim to essential being.

It is easy to see how necessary it is for the whole revolutionary movement to find both its empirical and its theoretical basis in the movement of private property or, to be exact, of the economy.

This material, immediately sensuous private property is the material, sensuous expression of estranged human life. Its movement—production and consumption—is the sensuous revelation of the movement of all previous production—i.e., the realization or reality of man. Religion, the family, the state, law, morality, science, art, etc., are only particular modes of production and therefore come under its general law. The positive supersession of private property, as the appropriation of human life, is therefore the positive supersession of all estrangement, and the return of man from religion, the family, the state, etc., to his human—i.e., social—existence. Religious estrangement as such takes place only in the sphere of consciousness, of man's inner life, but economic estrangement is that of real life—its supersession therefore embraces both aspects. Clearly the nature of the movement in different countries initially depends on whether the actual and acknowledged life of the people has its being more in consciousness or in the external world, in ideal or in real life. Communism begins with atheism (Owen), but atheism is initially far from being communism, and is for the most part an abstraction. The philanthropy of atheism is therefore at first nothing more than an abstract philosophical philanthropy, while that of communism is at once real and directly bent towards action.

We have seen how, assuming the positive supersession of private property, man produces man, himself and other men; how the object, which is the direct activity of his individuality, is at the same time his existence for other men, their existence and their existence for him. Similarly, however, both the material of labor and man as subject are the starting-point as well as the outcome of the movement (and the historical necessity of private-property lies precisely in the fact that they must be this starting-point). So the social character is the general character of the whole movement; just as society itself produces man as man, so it is produced by him. Activity and consumption, both in their content and in their mode of existence, are social activity and social consumption. The human essence of nature exists only for social man; for only here does nature exist for him as a bond with other men, as his existence for others and their existence for him, as the vital element of human reality; only here does it exist as the basis of his own human existence. Only here has his natural existence become his human existence and nature become man for him. Society is therefore the perfected unity in essence of man with nature, the true resurrection of nature, the realized naturalism of man and the realized humanism of nature. (Prostitution is only a particular expression of the universal prostitution of the worker, and since prostitution is a relationship which includes not only the prostituted but also the prostitutor—whose infamy is even greater—the capitalist is also included in this category.)

Social activity and social consumption by no means exist solely in the form of a directly communal activity and a directly communal consumption, even though communal activity and communal consumption—i.e., activity and consumption that express and confirm themselves directly in real association with other men—occur wherever that direct expression of sociality springs from the essential nature of the content of the activity and is appropriate to the nature of the consumption.

But even if I am active in the field of science, etc.—an activity which I am seldom able to perform in direct association with other men—I am still socially active because I am active as a man. It is not only the material of my activity—including even the language in which the thinker is active—which I receive as a social product. My own existence is social activity. Therefore what I create from myself I create for society, conscious of myself as a social being.

My universal consciousness is only the theoretical form of that whose living form is the real community, society, whereas at present universal consciousness is an abstraction from real life and as such in hostile opposition to it. Hence the activity of my universal consciousness—as activity—is my theoretical existence as a social being.

It is, above all, necessary to avoid once more establishing "society" as an abstraction over against the individual. The individual is the social being. His vital expression—even when it does not appear in the direct form of a communal expression, conceived in association with other men—is therefore an expression and confirmation of social life. Man's individual and species-life are not two distinct things, however much—and this is necessarily so—the mode of existence of individual life is a more particular or a more general mode of the species-life, or species-life a more particular or more general individual life.

As species-consciousness man confirms his real social life and merely repeats in thought his actual existence; conversely, species-being confirms itself in species-consciousness and exists for itself in its universality, as a thinking being.

Man, however much he may therefore be a particular individual—and it is just this particularity which makes him an individual totality, the ideal totality, the subjective existence of thought and experienced society for itself; he also exists in reality as the contemplation and true enjoyment of social existence and as a totality of vital human expression.

It is true that thought and being are distinct, but at the same time they are in unity with one another.

Death appears as the harsh victory of the species over the particular individual, and seemingly contradicts their unity; but the particular individual is only a particular species-being, and, as such, mortal.

(4) Just as private property is only the sensuous expression of the fact that man becomes objective for himself and at the same time becomes an alien and inhuman object for himself, that his expression of life is his alienation of life, and that his realization is a loss of reality, an alien reality, so the positive supersession of private property — i.e., the sensuous appropriation of the human essence and human life, of objective man and of human works by and for man — should not be understood only in the sense of direct, one-sided consumption, of possession, of having. Man appropriates his integral essence in an integral way, as a total man. All his human relations to the world — seeing, hearing, smelling, tasting, feeling, thinking, contemplating, sensing, wanting, acting, loving — in short, all the organs of his individuality, like the organs which are directly communal in form, are in their objective approach or in their approach to the object the appropriation of that object. This appropriation of human reality, their approach to the object, is the confirmation of human reality. (It is therefore just as varied as the determinations of the human essence and activities.) It is human effectiveness and human suffering, for suffering, humanly conceived, is an enjoyment of the self for man.

Private property has made us so stupid and one-sided that an object is only ours when we have it, when it exists for us as capital or when we directly possess, eat, drink, wear, inhabit it, etc., in short, when we use it. Although private property conceives all these immediate realizations of possession only as means of life; and the life they serve is the life of private property, labor, and capitalization.

Therefore all the physical and intellectual senses have been replaced by the simple estrangement of all these senses — the sense of having. So that it might give birth to its inner wealth, human nature had to be reduced to this absolute poverty.

The supersession of private property is therefore the complete emancipation of all human senses and attributes; but it is this emancipation precisely because these senses and attributes have become human, subjectively as well as objectively. The eye has become a human eye, just as its object has become a social, human object, made by man for man. The senses have therefore become theoreticians in their immediate praxis. They relate to the thing for its own sake, but the thing itself is an objective human relation to itself and to man, and vice versa. (In practice I can only relate myself to a thing in a human way if the thing is related in a human way to man.) Need or employment have therefore lost their egoistic nature, and nature has lost its mere utility in the sense that its use has become human use.

Similarly, senses and enjoyment of other men have become my own appropriation. Apart from these direct organs, social organs are therefore created in the form of society; for example, activity in direct association with others, etc., has become an organ of my life expressions and a mode of appropriation of human life.

Obviously the human eye takes in things in a different way from the crude non-human eye, the hum ear in a different way from the crude ear, etc.

To sum up: it is only when man's object becomes a human object or objective that man does not lose himself in that object. This is only possible when it becomes a social object for him and when he himself becomes a social being for himself, just as society becomes a being for him in this object.

On the one hand, therefore, it is only when objective reality universally becomes for man in society the reality of man's essential powers, becomes human reality, and thus the reality of his own essential powers, that all objects become for him the objectification of himself, objects that confirm and realize his individuality, his objects — i.e., he himself becomes the object. The manner in which they become his depends on the nature of the object and the nature of the essential power that corresponds to it; for it is just the determinateness of this relation that constitutes the particular, real mode of affirmation. An object is different for the eye from what it is for the ear, and the eye's object is different for from the ear's. The peculiarity of each essential power is precisely its peculiar essence, and thus also the peculiar mode of its objectification, of its objectively real, living being. Man is therefore affirmed in the objective world not only in thought but with all the senses.

On the other hand, let us look at the question in its subjective aspect: only music can awaken the musical sense in man and the most beautiful music has no sense for the unmusical ear, because my object can only be the confirmation of one of my essential powers – i.e., can only be for me insofar as my essential power exists for me as a subjective attribute (this is because the sense of an object for me extends only as far as my sense extends, only has sense for a sense that corresponds to that object). In the same way, and for the same reasons, the senses of social man are different from those of non-social man. Only through the objectively unfolded wealth of human nature can the wealth of subjective human sensitivity – a musical ear, an eye for the beauty of form, in short, senses capable of human gratification – be either cultivated or created. For not only the five senses, but also the so-called spiritual senses, the practical senses (will, love, etc.), in a word, the human sense, the humanity of the senses – all these come into being only through the existence of their objects, through humanized nature. The cultivation of the five senses is the work of all previous history. Sense which is a prisoner of crude practical need has only a restricted sense. For a man who is starving, the human form of food does not exist, only its abstract form exists; it could just as well be present in its crudest form, and it would be hard to say how this way of eating differs from that of animals. The man who is burdened with worries and needs has no sense for the finest of plays; the dealer in minerals sees only the commercial value, and not the beauty and peculiar nature of the minerals; he lacks a mineralogical sense; thus the objectification of the human essence, in a theoretical as well as a practical respect, is necessary both in order to make man's senses human and to create an appropriate human sense for the whole of the wealth of humanity and of nature.

Just as in its initial stages society is presented with all the material for this cultural development through the movement of private property, and of its wealth and poverty – both material and intellectual wealth and poverty – so the society that is fully developed produces man in all the richness of his being, the rich man who is profoundly and abundantly endowed with all the senses, as its constant reality. It can be seen how subjectiveness and objectivism, spiritualism and materialism, activity and passivity, lose their antithetical character, and hence their existence as such antithesis, only in the social condition; it can be seen how the resolution of the theoretical antitheses themselves is possible only in a practical way, only through the practical energy of man, and how their resolution is for that reason by no means only a problem of knowledge, but a real problem of life, a problem which philosophy was unable to solve precisely because it treated it as a purely theoretical problem.

It can be seen how the history of industry and the objective existence of industry as it has developed is the open book of the essential powers of man, man's psychology present in tangible form; up to now this history has not been grasped in its connection with the nature of man, but only in an external utilitarian aspect, for man, moving in the realm of estrangement, was only capable of conceiving the general existence of man—religion, or history in its abstract and universal form of politics, art, literature, etc.—as the reality of man's essential powers and as man's species-activity. In everyday, material industry (which can just as easily be considered as a part of that general development as that general development itself can be considered as a particular part of industry, since all human activity up to now has been labor—i.e., industry, self-estranged activity) we find ourselves confronted with the objectified powers of the human essence, in the form of sensuous, alien, useful objects, in the form of estrangement. A psychology for which this book, the most tangible and accessible part of history, is closed, can never become a real science with a genuine content. What indeed should we think of a science which primly abstracts from this large area of human labor, and fails to sense its own inadequacy, even though such an extended wealth of human activity says nothing more to it perhaps than what can be said in one word—"need", "common need"?

The natural sciences have been prolifically active and have gathered together an ever growing mass of material. But philosophy has remained just as alien to them as they have remained alien to philosophy. Their momentary union was only a fantastic illusion. The will was there, but not the means. Even historiography only incidentally takes account of natural science, which it sees as contributing to enlightenment, utility and a few great discoveries. But natural science has intervened in and transformed human life all the more practically through industry and has prepared the conditions for human emancipation, however much its immediate effect was to complete the process was to complete the process of dehumanization. Industry is the real historical relationship of nature, and hence of natural science, to man. If it is then conceived as the exoteric revelation of man's essential powers, the human essence of nature or the natural essence of man can also be understood. Hence natural science will lose its abstractly material, or rather idealist, orientation and become the basis of a human science, just as it has already become — though in an estranged form — the basis of actual human life. The idea of one basis for life and another for science is from the very outset a lie. Nature as it comes into being in human history — in the act of creation of human society — is the true nature of man; hence nature as it comes into being through industry, though in an estranged form, is true anthropological nature.

Sense perception (see Feuerbach) must be the basis of all science. Only when science starts out from sense perception in the dual form of sensuous consciousness and sensuous need — i.e., only when science starts out from nature — is it real science. The whole of history is a preparation, a development, for "man" to become the object of sensuous consciousness and for the needs of "man as man" to become sensuous needs. History itself is a real part of natural history and of nature's becoming man. Natural science will, in time, subsume the science of man, just as the science of man will subsume natural science: there will be one science.

Man is the immediate object of natural science; for immediate sensuous nature for man is, immediately, human sense perception (an identical expression) in the form of the other man who is present in his sensuous immediacy for him. His own sense perception only exists as human sense perception for himself through the other man. But nature is the immediate object of the science of man. Man's first object — man — is nature, sense perception; and the particular sensuous human powers, since they can find objective realization only in natural objects, can find self-knowledge only in the science of nature in general. The element of thought itself, the element of the vital expression of thought — language — is sensuous nature. The social reality of nature and human natural science or the natural science of man are identical expressions.

It can be seen how the rich man and the wealth of human need take the place of the wealth and poverty of political economy. The rich man is simultaneously the man in need of totality of vital human expression; he is the man in whom his own realization exists as inner necessity, as need. Given socialism, not only man's wealth but also his poverty acquire a human and hence a social significance. Poverty is the passive bond which makes man experience his greatest wealth — the other man — as need. The domination of the objective essences within me, the sensuous outburst of my essential activity, is passion, which here becomes the activity of my being.

(5) A being sees himself as independent only when he stands on his own feet, and he only stands on his own feet when he owes this existence to himself. A man who lives by the grace of another regards himself as a dependent being. But I live completely by the grace of another if I owe him not only the maintenance of my life, but also its creation, if he is the source of my life. My life is necessarily grounded outside itself if it is not my own creation. The creation is therefore an idea which is very hard to exorcize from the popular consciousness. This consciousness is incapable of comprehending the self-mediated being of nature and of man, since such a being contradicts all the palpable evidence of practical life.

The creation of the Earth receives a heavy blow from the science of geogeny — i.e., the science which depicts the formation of the Earth, its coming to be, as a process of self-generation. *Generatio aequivoca* (spontaneous generation) is the only practical refutation of the theory of creation.

Now, it is easy to say to a particular individual what Aristotle said: You were begotten by your father and your mother, which means that in you the mating of two human beings, a human species-act, produced another human being. Clearly, then, man also owes his existence to man in a physical sense. Therefore, you should not only keep sight of the one aspect, the infinite progression which leads you on to the question: "Who begot my father, his grandfather, etc.?" You should also keep in mind the circular movement sensuously perceptible in that progression whereby man reproduces himself in the act of begetting and thus always remains the subject. But you will reply: I grant you this circular movement, but you must also grant me the right to progress back to the question: Your question is itself a product of abstraction. Ask yourself how you arrived at that question. Ask yourself whether your question does not arise from a standpoint to which I cannot reply because it is a perverse one. Ask yourself whether that progression exists as such for rational thought. If you ask about the creation of nature and of man, then you are abstracting from nature and from man. You assume them as non-existent and want me to prove to you that they exist. My answer is: Give up your abstraction and you will them give up your question. But if you want to hold on to your abstraction, then do so consistently, and if you assume the non-existence of man and nature, then assume also your own non-existence, for you are also nature and man. Do not think and do not ask me questions, for as soon as you think and ask questions, your abstraction from the existence of nature and man has no meaning. Or are you such an egoist that you assume everything as non-existence and still want to exist yourself?

You can reply: I do not want to assume the nothingness of nature, etc. I am only asking how it arose, just as I might ask the anatomist about the formation of bones, etc.

But since for socialist man the whole of what is called world history is nothing more than the creation of man through human labor, and the development of nature for man, he therefore has palpable and incontrovertible proof of his self-mediated birth, of his process of emergence. Since the essentiality of man and nature, a man as the existence of nature for man and nature as the existence of man for man, has become practically and sensuously perceptible, the question of an alien being, being above nature and man—a question which implies an admission of the unreality of nature and of man—has become impossible in practice. Atheism, which is a denial of this unreality, no longer has any meaning, for atheism is a negation of God, through which negation it asserts the existence of man. But socialism as such no longer needs such mediation. Its starting point is the theoretically and practically sensuous consciousness of man and of nature as essential beings. It is the positive self-consciousness of man, no longer mediated through the abolition of religion, just as real life is positive reality no longer mediated through the abolition of private property, through communism. Communism is the act of positing as the negation of the negation, and is therefore a real phase, necessary for the next period of historical development, in the emancipation and recovery of mankind. Communism is the necessary form and the dynamic principle of the immediate future, but communism is not as such the goal of human development—the form of human society.

Need, Production And Division Of Labor
We have seen what significance the wealth of human needs has, on the presupposition of socialism, and consequently what significance a new mode of production and a new object of production have. A fresh confirmation of human powers and a fresh

enrichment of human nature. Under the system of private property their significance is reversed. Each person speculates on creating a new need in the other, with the aim of forcing him to make a new sacrifice, placing him in a new dependence and seducing him into a new kind of of enjoyment and hence into economic ruin. Each attempts to establish over the other an alien power, in the hope of thereby achieving satisfaction of his own selfish needs. With the mass of objects grows the realm of alien powers to which mn is subjected, and each new product is a new potentiality of mutual fraud and mutual pillage. Man becomes ever poorer as a man, and needs ever more money if he is to achieve mastery over the hostile being. The power of his money falls in inverse proportion to the volume of productions—i.e., his need grows as the power of money increases. The need for money is for that reason the real need created by the modern economic system, and the only need it creates. The quantity of money becomes more and more its sole important property. Just as it reduces everything to its own form of abstraction, so it reduces itself in the course of its own movement to something quantitative. Lack of moderation and intemperance become its true standard. Subjectively this is manifested partly in the fact that the expansion of production and needs becomes the inventive and ever calculating slave of inhuman, refined, unnatural and imaginary appetites—for private property does not know how to transform crude need into human need. Its idealism is fantasy, caprice, and infatuation. No eunuch flatters his despot more basely, or uses more infamous means to revive his flagging capacity for pleasure, in order to win a surreptitious favor for himself, than does the eunuch of industry, the manufacturer, in order to sneak himself a silver penny or two, or coax the gold from the pocket of his dearly beloved neighbor. Every product is a bait with which to entice the essence of the other, his money. Every real or potential need is a weakness which will tempt the fly onto the lime-twig. Universal exploitation of communal human nature. Just as each one of man's inadequacies is a bond with heaven, a way into his heart for the priest, so every need is an opportunity for stepping up to one's neighbor in sham friendship and saying to him: "Dear friend, I can give you want you need, but you know the terms. You know which ink you must use in signing yourself over to me. I shall cheat you while I provide your pleasure." He places himself at the disposal of his neighbor's most depraved fancies, panders to his needs, excites unhealthy appetites in him, and pounces on every weakness, so that he can then demand the money for his labor of love.

This estrangement partly manifests itself in the fact that the rent of needs and of the means of fulfilling them gives rise to a bestial degeneration and a complete, crude and abstract simplicity of need; or rather, that it merely reproduces itself in its opposite sense. Even the need for fresh air ceases to be a need for the worker. Man reverts once more to living in a cave, but the cave is now polluted by the mephitic and pestilential breath of civilization. Moreover, the worker has no more than a precarious right to live in it, for it is for him an alien power that can be daily withdrawn and from which, should he fail to pay, he can be evicted at any time. He actually has to pay for this mortuary. A dwelling in the light, which Prometheus describes in Aeschylus as one of the great gifts through which he transformed savages into men, ceases to exist for the worker. Light, ire, etc. — the simplest animal cleanliness — cases be a need for man. Dirt — this pollution and putrefaction of man, the sewage (this word is to be understood in its literal sense) of civilization — becomes an element of life for him. Universal unnatural neglect, putrefied nature, becomes an element of life for him. None of this sense exist any longer, either in their human form or in their inhuman form — i.e., not even in their animal form. The crudest modes (and instruments) of human labor reappear; for example, the tread-mill used by Roman slave has become the mode of production and mode of existence of many English workers. It is not only human needs which man lacks — even his animal needs cease to exist. The Irishman has only one need left — the need to eat, to eat potatoes, and, more precisely, to eat rotten potatoes, the worst kind of potatoes. But England and France already have a little Ireland in each of their industrial cities.. The savage and the animal at least have the need to hunt, to move about, etc., the need of companionship. The simplification of machinery and of labor is used to make workers out of human beings who are still growing, who are completely immature, out of children, while the worker himself becomes a neglected child. The machine accommodates itself to man's weakness, in order to turn weak man into a machine.

The fact that the multiplication of needs and of the means of fulfilling them gives rise to a lack of needs and of means is proved by the political economist (and by the capitalist — we invariably mean empirical businessmen when we refer to political economists, who are the scientific exposition and existence of the former) in the following ways:

(1) By reducing the worker's needs to the paltriest minimum necessary to maintain his physical existence and by reducing his activity to the most abstract mechanical movement. In so doing, the political economist declares that man has no other needs, either in the sphere of activity or in that of consumption. For even this life he calls human life and human existence.

(2) By taking as his standard — his universal standard, in the sense that it applies to the mass of men — the worst possible state of privation which life (existence) can know. He turns the worker into a being with neither needs nor senses and turn the worker's activity into a pure abstraction from all activity. Hence any luxury that the worker might enjoy is reprehensible, and anything that goes beyond the most abstract need — either in the form of passive enjoyment or active expression — appears to him as a luxury. Political economy, this science of wealth, is therefore at the same time the science of denial, of starvation, of saving, and it actually goes so far as to save man the need for fresh air or physical exercise. This science of the marvels of industry is at the same time the science of asceticism, and its true ideal is the ascetic but rapacious skinflint and the ascetic but productive slave. Its moral ideal is the worker who puts a part of his wages into savings, and it has even discovered a servile art which can dignify this charming little notion and present a sentimental version of it on the stage. It is therefore — for all its worldly and debauched appearance — a truly moral moral science, the most moral science of all. Self-denial, the denial of life and of all human needs, is its principal doctrine. The less you eat, drink, buy books, go to the theatre, go dancing, go drinking, think, love, theorize, sing, paint, fence, etc., the more you save and the greater will become that treasure which neither moths nor maggots can consume — your capital. The less you are, the less you give expression to your life, the more you have, the greater is your alienated life and the more you store up of your estranged life. Everything which the political economist takes from you in terms of life and humanity, he restores to you in the form of money and wealth, and everything which you are unable to do, your money can do for you: it can eat, drink, go dancing, go to the theatre, it can appropriate art, learning, historical curiosities, political power, it can travel, it is capable of doing all those thing for you; it can buy everything it is genuine wealth, genuine

ability. But for all that, it only likes to create itself, to buy itself, for after all everything else is its servant. And when I have the master I have the servant, and I have no need of his servant. So all passions and all activity are lost in greed. The worker is only permitted to have enough for him to live, and he is only permitted to live in order to have.

It is true that a controversy has arisen in the field of political economy. One school (Lauderdale, Malthus, etc.) advocates luxury and execrates thrift. The other (Say, Ricardo, etc.) advocates thrift and execrates luxury. But the former admits that it wants luxury in order to produce labor—i.e., absolute thrift; and the latter admits that it advocates thrift in order to produce wealth—i.e., luxury. The former has the romantic notion that greed alone should not regulate the consumption of the rich, and it contradicts its own laws when it forwards the idea of prodigality as a direct means of enrichment. The other side then advances earnest and detailed arguments to show that through prodigality I diminish rather than increase my possessions; but its supporters hypocritically refuse to admit that production is regulated by caprice and luxury; they forget the "refined needs" and forget that without consumption there can be no production; they forget that, through competition, production becomes more extensive and luxurious; they forget that it is use which determines the value of a thing, and that it is fashion which determines use; they want only "useful things" to be produced, but they forget that the production of too many useful things produces too many useless people. Both sides forget that prodigality and thrift, luxury and privation, wealth and poverty are equal.

And you must not only be parsimonious in gratifying your immediate senses, such as eating, etc. You must also be chary of participating in affairs of general interest, showing sympathy and trust, etc., if you want to be economical and if you want to avoid being ruined by illusions.

You must make everything which is yours venal—i.e., useful. I might ask the political economist: am I obeying economic laws if I make money by prostituting my body to the lust of another (in France, the factory workers call the prostitution of their wives and daughters the nth working hour, which is literally true), or if I sell my friend to the Moroccans, where they still had Christian slaves (and the direct sale of men in the form of trade in conscripts, etc., occurs in all civilized countries)? His answer will be: your acts do not contravene my laws, but you find out what Cousin Morality and Cousin Religion have to say about it; the morality and religion of my political economy have no objection to make, but... But who should I believe, then? Political economy or morality? The morality of political economy is gain, labor and thrift, sobriety—and yet political economy promises to satisfy my needs. The political economy of morality is the wealth of a good conscience, of virtue, etc. But how can I be virtuous if I do not exist? And how can I have a good conscience if I am not conscious of anything? It is inherent in the very nature of estrangement that each sphere imposes upon me a different and contrary standard; one standard for morality, one for political economy, and so on. This is because each of them is a particular estrangement of man and each is centred upon one particular area of estranged essential activity: each is related in an estranged way to the other... Thus M. Michael Chevalier accuses Ricardo of abstracting from morality. But Ricardo allows political economy to speak its own language. If this language is not that of morality, it is not the fault of Ricardo. M. Chevalier abstracts from political economy insofar as he moralizes, but he really and necessarily abstracts from morality insofar as he deals with political economy. The relationship of political economy to morality is either an arbitrary and contingent one which is neither founded nor scientific, a simulacrum, or it is essential and can only be the relationship of economic laws to morality. If such a relationship does not exist, or if the opposite is rather the case, can Ricardo do anything about it? Moreover, the opposition between political economy and morality is only an apparent one. It is both an opposition and not an opposition. Political economy merely gives expression to moral laws in its own way.

Absence of needs as the principle of political economy is most in its theory of population. There are too many people. Even the existence of man is a pure luxury, and if the worker is "moral" he will be economical in procreation. (Mill suggests public commendation of those who show themselves temperate in sexual matters and public rebukes of those who sin against this barrenness of marriage... Is this not the morality, the doctrine, of asceticism?) The production of people appears as a public disaster.

The meaning which production has for the wealthy is revealed in the meaning which it has for the poor. At the top, it always manifests itself in refined, concealed, and ambiguous way—as an appearance. At the bottom, it manifests itself in a crude, straightforward, and overt way—as a reality. The crude need of the worker is a much greater source of profit than the refined need of the rich. The basement dwellings in London bring in more for the landlords than the palaces—i.e., they constitute a greater wealth for him and, from an economic point of view, a greater social wealth.

Just as industry speculates on the refinement of needs, so too it speculated on their crudity. But the crudity on which it speculates is artificially produced, and its true manner of enjoyment is therefore self-stupefaction, this apparent satisfaction of need, this civilization within the crude barbarism of need. The English ginshops are, therefore, the symbolic representation of private property. Their luxury demonstrated to man the true relation of industrial luxury and wealth. For that reason, they are rightly the only Sunday enjoyment of the English people, and are at least treated mildly by the English police.

We have already seen how the political economist establishes the unity of labor and capital in a number of different ways:

(1) capital is accumulated labor;

(2) the purpose of capital within production—partly the reproduction of capital with profit, partly capital as raw material (material of labor) and partly as itself a working instrument (the machine is capital directly identified with labor) -- is productive labor;

(3) the worker is a piece of capital;

(4) wages belong to the costs of capital;

(5) for the worker, labor is the reproduction of his life capital;

(6) for the capitalist, it is a factor in the activity of his capital. Finally,

(7) the political economist postulates the original unity of capital and labor as the unity of capitalist and worker, which he sees as the original state of bliss. The fact that these two elements leap at each other's throats in the form of two persons is a contingent event for the political economist, and hence only to be explained by external factors (see Mill).

Those nations which are still dazzled by the sensuous glitter of precious metals and, therefore, make a fetish of metal money are not yet fully developed money nations. Compare England and France. The extent to which the solution of theoretical problems is a function of practice and is mediated through practice, and the extent to which true practice is the condition of a real and positive theory is shown, for example, in the case of fetish-worship. The sense perception of a fetish-worshipper is different from that of a Greek because his sensuous existence is different. The abstract hostility between sense and intellect is inevitable so long as the human sense (Sinn) for nature, the human significance of nature, and, hence, the natural sense of man, has not yet been produced by man's own labor.

Equality is nothing but a translation into French—i.e., into political form—of the German "Ich - Ich". Equality as the basis of communism is its political foundation. It is the same as when the German founds it on the fact that he sees man as universal self-consciousness. It goes without saying that the supersession of estrangement always emanates from the form of estrangement which is the dominant power—in Germany, self-consciousness; in France, equality, because politics; in England, real, material, practical need, which only measures itself against itself. It is from this point of view that Proudhon should be criticized and acknowledged.

If we characterize communism itself—which because of its character as negation of the negation, as appropriation of the human essence which is mediated with itself through the negation of private property, is not yet the true, self-generating position, but one generated by private property...

[words missing]

... the real estrangement of human life remains and is all the greater the more one is conscious of it as such, it can only be attained once communism is established. In order to supersede the idea of private property, the idea of communism is enough. In order to supersede private property as it actually exists, real communist activity is necessary. History will give rise to such activity, and the movement which we already know in thought to be a self-superseding movement will in reality undergo a very difficult and protracted process. But we must look upon it as a real advance that we have gained, at the outset, an awareness of the limits as well as the goal of this historical movement and are in a position to see beyond it.

When communist workmen gather together, their immediate aim is instruction, propaganda, etc. But at the same time, they acquire a new need—the need for society—and what appears as a means had become an end. This practical development can be most strikingly observed in the gatherings of French socialist workers. Smoking, eating, and drinking, etc., are no longer means of creating links between people. Company, association, conversation, which in turn has society as its goal, is enough for them. The brotherhood of man is not a hollow phrase, it is a reality, and the nobility of man shines forth upon us from their work-worn figures.

When political economy maintains that supply and demand always balance each other, it immediately forgets its own assertion that the supply of people (the theory of population) always exceeds the demand and that therefore the disproportion between supply and demand finds its most striking expression in what is the essential goal of production—the existence of man.

The extent to which money, which appears to be a means, is the true power and the sole end—the extent to which in general the means which gives me being and which appropriates for me alien and objective being, is an end in itself... is apparent from the fact that landed property, where the soil is the source of life, and the horse and the sword, where they are the true means of life, are also recognized as the actual political powers. In the Middle Ages, an Estate becomes emancipated as soon as it is allowed to bear a sword. Among nomadic peoples, it is the horse which makes one into a free man and a participant in the life of the community.

We said above that man is regressing to the cave dwelling, etc.— but in an estranged, repugnant form. The savage in his cave—an element of nature which is freely available for his use and shelter— does not experience his environment as alien; he feels just as much at home as a fish in water. But the poor man's basement dwelling is an uncongenial element, an "alien, restrictive power which only surrenders itself to him at the expense of his sweat and blood". He cannot look upon it as his home, as somewhere he can call his own. Instead, he finds himself in someone else's house, in an alien house, whose owner lies in wait for him every day, and evicts him if he fails to pay the rent. At the same time, he is aware of the difference in quality between his own dwelling and those other-worldly human dwellings which exist in the heaven of wealth.

Estrangement appears not only in the fact that the means of my life belong to another and that my desire is the inaccessible possession of another, but also in the fact that all things are other than themselves, that my activity is other than itself, and that finally—and this goes for the capitalists too—an inhuman power rules over everything.

There is one form of inactive and extravagant wealth, given over exclusively to pleasure, the owner of which is active as a merely ephemeral individual, rushing about erratically. He looks upon the slave labor of others, their human sweat and blood, as they prey of his desires, and regards man in general—including himself—as a futile and sacrificial being. He arrogantly looks down upon mankind, dissipating what would suffice to keep alive a hundred human beings, and propagates the infamous illusion that his unbridled extravagance and ceaseless, unproductive consumption is a condition of the labor, and, hence, subsistence of the others. For him, the realization of man's essential powers is simply the realization of his own disorderly existence, his whims, and his capricious and bizarre notions. But this wealth, which regards wealth as a mere means, worthy only of destruction, and which is therefore both slave and master, both generous and mean, capricious, conceited, presumptuous, refined, cultured, and ingenious—this wealth has not yet experienced wealth as an entirely alien power over itself; it sees in wealth nothing more than its own power, the final aim of which is not wealth but consumption...

[words missing]

... and the glittering illusion about the nature of wealth—an illusion which derives from its sensuous appearance—is confronted by the working, sober, prosaic, economical industrialist who is enlightened about the nature of wealth and who not only provides a wider range of opportunities for the other's self-indulgence and flatters him through his products—for his products are so many base compliments to the appetites of the spendthrift—but also manages to appropriate for himself in the only useful way the other's dwindling power. So if industrial wealth at first appears to be the product of extravagant, fantastic wealth, in its inherent course of development it actively supplants the latter. For the fall in the interest on money is a necessary consequence and result of industrial development. Therefore, the means of the extravagant rentier diminish daily in inverse proportion to the growing possibilities and temptations of pleasure. He must, therefore, either consume his capital himself, and in so doing bring about his own ruin, or become an industrial capitalist.... On the other hand, it is true that there is a direct and constant rise in the rent of land as a result of industrial development, but as we have already seen there inevitably comes a time when landed property, like every other kind of property, falls into the category of capital which reproduces itself with profit—and this is a result of the same industrial development. Therefore, even the extravagant landlord is forced either to consume his capital—i.e., ruin himself — or become the tenant farmer of his own property — an agricultural industrialist.

The decline in the rate of interest — which Proudhon regards as the abolition of capital and as a tendency towards the socialization of capital — is therefore rather a direct symptom of the complete victory of working capital over prodigal wealth — i.e., the transformation of all private property into industrial capital. It is the complete victory of private property over all those of its qualities which are still apparently human and the total subjugation of the property owner to the essence of private property — labor. To be sure, the industrial capitalist also seeks enjoyment. He does not by any means regress to an unnatural simplicity of need, but his enjoyment is only incidental, a means of relaxation; it is subordinated to production, it is a calculated and even an economical form of pleasure, for it is charged as an expense of capital; the sum dissipated may therefore not be in excess of what can be replaced by the reproduction of capital with profit. Enjoyment is, therefore, subsumed under capital, and the pleasure-seeking individual under the capitalizing individual, whereas earlier the contrary was the case. The decline in the rate of interest is therefore a symptom of the abolition of capital only insofar as it is a symptom of the growing domination of capital, of that growing estrangement which is hastening towards its own abolition. This is the only way in which that which exists affirms its opposite.

The wrangle among political economists about luxury and saving is therefore merely a wrangle between that section of political economy which has become aware of the nature of wealth and that section which is still imprisoned within romantic and anti-industrial memories. But neither of them knows how to express the object of the controversy in simple terms, and neither of them is therefore in a position to clinch the argument.

Furthermore, the rent of land qua rent of land has been abolished, for the argument of the Physiocrats, who say that the landowner is the only true producer, has been demolished by the political economists, who show that the landowner as such is the only completely unproductive rentier. Agriculture is a matter for the capitalist, who invests his capital in this way when he can expect to make a normal profit. The argument of the Physiocrats that landed property, as the only productive property, should alone pay state taxes and should therefore alone give its consent to them and take part in state affairs, is turned into the opposite argument that the tax on rent of land is the only tax on unproductive income and hence the only tax which does not harm national production. Naturally, it follows from this argument that the landowner can no longer derive political privileges from his position as principal tax-payer.

Everything which Proudhon interprets as the growing power of labor as against capital is simply the growing power of labor in the form of capital, industrial capital, as against capital which is not consumed as capital—i.e, industrially. And this development is on its way to victory—i.e., the victory of industrial capital.

Clearly, then, it is only when labor is grasped as the essence of private property that the development of the economy as such can be analyzed in its real determinateness.

Society, as it appears to the political economist, is civil society, in which each individual is a totality of needs and only exists for the other as the other exists for him—insofar as each becomes a means for the other. The political economist, like politics in its rights of man, reduces everything to man—i.e., to the individual, whom he divests of all his determinateness in order to classify him as a capitalist or a worker.

The division of labor is the economic expression of the social nature of labor within estrangement. Or, rather, since labor is only an expression of human activity within alienation, an expression of life as alienation of life, the division of labor is nothing more than the estranged, alienated positing of human activity as a real species-activity or as activity of man as a species-being.

Political economists are very unclear and self-contradictory about the essence of the division of labor, which was naturally seen as one of the main driving forces in the production of wealth as soon as labor was seem to be the essence of private property. That is to say, they are very unclear about human activity as species activity in this its estranged and alienated form.

Adam Smith: "The division of labor... is not originally the effect of any human wisdom.... It is the necessary, though very slow and gradual consequence of the propensity to truck, barter, and exchange one thing for another. Whether this propensity be one of those original principles of human nature... or whether, as seems more probably, it be the necessary consequence of the faculties of reason and of speech it belongs not to our present subject to inquire. It is common to all men, and to be found in no other race of animals.... In almost every other race of animals the individual when it is grown up to maturity is entirely independent.... But man has almost constant occasion for the help of his brethren, and it is in vain for him to expect it from their benevolence only. He will be more likely to prevail if he can interest their self-love in his favor, and show them that it is for their own advantage to do for him what he requires of them.... We address ourselves not to their humanity but to their self-love, and never talk to them of our own necessities but of their advantages."

"As it is by treaty, by barter, and by purchase that we obtain from one another the greater part of those mutual good offices that we stand in need of, so it is this same trucking disposition which originally gives occasion to the division of labor. In a tribe of hunters or shepherds a particular person makes bows and arrows, for example, with more readiness and dexterity than any other. He frequently exchanges them for cattle or for venison with his companions; and he finds at last that he can in this manner get more cattle and venison than if he himself went to the field to catch them. From a regard to his own interest, therefore, the making of bows and arrows grows to be his chief business..."

"The difference of natural talents in different men... is not... so much the cause as the effect of the division of labor.... Without the disposition to truck, barter, and exchange, every man must have procured to himself every necessary and conveniency of life which he wanted. All must have had... the same work to do, and there could have been no such difference of employment as could alone give occasion to any great difference of talent."

"As it is this disposition which forms that difference of talents... among men, so it is this same disposition which renders that difference useful. Many tribes of animals... of the same species derive from nature a much more remarkable distinction of genius than what, antecedent to custom and education, appears to take place among men. By nature a philosopher is not in genius and in disposition half so different from a street-porter, as a mastiff is from a greyhound, or a greyhound from a spaniel, or this last from a shepherd's dog. Those different tribes of animals, however, though all of the same species, are of scarce any use to one another. The strength of the mastiff is not, in the least, supported for example by the swiftness of the greyhound.... The effects of those geniuses and talents, for want of the power or disposition to barter and exchange, cannot be brought into a common stock, and do not in the least contribute to the better accommodation and conveniency of the species. Each animal is still obliged to support and defend itself, separately and independently, and derives no sort of advantage from that variety of talents with which nature has distinguished its fellows. Among men, on the contrary, the most dissimilar geniuses are of use to one another; the different produces of their respective talents, by the general disposition to truck, barter, and exchange, bring brought, as it were, into a common stock, where every man may purchase whatever part of the produce of other men's talents he has occasion for."

"As it is the power of exchanging that gives occasion to the division of labor, so the extent of this division must always be limited by the extent of that power, or in other words, by the extent of the market. When the market is very small, no person can have any encouragement to dedicate himself entirely to one employment, for want of the power to exchange all that surplus part of the produce of his own labor, which is over and above his own consumption, for such parts of the produce of other men's labor as he has occasion for." (Smith, I, p.12,13,14,15)

In an advanced state of society "every man thus lives by exchanging, or becomes in some measure a merchant, and the society itself grows to be what is properly a commercial society." (Smith, I, pp.20) (See Destutt de Tracy: "Society is a series of reciprocal exchanges; commerce contains the whole essence of society.") The accumulation of capitals increases with the division of labor, and vice-versa.

Thus far Adam Smith.

"If every family produced all that it consumed, society could keep going even if no exchange of any sort took place... Although it is not fundamental, exchange is indispensable in our advanced state of society... The division of labor is a skilful application of the powers of man; it increases society's production — its power and its pleasures — but it robs the individual, reduces the capacity of each person taken individually. Production cannot take place without exchange." (Smith, I, pp.76-7)

Thus J.-B. Say.

"The powers inherent in man are his intelligence and his physical capacity for work. Those which spring from the condition of society consist of the capacity to divide labor and to distribute different tasks among the different people... and the power to exchange mutual services and the products which constitute these means... The motive which induces a man to give his services to another is self-interest — he demands a recompense for the services rendered. The right of exclusive private property is indispensable to the establishment of exchange among men."

"Exchange and division of labor mutually condition each other." (*Theorie des richesses sociales, suivie d'une bibliographie de l'economie politique*, Paris, 1829, Vol. I, p.25f)

Thus Skarbek.

Mill presents developed exchange, trade, as a consequence of the division of labor.

"... the agency of man can be traced to very simple elements. He can, in fact, do nothing more than produce motion. He can move things towards one another; and he can separate them from one another; the properties of matter perform all the rest....

"In the employment of labor and machinery, it is often found that the effects can be increased by skilful distribution, by separating all those operations which have any tendency to impede one another, by bringing together all those operations which can be made in any way to aid one another. As men in general cannot perform many different operations with the same quickness and dexterity with which they can, by practice, learn to perform a few, it is always an advantage to limit as much as possible the number of operations imposed upon each. For dividing labor, and distributing the power of men and machinery, to the greatest advantage, it is in most cases necessary to operate upon large scale; in other words, to produce the commodities in great masses. It is this advantage which gives existence to the great manufactories; a few of which, placed in the most convenient situations, sometimes supply not one country, but many countries, with as much as they desire of the commodity produced." (James Mill, Elements of Political Economy, London, 1821, pp.5-9)

Thus Mill.

But all the modern political economists agree that division of labor and volume of production, division of labor and accumulation of capital, are mutually determining, and that only liberated private property, left to itself, is capable of producing the most effective and comprehensive division of labor.

Adam Smith's argument can be summed up as follows: the division of labor gives labor an infinite capacity to produce. It has its basis in the propensity to exchange and barter, a specifically human propensity which is probably not fortuitous but determined by the use of reason and of language. The motive of those engaged in exchange is not humanity but egoism. The diversity of human talents is more the effect than the cause of the division of labor—i.e., of exchange. Moreover, it is only on account of the latter that this diversity is useful. The particular qualities of the different races within a species of animal are by nature more marked than the difference between human aptitudes and activities. But since animals are not able to exchange, the diversity of qualities in animals of the same species but of different races does not benefit any individual animal. Animals are unable to combine the different qualities of their species; they are incapable of contributing anything to the common good and the common comfort of their species. This is not the case with men, whose most disparate talents and modes of activity are of benefit to each other, because they can gather together their different products in a common reserve from which each can make his purchases. Just as the division of labor stems from the propensity to exchange, so it grows and is limited by the extent of exchange, of the market. In developed conditions each man is a merchant and society is a trading association.

Say regards exchange as fortuitous and not basic. Society could exist without it. It becomes indispensable in an advanced state of society. Yet production cannot take place without it. The division of labor is a convenient, useful means, a skilful application of human powers for social wealth, but it is a diminution of the capacity of each man taken individually. This last remark is an advance of Say's part.

Skarbek distinguishes the individual powers inherent in man—intelligence and physical capacity for work—from those powers which are derived from society—exchange and division of labor, which mutually condition each other. But the necessary precondition of exchange is private property. Skarbek is here giving expression in objective form to what Smith, Say, Ricardo, etc., say when they designate egoism and private self-interest as the basis of exchange and haggling as the essential and adequate form of exchange.

Mill presents trade as a consequence of the division of labor. For him, human activity is reduced to mechanical movement. The division of labor and the use of machinery promote abundance of production. Each person must be allocated the smallest possible sphere of operations. The division of labor and the use of machinery, for their part, require the production of wealth en masse, which means a concentration of production. This is the reason for the big factories.

The consideration of the division of labor and exchange is of the highest interest, because they are the perceptibly alienated expressions of human activity and essential powers as species-activity and species-power.

To say that the division of labor and exchange are based on private property is simply to say that labor is the essence of private property—an assertion that the political economist is incapable of proving and which we intend to prove for him. It is precisely in the fact that the division of labor and exchange are configurations of private property that we find the proof, both that human life needed private property for its realization and that it now needs the abolition of private property.

The division of labor and exchange are the two phenomena on whose account the political economist brags about the social nature of his science, while in the same breath he unconsciously expresses the contradiction which underlies his science—the establishment of society through unsocial, particular interests.

The factors we have to consider are these: the propensity to exchange, which is grounded in egoism, is regarded as the cause or the reciprocal effect of the division of labor. Say regards exchange as not fundamental to the nature of society. Wealth and production are explained by the division of labor and exchange. The impoverishment and denaturing of individual activity by the division of labor are admitted. Exchange and division of labor are acknowledged as producers of the great diversity of human talents, a diversity which becomes useful because of exchange. Skarbek divides man's powers of production or essential powers into two parts:

(1) those which are individual and inherent in him, his intelligence and his special disposition or capacity for work; and

(2) those which are derived not from the real individual but from society, the division of labor and exchange.

Furthermore, the division of labor is limited by the market. HUman labor is simply mechanical movement; most of the work is done by the material properties of the objects. Each individual must be allocated the smallest number of operations possible. Fragmentation of labor and concentration of capital; the nothingness of individual production and the production of wealth en masse. Meaning of free private property in the division of labor.

Money

If man's feelings, passions, etc., are not merely anthropological characteristics in the narrower sense, but are truly ontological affirmations of his essence (nature), and if they only really affirm themselves insofar as their object exists sensuously for them, then it is clear:

(1) That their mode of affirmation is by no means one and the same, but rather that the different modes of affirmation constitute the particular character of their existence, of their life. The mode in which the object exists for them is the characteristic mode of their gratification.

(2) Where the sensuous affirmation is a direct annulment of the object in its independent form (eating, drinking, fashioning of objects, etc.), this is the affirmation of the object.

(3) Insofar as man, and hence also his feelings, etc., are human, the affirmation of the object by another is also his own gratification.

(4) Only through developed industry—i.e., through mediation of private property, does the ontological essence of human passion come into being, both in its totality and in its humanity; the science of man is, therefore, itself a product of the self-formation of man through practical activity.

(5) The meaning of private property, freed from its estrangement, is the existence of essential objects for man, both as objects of enjoyment and of activity.

Money, inasmuch as it possess the property of being able to buy everything and appropriate all objects, is the object most worth possessing. The universality of this property is the basis of money's omnipotence; hence, it is regarded as an omnipotent being... Money is the pimp between need and object, between life and man's means of life. But that which mediates my life also mediates the existence of other men for me. It is for me the other person.

"What, man! confound it, hands and feet And head and backside, all are yours! And what we take while life is sweet, Is that to be declared not ours? Six stallions, say, I can afford, Is not their strength my property? I tear along, a sporting lord, As if their legs belonged to me." (Goethe, Faust—Mephistopheles)

Shakespeare, in Timon of Athens: "Gold? Yellow, glittering, precious gold! No, gods, I am no idle votarist; roots, you clear heavens! Thus much of this will make black, white; foul, fair; Wrong, right; base, noble; old, young; coward, valiant. ... Why, this Will lug your priests and servants from your sides; Pluck stout men's pillows from below their heads: This yellow slave Will knit and break religions; bless th'accurst; Make the hoar leprosy adored; place thieves, And give them title, knee, and approbation, With senators on the bench: this is it That makes the wappen'd widow wed again; She whom the spital-house and ulcerous sores Would cast the gorge at, this embalms and spices To th'April day again. Come, damned earth, Thou common whore of mankind, that putt'st odds Among the rout of nations, I will make thee Do thy right nature."

And, later on:

"O thou sweet king-killer, and dear divorce 'Twixt natural son and sire! Thou bright defiler Of Hymen's purest bed! Thou valiant Mars! Thou ever young, fresh, loved and delicate wooer, Whose blush doth thaw the consecrated snow That lies on Dian's lap! Thous visible god, That solder'st close impossibilities, And mak'st them kiss! That speak'st with every tongue, To every purpose! O thou touch of hearts! Think, thy slave man rebels; and by thy virtue Set them into confounding odds, that beasts May have in world empire!"

Shakespeare paints a brilliant picture of the nature of money. To understand him, let us begin by expounding the passage from Goethe.

That which exists for me through the medium of money, that which I can pay for, i.e., that which money can buy, that am I, the possessor of money. The stronger the power of my money, the stronger am I. The properties of money are my, the possessor's, properties and essential powers. Therefore, what I am and what I can do is by no means determined by my individuality. I am ugly, but I can buy the most beautiful woman. Which means to say that I am not ugly, for the effect of ugliness, its repelling power, is destroyed by money. As an individual, I am lame, but money procures me 24 legs. Consequently, I am not lame. I am a wicked, dishonest, unscrupulous and stupid individual, but money is respected, and so also is its owner. Money is the highest good, and consequently its owner is also good. Moreover, money spares me the trouble of being dishonest, and I am therefore presumed to be honest. I am mindless, but if money is the true mind of all things, how can its owner be mindless? What is more, he can buy clever people for himself, and is not he who has power over clever people cleverer than them? Through money, I can have anything the human heart desires. Do I not possess all human abilities? Does not money therefore transform all my incapacities into their opposite?

If money is the bond which ties me to human life and society to me, which links me to nature and to man, is money not the bond of all bonds? Can it not bind and loose all bonds? Is it therefore not the universal means of separation? It is the true agent of separation and the true cementing agent, it is the chemical power of society.

Shakespeare brings out two properties of money in particular:

(1) It is the visible divinity, the transformation of all human and natural qualities into their opposites, the universal confusion and inversion of things; it brings together impossibilities.

(2) It is the universal whore, the universal pimp of men and peoples.

The inversion and confusion of all human and natural qualities, the bringing together of impossibilities, the divine power of money lies in its nature as the estranged and alienating species-essence of man which alienates itself by selling itself. It is the alienated capacity of mankind.

What I, as a man, do—i.e., what all my individual powers cannot do—I can do with the help of money. Money, therefore, transforms each of these essential powers into something which it is not, into its opposite.

If I desire a meal, or want to take the mail coach because I am not strong enough to make the journey on foot, money can provide me both the meal and the mail coach—i.e., it transfers my wishes from the realm of imagination, it translates them from their existence as thought, imagination, and desires, into their sensuous, real existence, from imagination into life, and from imagined being into real being. In this mediating role, money is the truly creative power.

Demand also exists for those who have no money, but their demand is simply a figment of the imagination. For me, or for any other third party, it has no effect, no existence. For me, it therefore remains unreal and without an object. The difference between effective demand based on money and ineffective demand based on my need, my passion, my desire, etc., is the difference between being and thinking, between a representation which merely exists within me and one which exists outside me as a real object.

If I have money for travel, I have no need—i.e., no real and self-realizing need—to travel. If I have a vocation to study, but no money for it, I have no vocation to study—i.e., no real, true vocation. But, if I really do not have any vocation to study, but have the will and the money, then I have an effective vocation do to so. Money, which is the external, universal means and power—derived not from man as man, and not from human society as society—to turn imagination into reality and reality into more imagination, similarly turns real human and natural powers into purely abstract representations, and therefore imperfections and phantoms—truly impotent powers which exist only in the individual's fantasy—into real essential powers and abilities. Thus characterized, money is the universal inversion of individualities, which it turns into their opposites and to whose qualities it attaches contradictory qualities.

Money, therefore, appears as an inverting power in relation to the individual and to those social and other bonds which claim to be essences in themselves. It transforms loyalty into treason, love into hate, hate into love, virtue into vice, vice into virtue, servant into master, master into servant, nonsense into reason, and reason into nonsense.

Since money, as the existing and active concept of value, confounds and exchanges everything, it is the universal confusion and exchange of all things, an inverted world, the confusion and exchange of all natural and human qualities.

He who can buy courage is brave, even if he is a coward. Money is not exchange for a particular quality, a particular thing, or for any particular one of the essential powers of man, but for the whole objective world of man and of nature. Seen from the standpoint of the person who possesses it, money exchanges every quality for every other quality and object, even if it is contradictory; it is the power which brings together impossibilities and forces contradictions to embrace.

If we assume man to be man, and his relation to the world to be a human one, then love can be exchanged only for love, trust for trust, and so on. If you wish to enjoy art, you must be an artistically educated person; if you wish to exercise influence on other men, you must be the sort of person who has a truly stimulating and encouraging effect on others. Each one of your relations to man—and to nature—must be a particular expression, corresponding to the object of your will, of your real individual life. If you love unrequitedly—i.e., if your love as love does not call forth love in return, if, through the vital expression of yourself as a loving person, you fail to become a loved person — then your love is impotent, it is a misfortune.

Critique Of Hegel's Dialectic And General Philosophy

This is, perhaps, the place to make a few remarks, by way of explanation and justification, about the Hegelian dialectic — both in general and in particular, as expounded in the Phenomenology and Logic, as well as about its relation to the modern critical movement.

Modern German criticism was so pre-occupied with the old world, and so entangled during the course of its development with its subject-matter, that it had a completely uncritical attitude to the method of criticism, and was completely unaware of the seemingly formal but in fact essential question of how we now stand in relation to the Hegelian dialectic. The lack of awareness about the relation of modern criticism to Hegelian philosophy in general and to the dialectic in particular has been so pronounced that critics like Strauss and Bruno Bauer are still, at least implicitly, imprisoned within Hegelian logic, the first completely so and the second in his *Synoptiker* (where, in opposition to Strauss, he substitutes the "self-consciousness" of abstract man for the substance of abstract nature) and even in his *Das entdeckte Christentum*. For example, in *Das entdeckte Christentum* we find the following passage:

"As if self-consciousness, in positing the world, that which is different, and in producing itself in that which it produces, since it then does away with the difference between what it has produced and itself and since it is only in the producing and in the movement that it is itself — as if it did not have its purpose in this movement," etc. (Bruno Bauer, *Das entdeckte Christentum, Eine Erinnerung an das achtzehnte Jahrhundert une ein Beitrag zur Krisis des neunzehnten*, Zurich and Winterthur, 1843, p.113)

Or again:

"They (the French Materialists) could not yet see that the movement of the universe only really comes to exist for itself and enters into unity with itself as the movement of self-consciousness." (Bauer, ibid., p.114 f.)

These expressions are not even different in their language from the Hegelian conception. They reproduce it word for word.

How little awareness there was of the relation to Hegel's dialectic while this criticism was under way (Bauer's *Synoptiker*), and how little even the completed criticism of the subject-matter contributed to such an awareness, is clear from Bauer's *Gute Sache der Freiheit*, where he dismisses Herr Gruppe's impertinent question "and now what will happen to logic?" by referring him to future Critics.

But, now that Feuerbach, both in his *"Thesen"* in the *Anekdota* and in greater detail in his *Philosophie der Zukunft*, has destroyed the foundations of the old dialectic and philosophy, that very school of Criticism, which was itself incapable of taking such a step but instead watched while it was taken, has proclaimed itself the pure, resolute, absolute Criticism which has achieved self-clarity, and in its spiritual pride has reduced the whole process of history to the relation between the rest of the world, which comes into the category of the "masses", and itself. It has assimilated all dogmatic antitheses into the one dogmatic antithesis between its own sagacity and the stupidity of the world, between the critical Christ and mankind — the "rabble". It has daily and hourly demonstrated its own excellence against the mindlessness of the masses and has finally announced that the critical Day of Judgment is drawing near, when the whole of fallen humanity will be arrayed before it and divided into groups, whereupon each group will receive its certificate of poverty. The school of Criticism has made known in print its superiority to human feelings and the world, above which it sits enthroned in sublime solitude, with nothing but an occasional roar of sarcastic laughter from its Olympian lips. After all these delightful capers of idealism (Young Hegelianism) which is expiring in the form of Criticism, it (the critical school) has not once voiced so much as a suspicion of the need for a critical debate with its progenitor, the Hegelian dialectic. It has not even indicated a critical attitude to Feuerbach's dialectic. A completely uncritical attitude towards itself.

Feuerbach is the only person who has a serious and critical attitude to the Hegelian dialectic and who has made real discoveries in this field. He is the true conqueror of the old philosophy. The magnitude of his achievement and the quiet simplicity with which he present to to the world are in marked contrast to the others.

Feuerbach's great achievement is:

(1) To have shown that philosophy is nothing more than religion brought into thought and developed in thought, and that it is equally to be condemned as another form and mode of existence of the estrangement of man's nature.

(2) To have founded true materialism and real science by making the social relation of "man to man" the basic principle of this theory.

(3) To have opposed to the negation of the negation, which claims to be the absolute positive, the positive which is based upon itself and positively grounded in itself.

Feuerbach explains the Hegelian dialectic, and in so doing justifies taking the positive, that is sensuously ascertained, as his starting-point, in the following way:

Hegel starts out from the estrangement of substance (in logical terms: from the infinite, the abstractly universal), from the absolute and fixed abstraction. In ordinary language, he starts out from religion and theology.

Secondly, he supercedes the infinite and posits the actual, the sensuous, the real, the finite, the particular. (Philosophy as supersession of religion and theology.)

Thirdly, he once more supersedes the positive, and restores the abstraction, the infinite. Restoration of religion and theology.

Feuerbach, therefore, conceives the negation of the negation only as a contradiction of philosophy with itself, as philosophy which affirms theology (supersession, etc.) after having superseded it and, hence, affirms it in opposition to itself.

The positing or self-affirmation and self-confirmation present in the negation of the negation is regarded as a positing which is not yet sure of itself, which is still preoccupied with its opposite, which doubts itself and therefore stands in need of proof, which does not prove itself through its own existence, which is not admitted. It is, therefore, directly counterposed to that positing which is sensuously ascertained and grounded in itself. (Feuerbach sees negation of the negation, the concrete concept, as thought which surpasses itself in thought and as thought which strives to be direct awareness, nature, reality.)

But, since he conceives the negation of the negation from the aspect of the positive relation contained within it as the true and only positive and from the aspect of the negative relation contained within it as the only true act and self-realizing act of all being, Hegel has merely discovered the abstract, logical, speculative expression of the movement of history. This movement of history is not yet the real history of man as a given subject, it is simply the process of his creation, the history of his emergence. We shall explain both the abstract form of this movement and the difference between Hegel's conception of this process and that of modern criticism as formulated in Feuerbach's *Das Wesen des Christentums*, or, rather, the critical form of a movement which in Hegel is still uncritical.

Let us take a look at Hegel's system. We must begin with his *Phenomenology*, which is the true birthplace and secret of the Hegelian philosophy.

Phenomenology

A. Self-consciousness

1. Consciousness. (a) Certainty in sense experience, or the "this" and meaning. (b) Perception or the thing with its properties and illusion. (c) Power and understanding, phenomena and the super-sensible world.

2. Self-consciousness. The truth of certainty of oneself.

(a) Independence and dependence of self-consciousness (b) Freedom of self-consciousness. Stoicism, scepticism, the unhappy consciousness.

3. Reason. Certainty and truth.

(a) Observational reason; observation of nature and of self-consciousness. (b) Realization of rational self-consciousness through itself. Pleasure and necessity. The law of the heart and the madness of self-conceit. Virtue and the way of the world. (c) Individuality which is real in and for itself. The spiritual animal kingdom and deception or the thing itself. Legislative reason. Reason which tests laws.

B. Mind.

1. True mind, morality. 2. Self-estranged mind, culture. 3. Mind certain of itself, morality.

C. Religion. Natural religion, the religion of art, revealed religion.

D. Absolute knowledge.

Hegel's *Encyclopaedia* begins with logic, with pure speculative thought, and ends with absolute knowledge, with the self-conscious, self-comprehending philosophical or absolute mind — i.e., super-human, abstract mind. In the same way, the whole of the *Encyclopaedia* is nothing but the extended being or philosophical mind, its self-objectification; and the philosophical mind is nothing but the estranged mind of the world thinking within its self-estrangement — i.e., conceiving itself abstractly. Logic is the currency of the mind, the speculative thought-value of man and of nature, their essence which has become completely indifferent to all real determinateness and hence unreal, alienated thought, and therefore though which abstract from nature and from real man; abstract thought. The external character of this abstract thought... nature as it is for this abstract thought. Nature is external to it, its loss of self; it grasps nature externally, as abstract thought, but as alienated abstract thought. Finally mind, which is thought returning to its birthplace and which as anthropological, phenomenological, psychological, moral, artistic-religious mind, is not valid for itself until it finally discovers and affirms itself as absolute knowledge and therefore as absolute, i.e., abstract mind, receives its conscious and appropriate existence. For its real existence is abstraction.

Hegel commits a double error.

The first appears most clearly in the *Phenomenology*, which is the birthplace of Hegelian philosophy. When, for example, Hegel conceives wealth, the power of the state, etc., as entities estranged from the being of man, he conceives them only in their thought form... They are entities of thought, and therefore simply an estrangement of pure—i.e., abstract—philosophical thought. Therefore, the entire movement ends with absolute knowledge. What these objects are estranged from and what they confront with their claim to reality is none other than abstract thought. The philosopher—himself an abstract form of estranged man—sets himself up as the yardstick of the estranged world. The entire history of alienation, and the entire retraction of this alienation, is, therefore, nothing more than the history of the production of abstract (i.e., absolute), though, of logical, speculative thought. Estrangement, which thus forms the real interest of this alienation and its super-session, is the opposition of in itself and for itself, of consciousness and self-consciousness, of object and subject—i.e., the opposition within thought itself of abstract thought and sensuous reality, or real sensuousness. All other oppositions and the movements of these oppositions are only the appearance, the mask, the exoteric form of these two opposites which are alone important and which form the meaning of these other, profane oppositions. It is not the fact that the human essence objectifies itself in an inhuman way, in opposition to itself, but that it objectifies itself in distinction from and in opposition to abstract thought, which constitutes the essence of estrangement as it exists and as it is to be superseded.

The appropriation of man's objectified and estranged essential powers is, therefore, firstly only an appropriation which takes place in consciousness, in pure thought—i.e., in abstraction. In the *Phenomenology*, therefore, despite its thoroughly negative and critical appearance, and despite the fact that its criticism is genuine and often well ahead of its time, the uncritical positivism, and equally uncritical idealism of Hegel's later works, the philosophical dissolution and restoration of the empirical world, is already to be found in its latent form, in embryo, as a potentiality and a secret. Secondly, the vindication of the objective world for man—e.g., the recognition that sensuous consciousness is not abstractly sensuous consciousness, but humanly sensuous consciousness; that religion, wealth, etc., are only the estranged reality of human objectification, of human essential powers born into work, and therefore only the way to true human reality—this appropriation, or the insight into this process, therefore appears in Hegel in such a way that sense perception, religion, the power of the state, etc., are spiritual entities, for mind alone is the true essence of man, and the true form of mind is the thinking mind, the logical, speculative mind. The humanity of nature and of nature as produced by history, of man's products, is apparent from the fact that they are products of abstract mind and therefore factors of the mind, entities of thought. The *Phenomenology* is therefore concealed and mystifying criticism, criticism which has not attained self-clarity; but insofar as it grasps the estrangement of man—even though man appears only in the form of mind—all the elements of criticism are concealed within it, and often prepared and worked out in a way that goes far beyond Hegel's own point of view. The "unhappy consciousness", the "honest consciousness", the struggle of the "noble and base consciousness", etc., etc., these separate sections contain the critical elements—but still in estranged form—of entire spheres, such as religion, the state, civil life and so fort. Just as the entity, the object, appears as a thought-entity, so also the subject is always consciousness of self-consciousness; or rather, the object appears only as abstract consciousness and men only as self-consciousness. The various forms of estrangement which occur are therefore merely different forms of consciousness and self-consciousness. Since abstract consciousness, which is how the object is conceived, is in itself only one moment in the differentiation of self-consciousness, the result of the movement is the identity of self-consciousness and consciousness, absolute knowledge, the movement of abstract thought no longer directed outwards but proceeding only within itself; i.e., the result is the dialectic of pure thought.

The importance of Hegel's *Phenomenology* and its final result—the dialectic of negativity as the moving and producing principle—lies in the fact that Hegel conceives the self-creation of man as a process, objectification as loss of object, as alienation and as supersession of this alienation; that he therefore grasps the nature of labor and conceives objective man—true, because real man—as the result of his own labor. The real, active relation of man to himself as a species-being, or the realization of himself as a real species-being—i.e., as a human being, is only possible if he really employs all this species-powers—which again is only possible through the cooperation of mankind and as a result of history—and treats them as objects, which is at first only possible in the form of estrangement.

We shall now demonstrate, in detail, the one-sidedness and the limitations of Hegel, as observed in the closing chapter of the *Phenomenology*. This chapter ("Absolute Knowledge") contains the concentrated essence of the *Phenomenology*, its relation to the dialectic, and Hegel's consciousness of both and their interrelations.

For the present, let us observe that Hegel adopts the standpoint of modern political economy. He sees labor as the essence, the self-confirming essence, of man; he sees only the positive and not the negative side of labor. Labor is man's coming to be for himself within alienation or as an alienated man. The only labor Hegel knows and recognizes is abstract mental labor. So that which above all constitutes the essence of philosophy—the alienation of man who knows himself or alienated science that thinks itself—Hegel grasps as its essence, and is therefore able to bring together the separate elements of previous philosophies and present his own philosophy as the philosophy. What other philosophers did—that they conceived separate moments of nature and of man's life as moments of self-consciousness, indeed, of abstract self-consciousness—this Hegel knows by doing philosophy. Therefore, his science is absolute.

Let us now proceed to our subject.

"Absolute Knowledge." The last chapter of the *Phenomenology*.

The main point is that the object of consciousness is nothing else but self-consciousness, or that the object is only objectified self-consciousness, self-consciousness as object. (The positing of man = self-consciousness.)

It is, therefore, a question of surmounting the object of consciousness. Objectivity as such is seen as an estranged human relationship which does not correspond to human nature, to self-consciousness. The reappropriation of the objective essence of man, produced in the form of estrangement as something alien, therefore means transcending not only estrangement but also objectivity. That is to say, man is regarded as a non-objective, spiritual being.

Hegel describes the process of surmounting the object of consciousness in the following way:

The object does not only show itself as returning into the self, (according to Hegel that is a one-sided conception of the movement, a conception which grasps only one side). Man is equated with self. But the self is only abstractly conceived man, man produced by abstraction. Man is self. His eyes, his ears, etc., have the quality of self; each one of his essential powers has this quality of self. But therefore it is quite wrong to say that self-consciousness has eyes, ears, essential powers. Self-consciousness is rather a quality of human nature, of the human eye, etc.; human nature is not a quality of self-consciousness.

The self abstracted and fixed for itself is man as abstract egoist, egoism raised to its pure abstraction in thought. (We shall come back to this later.)

For Hegel, human nature, man, is equivalent to self-consciousness. All estrangement of human nature is therefore nothing but estrangement of self-consciousness not as the expression, reflected in knowledge and in thought, of the real estrangement of human nature. On the contrary, actual estrangement, estrangement which appears real, is in its innermost hidden nature—which philosophy first brings to light—nothing more than the appearance of the estrangement of real human nature, of self-consciousness. The science which comprehends this is therefore called phenomenology. All reappropriation of estranged objective being, therefore, appears as an incorporation into self-consciousness; the man who takes hold of his being is only the self-consciousness which takes hold of objective being. The return of the object into the self is therefore the reappropriation of the object.

Expressed comprehensively, the surmounting of the object of consciousness means:

(1) That the object as such presents itself to consciousness as something disappearing.

(2) That it is the alienation of self-consciousness which establishes thingness.

(3) That this alienation has not only a negative but also a positive significance. (4) That this significance is not only for us or in itself, but for self-consciousness itself.

(5) For self-consciousness the negative of the object, its own supersession of itself, has a positive significance—or self-consciousness knows the nullity of the object—in that self-consciousness alienates itself, for in this alienation it establishes itself as object of establishes the object as itself, for the sake of the indivisible unity of being-for-itself.

(6) On the other hand, this other moment is also present in the process, namely, that self-consciousness has superseded and taken back into itself this alienation and objectivity, and is therefore at home in its other-being as such.

(7) This is the movement of consciousness, and consciousness is therefore the totality of its moments.

(8) Similarly, consciousness must have related itself to the object in terms of the totality of its determinations, and have grasped it in terms of each of them. This totality of determinations make the object intrinsically a spiritual being, and it becomes that in reality for consciousness through the apprehending of each one of these determinations as determinations of self or through what we earlier called the spiritual attitude towards them.

As to (1)

That the object as such presents itself to consciousness as something disappearing is the above-mentioned return of the object into self.

As to (2)

The alienation of self-consciousness establishes thingness. Because man is equivalent to self-consciousness, his alienated objective being or thingness (that which is an object for him, and the only true object for him is that which is an essential object—i.e., his objective essence; since it is not real man, and therefore not nature, for man is human nature, who becomes as such the subject, but only the abstraction of man, self-consciousness, thingness can only be alienated self-consciousness) is the equivalent of alienated self-consciousness, and thingness is established by this alienation. It is entirely to be expected that a living, natural being equipped and endowed with objective— i.e., material—essential powers should have real natural objects for the objects of its being, and that its self-alienation should take the form of the establishment of a real, objective world, but as something external to it, a world which does not belong to its being and which overpowers it. There is nothing incomprehensible or mysterious about that. It would only be mysterious if the contrary were true. But it is equally clear that a self-consciousness, through its alienation, can only establish thingness — i.e., and abstract thing, a thing of abstraction and not a real thing. It is also clear that thingness is therefore in no way something independent or substantial vis-a-vis self-consciousness; it is a mere creature, a postulate of self-consciousness. And what is postulated, instead of confirming itself, is only a confirmation of the act of postulating; an act which, for a single moment, concentrates its energy as product and apparently confers upon that product — but only for a moment — the role of an independent, real being.

When real, corporeal man, his feet firmly planted on the solid earth and breathing all the powers of nature, establishes his real, objective essential powers as alien objects by externalization, it is not the establishing which is subject; it is the subjectivity of objective essential powers whose action must therefore be an objective one. An objective being acts objectively, and it would not act objectively is objectivity were not an inherent part of its essential nature. It creates and establishes only objects because it is established by objects, because it is fundamentally nature. In the act of establishing, it, therefore, does not descend from its "pure activity" to the creation of objects; on the contrary, its objective product simply confirms its objective activity, its activity as the activity of an objective, natural being.

Here we see how the constant naturalism or humanism differs both from idealism and materialism and is at the same time their unifying truth. We also see that only naturalism is capable of comprehending the process of world history.

Man is directly a natural being. As a natural being, and as a living natural being, he is on the one hand equipped with natural powers, with vital powers, he is an active natural being; these powers exist in him as dispositions and capacities, as drives. On the other hand, as a natural, corporeal, sensuous, objective being, he is a suffering, conditioned, and limited being, like animals and plants. that is to say, the objects of his drives exist outside him as objects independent of him; but these objects are objects of his need, essential objects, indispensable to the exercise and confirmation of his essential powers. To say that man is a corporeal, living, real, sensuous, objective being with natural powers means that he has real, sensuous objects as the object of his being and of his vital expression, or that he can only express his life in real, sensuous objects. To be objective, natural, and sensuous, and to have object, nature, and sense outside oneself, or to be oneself object, nature, and sense for a third person is one and the same thing. Hunger is a natural need; it therefore requires a nature and an object outside itself in order to satisfy and still itself. Hunger is the acknowledged need of my body for an object which exists outside itself and which is indispensable to its integration and to the expression of its essential nature. The Sun is an object for the plant, an indispensable object with confirms its life, just as the plant is an object for the Sun, as expression of its life-awakening power and its objective essential power.

A being which does not have its nature outside itself is not a natural being and plays no part in the system of nature. A being which has no object outside it, it would exist in a condition of solitude. For as soon as there are objects outside me, as soon as I am not alone, I am another, a reality other than the object outside me. For this third object I am therefore a reality other than it—i.e., its object. A being which is not the object of another being therefore presupposes that no objective being exists. As soon as I have an object, this object has me for its object. But a non-objective being is an unreal, non-sensuous, merely thought—i.e., merely conceived—being, a being of abstraction. To be sensuous—i.e., to be real—is to be an object of sense, a sensuous object, and thus to have sensuous objects outside oneself, objects of one's sense perception. To be sensuous is to suffer (to be subjected to the actions of another).

Man as an objective sensuous being is therefore a suffering being, and because he feels his suffering, he is a passionate being. Passion is man's essential power vigorously striving to attain its object.

But man is not only a natural being; he is a human natural being; i.e., he is a being for himself and hence a species-being, as which he must confirm and realize himself both in his being and in his knowing. Consequently, human objects are not natural objects as they immediately present themselves, nor is human sense, in its immediate and objective existence, human sensibility and human objectivity. Neither objective nor subjective nature is immediately present in a form adequate to the human being. And as everything natural must come into being, so man also has his process of origin in history. But for him history is a conscious process, and hence one which consciously superseded itself. History is the true natural history of man. (We shall return to this later.)

Thirdly, since this establishing of thingness is itself only an appearance, n act which contradicts the nature of pure activity, it must be superseded once again and thingness must be denied.

As to 3, 4, 5, 6.

(3) This alienation of consciousness has not only a negative but also a positive significance, and (4) it has this positive significance not only for us or in itself, but for consciousness itself.

(5) For self-consciousness, the negative of the object or its own supersession of itself has a positive significance — or self-consciousness knows the nullity of the object — in that self-consciousness alienates itself, for in this alienation it knows itself as object or, for the sake of the indivisible unity of being-for-itself, the object as itself.

(6) On the other hand, the other moment is also present in the process, namely, that self-consciousness has superseded and taken back into itself this alienation and objectivity, and is therefore at home in its other-being as such.

To recapitulate. The appropriation of estranged objective being or the supersession of objectivity in the form of estrangement — which must proceed from indifferent otherness to real, hostile estrangement — principally means for Hegel the supersession of objectivity, since it is not the particular character of the object but its objective character which constitutes the offense and the estrangement as far as self-consciousness is concerned. The object is therefore negative, self-superseding, a nullity. This nullity of the object has not only a negative but also a positive significance for consciousness, for it is precisely the self-confirmation of its non-objectivity and abstraction. For consciousness itself, the nullity of the object therefore has a positive significance because it knows this nullity, the objective being, as its self-alienation, because it knows that this nullity exists only as a result of its own self-alienation...

The way in which consciousness is, and in which something is for it, is knowing. Knowing is its only act. Hence, something comes to exist for consciousness insofar as it knows that something. Knowing is its only objective relationship. It knows the nullity of the object — i.e., that the object is not direct from it, the non-existence of the object for it, in that it knows the object as its own self-alienation; that is, it knows itself — i.e., it knows knowing, considered as an object — in that the object is only the appearance of an object, an illusion, which in essence is nothing more than knowing itself which has confronted itself with itself and hence a nullity, a something which has no objectivity outside knowing. Knowing knows that when it relates itself to an object it is only outside itself, alienates itself; that it only appears to itself as an object, or rather, that what appears to it as an object is only itself.

On the other hand, says, Hegel, this other moment is also present in the process, namely, that self-consciousness has superseded and taken back into itself this alienation and objectivity, and is therefore at home in its other-being as such.

This discussion is a compendium of all the illusions of speculation.

Firstly, consciousness — self-consciousness — is at home in its other-being as such. It is therefore, if we here abstract from Hegel's abstraction and talk instead of self-consciousness, of the self-consciousness of man, at home in its other-being as such. This implies, for one thing, that consciousness — knowing as knowing, thinking as thinking — claims to be the direct opposite of itself, claims to be the sensuous world, reality, life — thought over-reaching itself in thought (Feuerbach). This aspect is present insofar as consciousness as mere consciousness is offended not by estranged objectivity but by objectivity as such.

Secondly, it implies that self-conscious man, insofar as he has acknowledged and superseded the spiritual world, or the general spiritual existence of his world, as self-alienation, goes on to reaffirm it in this alienated form and presents it as his true existence, restores it and claims to be at home in his other-being as such. Thus, for example, having superseded religion and recognized it as a product of self-alienation, he still finds himself confirmed in religion as religion. Here is the root of Hegel's false positivism or of his merely apparent criticism; it is what Feuerbach calls the positing, negating, and re-establishing of religion or theology, but it needs to be conceived in a more general way. So reason is at home in unreason as unreason. Man, who has realized that in law, politics, etc., he leads an alienated life as such. Self-affirmation, self-confirmation in contradiction with itself and with the knowledge and the nature of the object is therefore true knowledge and true life.

Therefore there can no longer be any question abut a compromise on Hegel's part with religion, the state, etc., since this untruth is the untruth of his principle.

If I know religion as alienated human self-consciousness, then what I know in it as religion is not my self-consciousness but my alienated self-consciousness confirmed in it. Thus I know that the self-consciousness which belongs to the essence of my own self is confirmed not in religion but in the destruction and supersession of religion.

In Hegel, therefore, the negation of the negation is not the confirmation of true being through the negation of apparent being. It is the confirmation of apparent being or self-estranged being in its negation, or the negation of this apparent being as an objective being residing outside man and independent of him and its transformation into the subject.

The act of superseding therefore plays a special role in which negation and preservation (affirmation) are brought together.

Thus, for example, in Hegel's *Philosophy of Right*, private right superseded equals morality, morality superseded equals family, family superseded equals civil society, civil society superseded equals state, and state superseded equals world history. In reality, private right, morality, family, civil society, state, etc., continue to exist, but have become moments and modes of human existence which are meaningless in isolation but which mutually dissolve and engender one another. They are moments of movement.

In their real existence this character of mobility is hidden. It first appears, is first revealed, in thought and in philosophy. Hence, my true religious existence is my existence in the philosophy of religion, my true political existence is my existence in the philosophy of right, my true natural existence is my existence in the philosophy of nature, my true artistic existence is my existence in the philosophy of art and my true human existence is my existence in philosophy. Similarly, the true existence of religion, state, nature, and art is the philosophy of religion, nature, the state and art. But if the philosophy of religions, etc., is for me the true existence of religion, then I am truly religious only as a philosopher of religion, and I therefore deny real religiosity and the really religious man. But at the same time I confirm them, partly in my own existence or in the alien existence which I oppose to them — for this is merely their philosophical expression — and partly in their particular and original form, for I regard them as merely apparent other-being, as allegories, forms of their own true existence concealed under sensuous mantles—i.e. forms of my philosophical existence.

Similarly, quality superseded equals quantity, quantity superseded equals measure, measure superseded equals essence, essence superseded equals appearance, appearance superseded equals reality, reality superseded equals the concept, the concept superseded equals objectivity, objectivity superseded, equals the absolute idea, the absolute idea superseded equals nature, nature superseded equals subjective spirit, subjective spirit superseded equals ethical objective spirit, ethical spirit superseded equals art, art superseded equals religion, religion superseded equals absolute knowledge.

On the one hand, this act of superseding is the act of superseding an entity of thought; thus, private property as thought is superseded in the thought of morality. And because thought imagines itself to be the direct opposite of itself—i.e., sensuous reality—and therefore regards its own activity as sensuous, real activity, this supersession in thought, which leaves its object in existence in reality, thinks it has actually overcome it. On the other hand, since the object has now become a moment of thought for the thought which is doing the superseding, it is regarded in its real existence as a continuation of thought, so self-consciousness, of abstraction.

From one aspect the existence which Hegel superseded in philosophy is therefore not real religion, state, nature, but religion already in the form of an object of knowledge—i.e., dogmatics; hence also jurisprudence, political science, and natural science. From this aspect, he therefore stands in opposition both to the actual being and to the immediate non-philosophical science or non-philosophical concepts of being. He therefore contradicts their current conceptions.

From the other aspect the man who is religious, etc., can find his final confirmation in Hegel.

We should now examine the positive moments of the Hegelian dialectic, within the determining limits of estrangement.

(a) The act of superseding as an objective movement which re-absorbs alienation into itself. This is the insight, expressed within estrangement, into the appropriation of objective being through the supersession of its alienation; it is the estranged insight into the real objectification of man, into the real appropriation of his objective being through the destruction of the estranged character of the objective world, through the supersession of its estranged mode of existence, just as atheism as the supersession of God is the emergence of theoretical humanism, and communism as the supersession of private property the vindication of real human life as man's property, the emergence of practical humanism. Atheism is humanism mediated with itself through the supersession of religion; communism is humanism mediated with itself through the supersession of private property. Only when we have superseded this mediation—which is, however, a necessary precondition—will positive humanism, positively originating in itself, come into being.

But atheism and communism are no flight, no abstraction, no loss of the objective world created by man or of his essential powers projected into objectivity. No impoverished regression to unnatural, primitive simplicity. They are rather the first real emergence, the realization become real for man, of his essence as something real.

Therefore, in grasping the positive significance of the negation which has reference to itself, even if once again in estranged form, Hegel grasps man's self-estrangement alienation of being, loss of objectivity, and loss of reality as self-discovery, expression of being, objectification and realization. In short, he sees labor—within abstraction—as man's act of self-creation and man's relation to himself as an alien being and the manifestation of himself as an alien being as the emergence of species-consciousness and species-life.

(b) But in Hegel, apart from or rather as a consequence of the inversion we have already described, this act appears, firstly, to be merely formal because it is abstract and because human nature itself is seen only as abstract thinking being, as self-consciousness.

And secondly, because the conception is formal and abstract, the supersession of alienation becomes a confirmation of alienation. In other words, Hegel sees this movement of self-creation and self-objectification in the form of self-alienation and self-estrangement as the absolute and hence the final expression of human life which has itself as its aim, is at rest in itself and has attained its own essential nature.

This movement in its abstract form as dialectic is therefore regarded as truly human life. And since it is still an abstraction, an estrangement of human life, it is regarded as a divine process, but as the divine process of man. It is man's abstract, pure, absolute being (as distinct from himself), which itself passes through this process.

Thirdly, this process must have a bearer, a subject; but the subject comes into being only as the result; this result, the subject knowing itself as absolute self-consciousness, is therefore God, absolute spirit, the self-knowing and self-manifesting idea. Real man and real nature become mere predicates, symbols of this hidden, unreal man and this unreal nature. Subject and predicate therefore stand in a relation of absolute inversion to one another; a mystical subject-object or subjectivity encroaching upon the object, the absolute subject as a process, as a subject which alienates itself and returns to itself from alienation, while at the same time re-absorbing this alienation, and the subject as this process; pure, ceaseless revolving within itself.

First, the formal and abstract conception of man's act of self-creation of self-objectification.

Because Hegel equates man with self-consciousness, the estranged object, the estranged essential reality of man is nothing but consciousness, nothing but the thought of estrangement, its abstract and hence hollow and unreal expression, negation. The supersession of alienation is therefore likewise nothing but an abstract, hollow supersession of that hollow abstraction, the negation of the negation. The inexhaustible, vital, sensuous, concrete activity of self-objectification is therefore reduced to its mere abstraction, absolute negativity, an abstraction which is then given permanent form as such and conceived as independent activity, as activity itself. Since this so-called negativity is nothing more than the abstract, empty form of that real living act, its content can only be a formal content, created by abstraction from all content. Consequently there are general, abstract forms of abstraction which fit every content and are therefore indifferent to all content: forms of thought and logical categories torn away from real mind and real nature. (We shall expound the logical content of absolute negativity later.)

Hegel's positive achievement in his speculative logic is to present determinate concepts, the universal fixed thought-forms in their independence of nature and mind, as a necessary result of the universal estrangement of human existence, and thus also of human thought, and to comprehend them as moments in the process of abstraction. For example, being superseded is essence, essence superseded is the concept, the concept superseded is... the absolute idea. But what is the absolute idea? It is compelled to supersede its own self again, if it does not wish to go through the whole act of abstraction once more from the beginning and to reconcile itself to being a totality of abstraction which comprehends itself as abstraction knows itself to be nothing; it must relinquish itself, the abstraction, and so arrives at something which is its exact opposite, nature. Hence the whole of the Logic is proof of the fact that abstract thought is nothing for itself, that the absolute idea is nothing for itself, and that only nature is something.

The absolute idea, the abstract idea which "considered from the aspect of its unity with itself in intuition", and which "in its own absolute truth resolves to let the moment of it s particularity or of initial determination and other-being, the immediate-idea, as its reflection, issue freely from itself as nature", this whole idea, which conducts itself in such a strange and baroque fashion, and which has caused the Hegelians such terrible headaches, is purely and simply abstraction—i.e., the abstract thinker; abstraction which, taught by experience and enlightened as to its own truth, resolves under various conditions—themselves false and still abstract—to relinquish itself and to establish its other-being, the particular, the determinate, in place of its self-pervasion, non-being, universality, and indeterminateness; to let nature, which is concealed within itself as a mere abstraction, as a thing of things, issue freely from itself—i.e., to abandon abstractions and to take a look at nature, which exists free from abstraction. The abstract idea, which directly becomes intuition, is quite simply nothing more than abstract thought which relinquishes itself and decides to engage in intuiting. This entire transition from logic to philosophy of nature is nothing more than the transition—so difficult for the abstract thinker to effect, and hence described by him in such a bizarre manner—from abstracting to intuiting. The mystical feeling which drives the philosopher from abstract thinking to intuition is boredom, the longing for a content.

The man estranged from himself is also the thinker estranged from his essence—i.e., from his natural and human essence. His thoughts are therefore fixed phantoms existing outside nature and man. In his Logic, Hegel has locked up all these phantoms, conceiving each of them firstly as negative—i.e., as alienation of human thought—and secondly as negation of the negation—i.e., as supersession of this alienation, as a real expression of human thought. But since this negation of the negation is itself still trapped in estrangement, what this amounts to is in part a failure to move beyond the final stage, the stage of self-reference in alienation, which is the true existence of these phantoms.

(That is, Hegel substitutes the act of abstraction revolving within itself for these fixed abstractions; in so doing he has the merit, first of all, of having revealed the source of all these inappropriate concepts which originally belonged to separate philosophers, of having combined them and of having created as the object of criticism the exhaustive range of abstraction rather than one particular abstraction. We shall later see why Hegel separates thought from the subject; but it is already clear that if man is not human, then the expression of his essential nature cannot be human, and therefore that thought itself could not be conceived as an expression of man's being, of man as a human and natural subject, with eyes, ears, etc., living in society, in the world, and in nature.)

Insofar as this abstraction apprehends itself and experiences an infinite boredom with itself, we find in Hegel an abandonment of abstract thought which moves solely within thought, which has no eyes, teeth, ears, anything, and a resolve to recognize nature as being and to go over to intuition.

But nature, too, taken abstractly, for itself, and fixed in its separation from man, is nothing for man. It goes without saying that the abstract thinker who decides on intuition, intuits nature abstractly. Just as nature lay enclosed in the thinker in a shape which even to him was shrouded and mysterious, as an absolute idea, a thing of thought, so what he allowed to come forth from himself was simply this abstract nature, nature as a thing of thought—but with the significance now of being the other-being of thought, real, intuited nature as distinct from abstract thought. Or, to put it in human terms, the abstract thinker discovers from intuiting nature that the entities which he imagined he was creating out of nothing, out of pure abstraction, in a divine dialectic, as the pure products of the labor of thought living and moving within itself and never looking out into reality, are nothing more than abstractions from natural forms. The whole of nature only repeats to him in a sensuous, external form the abstractions of logic. He analyzes nature and these abstractions again. His intuiting of nature is therefore only the act of confirmation of his abstraction from the intuition of nature, a conscious re-enactment of the process by which he produced his abstraction. Thus, for example, Time is equated with Negativity referred to itself. In the natural form, superseded Movement as Matter corresponds to superseded Becoming as Being. Light is the natural form of Reflection-in-itself. Body as Moon and Comet is the natural form of the antithesis which, according to the Logic, is the positive grounded upon itself and the negative grounded upon itself. The Earth is the natural form of the logical ground, as the negative unity of the antithesis, etc.

Nature as nature—i.e., insofar as it is sensuously distinct from the secret sense hidden within it—nature separated and distinct from these abstractions is nothing, a nothing proving itself to be nothing, it is devoid of sense, or only has the sense of an externality to be superseded.

"In the finite-teleological view is to be found the correct premise that nature does not contain the absolute end within itself."

Its end is the confirmation of abstraction.

"Nature has revealed itself as the idea in the form of other-being. Since the idea in this form is the negative of itself, or external to itself, nature is not only external relative to this idea, but externality constitutes the form in which it exists as nature." (Hegel p.225)

"For us, mind has nature as its premise, since it is nature's truth and, therefore, its absolute primus. In this truth, nature has disappeared, and mind has yielded as the idea which has attained being-for-itself, whose object as well as subject is the concept. This identity is absolute negativity, for, whereas in nature the concept has its perfect external objectivity, in this its alienation has been superseded and the concept has become identical with itself. It is this identity only in that it is a return from nature."

"Revelation, as the abstract idea, is unmediated transition to, the coming-to-be, nature; as the revelation of the mind which is free it is the establishing of nature as its own world; an establishing which, as reflection, is at the same time a presupposing of the world as independently existing nature. Revelation in its concept is the creation of nature as the mind's being, in which it procures the affirmation and truth of its freedom."

"The absolute is mind; this is the highest definition of the absolute."

Communist Manifesto

Introduction

A spectre is haunting Europe — the spectre of communism. All the powers of old Europe have entered into a holy alliance to exorcise this spectre: Pope and Tsar, Metternich and Guizot, French Radicals and German police-spies.

Where is the party in opposition that has not been decried as communistic by its opponents in power? Where is the opposition that has not hurled back the branding reproach of communism, against the more advanced opposition parties, as well as against its reactionary adversaries?

Two things result from this fact:

Communism is already acknowledged by all Europe's powers to be itself a Power.

It is high time that Communists should openly, in the face of the whole world, publish their views, their aims, their tendencies, and meet this nursery tale of the spectre of communism with a manifesto of the party itself.

To this end, Communists of various nationalities have assembled in London and sketched the following manifesto, to be published in the English, French, German, Italian, Flemish and Danish languages.

Chapter I: Bourgeois and Proletarians

The history of all hitherto existing society is the history of class struggles.

Freeman and slave, patrician and plebeian, lord and serf, guild-master and journeyman, in a word, oppressor and oppressed, stood in constant opposition to one another, carried on an uninterrupted, now hidden, now open fight, a fight that each time ended, either in a revolutionary reconstitution of society at large, or in the common ruin of the contending classes.

In the earlier epochs of history, we find almost everywhere a complicated arrangement of society into various orders, a manifold gradation of social rank. In ancient Rome we have patricians, knights, plebeians, slaves; in the Middle Ages, feudal lords, vassals, guild-masters, journeymen, apprentices, serfs; in almost all of these classes, again, subordinate gradations.

The modern bourgeois society that has sprouted from the ruins of feudal society has not done away with class antagonisms. It has but established new classes, new conditions of oppression, new forms of struggle in place of the old ones.

Our epoch, the epoch of the bourgeoisie, possesses, however, this distinct feature: it has simplified class antagonisms. Society as a whole is more and more splitting up into two great hostile camps, into two great classes directly facing each other—bourgeoisie and proletariat.

From the serfs of the Middle Ages sprang the chartered burghers of the earliest towns. From these burgesses the first elements of the bourgeoisie were developed.

The discovery of America, the rounding of the Cape, opened up fresh ground for the rising bourgeoisie. The East-Indian and Chinese markets, the colonization of America, trade with the colonies, the increase in the means of exchange and in commodities generally, gave to commerce, to navigation, to industry, an impulse never before known, and thereby, to the revolutionary element in the tottering feudal society, a rapid development.

The feudal system of industry, in which industrial production was monopolized by closed guilds, now no longer suffices for the growing wants of the new markets. The manufacturing system took its place. The guild-masters were pushed aside by the manufacturing middle class; division of labor between the different corporate guilds vanished in the face of division of labor in each single workshop.

Meantime, the markets kept ever growing, the demand ever rising. Even manufacturers no longer sufficed. Thereupon, steam and machinery revolutionized industrial production. The place of manufacture was taken by the giant, Modern Industry; the place of the industrial middle class by industrial millionaires, the leaders of the whole industrial armies, the modern bourgeois.

Modern industry has established the world market, for which the discovery of America paved the way. This market has given an immense development to commerce, to navigation, to communication by land. This development has, in turn, reacted on the extension of industry; and in proportion as industry, commerce, navigation, railways extended, in the same proportion the bourgeoisie developed, increased its capital, and pushed into the background every class handed down from the Middle Ages.

We see, therefore, how the modern bourgeoisie is itself the product of a long course of development, of a series of revolutions in the modes of production and of exchange.

Each step in the development of the bourgeoisie was accompanied by a corresponding political advance in that class. An oppressed class under the sway of the feudal nobility, an armed and self-governing association of medieval commune: here independent urban republic (as in Italy and Germany); there taxable "third estate" of the monarchy (as in France); afterward, in the period of manufacturing proper, serving either the semi-feudal or the absolute monarchy as a counterpoise against the nobility, and, in fact, cornerstone of the great monarchies in general—the bourgeoisie has at last, since the establishment of Modern Industry and of the world market, conquered for itself, in the modern representative state, exclusive political sway. The executive of the modern state is but a committee for managing the common affairs of the whole bourgeoisie.

The bourgeoisie, historically, has played a most revolutionary part.

The bourgeoisie, wherever it has got the upper hand, has put an end to all feudal, patriarchal, idyllic relations. It has pitilessly torn asunder the motley feudal ties that bound man to his "natural superiors", and has left no other nexus between man and man than naked self-interest, than callous "cash payment". It has drowned out the most heavenly ecstasies of religious fervour, of chivalrous enthusiasm, of philistine sentimentalism, in the icy water of egotistical calculation. It has resolved personal worth into exchange value, and in place of the numberless indefeasible chartered freedoms, has set up that single, unconscionable freedom—Free Trade. In one word, for exploitation, veiled by religious and political illusions, it has substituted naked, shameless, direct, brutal exploitation.

The bourgeoisie has stripped of its halo every occupation hitherto honored and looked up to with reverent awe. It has converted the physician, the lawyer, the priest, the poet, the man of science, into its paid wage laborers.

The bourgeoisie has torn away from the family its sentimental veil, and has reduced the family relation into a mere money relation.

The bourgeoisie has disclosed how it came to pass that the brutal display of vigour in the Middle Ages, which reactionaries so much admire, found its fitting complement in the most slothful indolence. It has been the first to show what man's activity can bring about. It has accomplished wonders far surpassing Egyptian pyramids, Roman aqueducts, and Gothic cathedrals; it has conducted expeditions that put in the shade all former exoduses of nations and crusades.

The bourgeoisie cannot exist without constantly revolutionizing the instruments of production, and thereby the relations of production, and with them the whole relations of society. Conservation of the old modes of production in unaltered form, was, on the contrary, the first condition of existence for all earlier industrial classes. Constant revolutionizing of production, uninterrupted disturbance of all social conditions, everlasting uncertainty and agitation distinguish the bourgeois epoch from all earlier ones. All fixed, fast frozen relations, with their train of ancient and venerable prejudices and opinions, are swept away, all new-formed ones become antiquated before they can ossify. All that is solid melts into air, all that is holy is profaned, and man is at last compelled to face with sober senses his real condition of life and his relations with his kind.

The need of a constantly expanding market for its products chases the bourgeoisie over the entire surface of the globe. It must nestle everywhere, settle everywhere, establish connections everywhere.

The bourgeoisie has, through its exploitation of the world market, given a cosmopolitan character to production and consumption in every country. To the great chagrin of reactionaries, it has drawn from under the feet of industry the national ground on which it stood. All old-established national industries have been destroyed or are daily being destroyed. They are dislodged by new industries, whose introduction becomes a life and death question for all civilized nations, by industries that no longer work up indigenous raw material, but raw material drawn from the remotest zones; industries whose products are consumed, not only at home, but in every quarter of the globe. In place of the old wants, satisfied by the production of the country, we find new wants, requiring for their satisfaction the products of distant lands and climes. In place of the old local and national seclusion and self-sufficiency, we have intercourse in every direction, universal inter-dependence of nations. And as in material, so also in intellectual production. The intellectual creations of individual nations become common property. National one-sidedness and narrow-mindedness become more and more impossible, and from the numerous national and local literatures, there arises a world literature.

The bourgeoisie, by the rapid improvement of all instruments of production, by the immensely facilitated means of communication, draws all, even the most barbarian, nations into civilization. The cheap prices of commodities are the heavy artillery, with which it batters down all Chinese walls, with which it forces the barbarians' intensely obstinate hatred of foreigners to capitulate. It compels all nations, on pain of extinction, to adopt the bourgeois mode of production; it compels them to introduce what it calls civilization into their midst, i.e., to become bourgeois themselves. In one word, it creates a world after its own image.

The bourgeoisie has subjected the country to the rule of the towns. It has created enormous cities, has greatly increased the urban population as compared with the rural, and has thus rescued a considerable part of the population from the idiocy of rural life. Just as it has made the country dependent on the towns, so it has made barbarian and semi-barbarian countries dependent on the civilized ones, nations of peasants on nations of bourgeois, the East on the West.

The bourgeoisie keeps more and more doing away with the scattered state of the population, of the means of production, and of property. It has agglomerated population, centralized the means of production, and has concentrated property in a few hands. The necessary consequence of this was political centralization. Independent, or but loosely connected provinces, with separate interests, laws, governments, and systems of taxation, became lumped together into one nation, with one government, one code of laws, one national class interest, one frontier, and one customs tariff.

The bourgeoisie, during its rule of scarce one hundred years, has created more massive and more colossal productive forces than have all preceding generations together. Subjection of nature's forces to man, machinery, application of chemistry to industry and agriculture, steam navigation, railways, electric telegraphs, clearing of whole continents for cultivation, canalization or rivers, whole populations conjured out of the ground—what earlier century had even a presentiment that such productive forces slumbered in the lap of social labor?

We see then: the means of production and of exchange, on whose foundation the bourgeoisie built itself up, were generated in feudal society. At a certain stage in the development of these means of production and of exchange, the conditions under which feudal society produced and exchanged, the feudal organization of agriculture and manufacturing industry, in one word, the feudal relations of property became no longer compatible with the already developed productive forces; they became so many fetters. They had to be burst asunder; they were burst asunder.

Into their place stepped free competition, accompanied by a social and political constitution adapted in it, and the economic and political sway of the bourgeois class.

A similar movement is going on before our own eyes. Modern bourgeois society, with its relations of production, of exchange and of property, a society that has conjured up such gigantic means of production and of exchange, is like the sorcerer who is no longer able to control the powers of the nether world whom he has called up by his spells. For many a decade past, the history of industry and commerce is but the history of the revolt of modern productive forces against modern conditions of production, against the property relations that are the conditions for the existence of the bourgeois and of its rule. It is enough to mention the commercial crises that, by their periodical return, put the existence of the entire bourgeois society on its trial, each time more threateningly. In these crises, a great part not only of the existing products, but also of the previously created productive forces, are periodically destroyed. In these crises, there breaks out an epidemic that, in all earlier epochs, would have seemed an absurdity—the epidemic of over-production. Society suddenly finds itself put back into a state of momentary barbarism; it appears as if a famine, a universal war of devastation, had cut off the supply of every means of subsistence; industry and commerce seem to be destroyed. And why? Because there is too much civilization, too much means of subsistence, too much industry, too much commerce. The productive forces at the disposal of society no longer tend to further the development of the conditions of bourgeois property; on the contrary, they have become too powerful for these conditions, by which they are fettered, and so soon as they overcome these fetters, they bring disorder into the whole of bourgeois society, endanger the existence of bourgeois property. The conditions of bourgeois society are too narrow to comprise the wealth created by them. And how does the bourgeoisie get over these crises? On the one hand, by enforced destruction of a mass of productive forces; on the other, by the conquest of new markets, and by the more thorough exploitation of the old ones. That is to say, by paving the way for more extensive and more destructive crises, and by diminishing the means whereby crises are prevented.

The weapons with which the bourgeoisie felled feudalism to the ground are now turned against the bourgeoisie itself.

But not only has the bourgeoisie forged the weapons that bring death to itself; it has also called into existence the men who are to wield those weapons—the modern working class—the proletarians.

In proportion as the bourgeoisie, i.e., capital, is developed, in the same proportion is the proletariat, the modern working class, developed—a class of laborers, who live only so long as they find work, and who find work only so long as their labor increases capital. These laborers, who must sell themselves piecemeal, are a commodity, like every other article of commerce, and are consequently exposed to all the vicissitudes of competition, to all the fluctuations of the market.

Owing to the extensive use of machinery, and to the division of labor, the work of the proletarians has lost all individual character, and, consequently, all charm for the workman. He becomes an appendage of the machine, and it is only the most simple, most monotonous, and most easily acquired knack, that is required of him. Hence, the cost of production of a workman is restricted, almost entirely, to the means of subsistence that he requires for maintenance, and for the propagation of his race. But the price of a commodity, and therefore also of labor, is equal to its cost of production. In proportion, therefore, as the repulsiveness of the work increases, the wage decreases. What is more, in proportion as the use of machinery and division of labor increases, in the same proportion the burden of toil also increases, whether by prolongation of the working hours, by the increase of the work exacted in a given time, or by increased speed of machinery, etc.

Modern Industry has converted the little workshop of the patriarchal master into the great factory of the industrial capitalist. Masses of laborers, crowded into the factory, are organized like soldiers. As privates of the industrial army, they are placed under the command of a perfect hierarchy of officers and sergeants. Not only are they slaves of the bourgeois class, and of the bourgeois state; they are daily and hourly enslaved by the machine, by the overlooker, and, above all, in the individual bourgeois manufacturer himself. The more openly this despotism proclaims gain to be its end and aim, the more petty, the more hateful and the more embittering it is.

The less the skill and exertion of strength implied in manual labor, in other words, the more modern industry becomes developed, the more is the labor of men superseded by that of women. Differences of age and sex have no longer any distinctive social validity for the working class. All are instruments of labor, more or less expensive to use, according to their age and sex.

No sooner is the exploitation of the laborer by the manufacturer, so far at an end, that he receives his wages in cash, than he is set upon by the other portion of the bourgeoisie, the landlord, the shopkeeper, the pawnbroker, etc.

The lower strata of the middle class—the small tradespeople, shopkeepers, and retired tradesmen generally, the handicraftsmen and peasants—all these sink gradually into the proletariat, partly because their diminutive capital does not suffice for the scale on which Modern Industry is carried on, and is swamped in the competition with the large capitalists, partly because their specialized skill is rendered worthless by new methods of production. Thus, the proletariat is recruited from all classes of the population.

The proletariat goes through various stages of development. With its birth begins its struggle with the bourgeoisie. At first, the contest is carried on by individual laborers, then by the work of people of a factory, then by the operative of one trade, in one locality, against the individual bourgeois who directly exploits them. They direct their attacks not against the bourgeois condition of production, but against the instruments of production themselves; they destroy imported wares that compete with their labor, they smash to pieces machinery, they set factories ablaze, they seek to restore by force the vanished status of the workman of the Middle Ages.

At this stage, the laborers still form an incoherent mass scattered over the whole country, and broken up by their mutual competition. If anywhere they unite to form more compact bodies, this is not yet the consequence of their own active union, but of the union of the bourgeoisie, which class, in order to attain its own political ends, is compelled to set the whole proletariat in motion, and is moreover yet, for a time, able to do so. At this stage, therefore, the proletarians do not fight their enemies, but the enemies of their enemies, the remnants of absolute monarchy, the landowners, the non-industrial bourgeois, the petty bourgeois. Thus, the whole historical movement is concentrated in the hands of the bourgeoisie; every victory so obtained is a victory for the bourgeoisie.

But with the development of industry, the proletariat not only increases in number; it becomes concentrated in greater masses, its strength grows, and it feels that strength more. The various interests and conditions of life within the ranks of the proletariat are more and more equalized, in proportion as machinery obliterates all distinctions of labor, and nearly everywhere reduces wages to the same low level. The growing competition among the bourgeois, and the resulting commercial crises, make the wages of the workers ever more fluctuating. The increasing improvement of machinery, ever more rapidly developing, makes their livelihood more and more precarious; the collisions between individual workmen and individual bourgeois take more and more the character of collisions between two classes. Thereupon, the workers begin to form combinations (trade unions) against the bourgeois; they club together in order to keep up the rate of wages; they found permanent associations in order to make provision beforehand for these occasional revolts. Here and there, the contest breaks out into riots.

Now and then the workers are victorious, but only for a time. The real fruit of their battles lie not in the immediate result, but in the ever expanding union of the workers. This union is helped on by the improved means of communication that are created by Modern Industry, and that place the workers of different localities in contact with one another. It was just this contact that was needed to centralize the numerous local struggles, all of the same character, into one national struggle between classes. But every class struggle is a political struggle. And that union, to attain which the burghers of the Middle Ages, with their miserable highways, required centuries, the modern proletarian, thanks to railways, achieve in a few years.

This organization of the proletarians into a class, and, consequently, into a political party, is continually being upset again by the competition between the workers themselves. But it ever rises up again, stronger, firmer, mightier. It compels legislative recognition of particular interests of the workers, by taking advantage of the divisions among the bourgeoisie itself. Thus, the Ten-Hours Bill in England was carried.

Altogether, collisions between the classes of the old society further in many ways the course of development of the proletariat. The bourgeoisie finds itself involved in a constant battle. At first with the aristocracy; later on, with those portions of the bourgeoisie itself, whose interests have become antagonistic to the progress of industry; at all time with the bourgeoisie of foreign countries. In all these battles, it sees itself compelled to appeal to the proletariat, to ask for help, and thus to drag it into the political arena. The bourgeoisie itself, therefore, supplies the proletariat with its own elements of political and general education, in other words, it furnishes the proletariat with weapons for fighting the bourgeoisie.

Further, as we have already seen, entire sections of the ruling class are, by the advance of industry, precipitated into the proletariat, or are at least threatened in their conditions of existence. These also supply the proletariat with fresh elements of enlightenment and progress.

Finally, in times when the class struggle nears the decisive hour, the progress of dissolution going on within the ruling class, in fact within the whole range of old society, assumes such a violent, glaring character, that a small section of the ruling class cuts itself adrift, and joins the revolutionary class, the class that holds the future in its hands. Just as, therefore, at an earlier period, a section of the nobility went over to the bourgeoisie, so now a portion of the bourgeoisie goes over to the proletariat, and in particular, a portion of the bourgeois ideologists, who have raised themselves to the level of comprehending theoretically the historical movement as a whole.

Of all the classes that stand face to face with the bourgeoisie today, the proletariat alone is a genuinely revolutionary class. The other classes decay and finally disappear in the face of Modern Industry; the proletariat is its special and essential product.

The lower middle class, the small manufacturer, the shopkeeper, the artisan, the peasant, all these fight against the bourgeoisie, to save from extinction their existence as fractions of the middle class. They are therefore not revolutionary, but conservative. Nay, more, they are reactionary, for they try to roll back the wheel of history. If, by chance, they are revolutionary, they are only so in view of their impending transfer into the proletariat; they thus defend not their present, but their future interests; they desert their own standpoint to place themselves at that of the proletariat.

The "dangerous class", the social scum, that passively rotting mass thrown off by the lowest layers of the old society, may, here and there, be swept into the movement by a proletarian revolution; its conditions of life, however, prepare it far more for the part of a bribed tool of reactionary intrigue.

In the condition of the proletariat, those of old society at large are already virtually swamped. The proletarian is without property; his relation to his wife and children has no longer anything in common with the bourgeois family relations; modern industry labor, modern subjection to capital, the same in England as in France, in America as in Germany, has stripped him of every trace of national character. Law, morality, religion, are to him so many bourgeois prejudices, behind which lurk in ambush just as many bourgeois interests.

All the preceding classes that got the upper hand sought to fortify their already acquired status by subjecting society at large to their conditions of appropriation. The proletarians cannot become masters of the productive forces of society, except by abolishing their own previous mode of appropriation, and thereby also every other previous mode of appropriation. They have nothing of their own to secure and to fortify; their mission is to destroy all previous securities for, and insurances of, individual property.

All previous historical movements were movements of minorities, or in the interest of minorities. The proletarian movement is the self-conscious, independent movement of the immense majority, in the interest of the immense majority. The proletariat, the lowest stratum of our present society, cannot stir, cannot raise itself up, without the whole super incumbent strata of official society being sprung into the air.

Though not in substance, yet in form, the struggle of the proletariat with the bourgeoisie is at first a national struggle. The proletariat of each country must, of course, first of all settle matters with its own bourgeoisie.

In depicting the most general phases of the development of the proletariat, we traced the more or less veiled civil war, raging within existing society, up to the point where that war breaks out into open revolution, and where the violent overthrow of the bourgeoisie lays the foundation for the sway of the proletariat.

Hitherto, every form of society has been based, as we have already seen, on the antagonism of oppressing and oppressed classes. But in order to oppress a class, certain conditions must be assured to it under which it can, at least, continue its slavish existence. The serf, in the period of serfdom, raised himself to membership in the commune, just as the petty bourgeois, under the yoke of the feudal absolutism, managed to develop into a bourgeois. The modern laborer, on the contrary, instead of rising with the process of industry, sinks deeper and deeper below the conditions of existence of his own class. He becomes a pauper, and pauperism develops more rapidly than population and wealth. And here it becomes evident that the bourgeoisie is unfit any longer to be the ruling class in society, and to impose its conditions of existence upon society as an overriding law. It is unfit to rule because it is incompetent to assure an existence to its slave within his slavery, because it cannot help letting him sink into such a state, that it has to feed him, instead of being fed by him. Society can no longer live under this bourgeoisie, in other words, its existence is no longer compatible with society.

The essential conditions for the existence and for the sway of the bourgeois class is the formation and augmentation of capital; the condition for capital is wage labor. Wage labor rests exclusively on competition between the laborers. The advance of industry, whose involuntary promoter is the bourgeoisie, replaces the isolation of the laborers, due to competition, by the revolutionary combination, due to association. The development of Modern Industry, therefore, cuts from under its feet the very foundation on which the bourgeoisie produces and appropriates products. What the bourgeoisie therefore produces, above all, are its own grave-diggers. Its fall and the victory of the proletariat are equally inevitable.

Chapter II: Proletarians and Communists

In what relation do the Communists stand to the proletarians as a whole?

The Communists do not form a separate party opposed to the other working-class parties.

They have no interests separate and apart from those of the proletariat as a whole.

They do not set up any sectarian principles of their own, by which to shape and mold the proletarian movement.

The Communists are distinguished from the other working-class parties by this only:

(1) In the national struggles of the proletarians of the different countries, they point out and bring to the front the common interests of the entire proletariat, independently of all nationality.

(2) In the various stages of development which the struggle of the working class against the bourgeoisie has to pass through, they always and everywhere represent the interests of the movement as a whole.

The Communists, therefore, are on the one hand practically, the most advanced and resolute section of the working-class parties of every country, that section which pushes forward all others; on the other hand, theoretically, they have over the great mass of the proletariat the advantage of clearly understanding the lines of march, the conditions, and the ultimate general results of the proletarian movement.

The immediate aim of the Communists is the same as that of all other proletarian parties: Formation of the proletariat into a class, overthrow of the bourgeois supremacy, conquest of political power by the proletariat.

The theoretical conclusions of the Communists are in no way based on ideas or principles that have been invented, or discovered, by this or that would-be universal reformer.

They merely express, in general terms, actual relations springing from an existing class struggle, from a historical movement going on under our very eyes. The abolition of existing property relations is not at all a distinctive feature of communism.

All property relations in the past have continually been subject to historical change consequent upon the change in historical conditions.

The French Revolution, for example, abolished feudal property in favor of bourgeois property.

The distinguishing feature of communism is not the abolition of property generally, but the abolition of bourgeois property. But modern bourgeois private property is the final and most complete expression of the system of producing and appropriating products that is based on class antagonisms, on the exploitation of the many by the few.

In this sense, the theory of the Communists may be summed up in the single sentence: Abolition of private property.

We Communists have been reproached with the desire of abolishing the right of personally acquiring property as the fruit of a man's own labor, which property is alleged to be the groundwork of all personal freedom, activity and independence.

Hard-won, self-acquired, self-earned property! Do you mean the property of petty artisan and of the small peasant, a form of property that preceded the bourgeois form? There is no need to abolish that; the development of industry has to a great extent already destroyed it, and is still destroying it daily.

Or do you mean the modern bourgeois private property?

But does wage labor create any property for the laborer? Not a bit. It creates capital, i.e., that kind of property which exploits wage labor, and which cannot increase except upon conditions of begetting a new supply of wage labor for fresh exploitation. Property, in its present form, is based on the antagonism of capital and wage labor. Let us examine both sides of this antagonism.

To be a capitalist, is to have not only a purely personal, but a social status in production. Capital is a collective product, and only by the united action of many members, nay, in the last resort, only by the united action of all members of society, can it be set in motion.

Capital is therefore not only personal; it is a social power.

When, therefore, capital is converted into common property, into the property of all members of society, personal property is not thereby transformed into social property. It is only the social character of the property that is changed. It loses its class character.

Let us now take wage labor.

The average price of wage labor is the minimum wage, i.e., that quantum of the means of subsistence which is absolutely requisite to keep the laborer in bare existence as a laborer. What, therefore, the wage laborer appropriates by means of his labor merely suffices to prolong and reproduce a bare existence. We by no means intend to abolish this personal appropriation of the products of labor, an appropriation that is made for the maintenance and reproduction of human life, and that leaves no surplus wherewith to command the labor of others. All that we want to do away with is the miserable character of this appropriation, under which the laborer lives merely to increase capital, and is allowed to live only in so far as the interest of the ruling class requires it.

In bourgeois society, living labor is but a means to increase accumulated labor. In communist society, accumulated labor is but a means to widen, to enrich, to promote the existence of the laborer.

In bourgeois society, therefore, the past dominates the present; in communist society, the present dominates the past. In bourgeois society, capital is independent and has individuality, while the living person is dependent and has no individuality.

And the abolition of this state of things is called by the bourgeois, abolition of individuality and freedom! And rightly so. The abolition of bourgeois individuality, bourgeois independence, and bourgeois freedom is undoubtedly aimed at.

By freedom is meant, under the present bourgeois conditions of production, free trade, free selling and buying.

But if selling and buying disappears, free selling and buying disappears also. This talk about free selling and buying, and all the other "brave words" of our bourgeois about freedom in general, have a meaning, if any, only in contrast with restricted selling and buying, with the fettered traders of the Middle Ages, but have no meaning when opposed to the communist abolition of buying and selling, or the bourgeois conditions of production, and of the bourgeoisie itself.

You are horrified at our intending to do away with private property. But in your existing society, private property is already done away with for nine-tenths of the population; its existence for the few is solely due to its non-existence in the hands of those nine-tenths. You reproach us, therefore, with intending to do away with a form of property, the necessary condition for whose existence is the non-existence of any property for the immense majority of society.

In one word, you reproach us with intending to do away with *your* property. Precisely so; that is just what we intend.

From the moment when labor can no longer be converted into capital, money, or rent, into a social power capable of being monopolized, i.e., from the moment when individual property can no longer be transformed into bourgeois property, into capital, from that moment, you say, individuality vanishes.

You must, therefore, confess that by "individual" you mean no other person than the bourgeois, than the middle-class owner of property. This person must, indeed, be swept out of the way, and made impossible.

Communism deprives no man of the power to appropriate the products of society; all that it does is to deprive him of the power to subjugate the labor of others by means of such appropriations.

It has been objected that upon the abolition of private property, all work will cease, and universal laziness will overtake us.

According to this, bourgeois society ought long ago to have gone to the dogs through sheer idleness; for those who acquire anything, do not work. The whole of this objection is but another expression of the tautology: There can no longer be any wage labor when there is no longer any capital.

All objections urged against the communistic mode of producing and appropriating material products, have, in the same way, been urged against the communistic mode of producing and appropriating intellectual products. Just as to the bourgeois, the disappearance of class property is the disappearance of production itself, so the disappearance of class culture is to him identical with the disappearance of all culture.

That culture, the loss of which he laments, is, for the enormous majority, a mere training to act as a machine.

But don't wrangle with us so long as you apply, to our intended abolition of bourgeois property, the standard of your bourgeois notions of freedom, culture, law, etc. Your very ideas are but the outgrowth of the conditions of your bourgeois production and bourgeois property, just as your jurisprudence is but the will of your class made into a law for all, a will whose essential character and direction are determined by the economical conditions of existence of your class.

The selfish misconception that induces you to transform into eternal laws of nature and of reason the social forms stringing from your present mode of production and form of property — historical relations that rise and disappear in the progress of production — this misconception you share with every ruling class that has preceded you. What you see clearly in the case of ancient property, what you admit in the case of feudal property, you are of course forbidden to admit in the case of your own bourgeois form of property.

Abolition of the family! Even the most radical flare up at this infamous proposal of the Communists.

On what foundation is the present family, the bourgeois family, based? On capital, on private gain. In its completely developed form, this family exists only among the bourgeoisie. But this state of things finds its complement in the practical absence of the family among proletarians, and in public prostitution.

The bourgeois family will vanish as a matter of course when its complement vanishes, and both will vanish with the vanishing of capital.

Do you charge us with wanting to stop the exploitation of children by their parents? To this crime we plead guilty.

But, you say, we destroy the most hallowed of relations, when we replace home education by social.

And your education! Is not that also social, and determined by the social conditions under which you educate, by the intervention direct or indirect, of society, by means of schools, etc.? The Communists have not intended the intervention of society in education; they do but seek to alter the character of that intervention, and to rescue education from the influence of the ruling class.

The bourgeois claptrap about the family and education, about the hallowed correlation of parents and child, becomes all the more disgusting, the more, by the action of Modern Industry, all the family ties among the proletarians are torn asunder, and their children transformed into simple articles of commerce and instruments of labor.

But you Communists would introduce community of women, screams the bourgeoisie in chorus.

The bourgeois sees his wife a mere instrument of production. He hears that the instruments of production are to be exploited in common, and, naturally, can come to no other conclusion that the lot of being common to all will likewise fall to the women.

He has not even a suspicion that the real point aimed at is to do away with the status of women as mere instruments of production.

For the rest, nothing is more ridiculous than the virtuous indignation of our bourgeois at the community of women which, they pretend, is to be openly and officially established by the Communists. The Communists have no need to introduce free love; it has existed almost from time immemorial.

Our bourgeois, not content with having wives and daughters of their proletarians at their disposal, not to speak of common prostitutes, take the greatest pleasure in seducing each other's wives.

Bourgeois marriage is, in reality, a system of wives in common and thus, at the most, what the Communists might possibly be reproached with is that they desire to introduce, in substitution for a hypocritically concealed, an openly legalized system of free love. For the rest, it is self-evident that the abolition of the present system of production must bring with it the abolition of free love springing from that system, i.e., of prostitution both public and private.

The Communists are further reproached with desiring to abolish countries and nationality.

The working men have no country. We cannot take from them what they have not got. Since the proletariat must first of all acquire political supremacy, must rise to be the leading class of the nation, must constitute itself the nation, it is, so far, itself national, though not in the bourgeois sense of the word.

National differences and antagonism between peoples are daily more and more vanishing, owing to the development of the bourgeoisie, to freedom of commerce, to the world market, to uniformity in the mode of production and in the conditions of life corresponding thereto.

The supremacy of the proletariat will cause them to vanish still faster. United action of the leading civilized countries at least is one of the first conditions for the emancipation of the proletariat.

In proportion as the exploitation of one individual by another will also be put an end to, the exploitation of one nation by another will also be put an end to. In proportion as the antagonism between classes within the nation vanishes, the hostility of one nation to another will come to an end.

The charges against communism made from a religious, a philosophical and, generally, from an ideological standpoint, are not deserving of serious examination.

Does it require deep intuition to comprehend that man's ideas, views, and conception, in one word, man's consciousness, changes with every change in the conditions of his material existence, in his social relations and in his social life?

What else does the history of ideas prove, than that intellectual production changes its character in proportion as material production is changed? The ruling ideas of each age have ever been the ideas of its ruling class.

When people speak of the ideas that revolutionize society, they do but express that fact that within the old society the elements of a new one have been created, and that the dissolution of the old ideas keeps even pace with the dissolution of the old conditions of existence.

When the ancient world was in its last throes, the ancient religions were overcome by Christianity. When Christian ideas succumbed in the eighteenth century to rationalist ideas, feudal society fought its death battle with the then revolutionary bourgeoisie. The ideas of religious liberty and freedom of conscience merely gave expression to the sway of free competition within the domain of knowledge.

"Undoubtedly," it will be said, "religious, moral, philosophical, and juridicial ideas have been modified in the course of historical development. But religion, morality, philosophy, political science, and law, constantly survived this change."

"There are, besides, eternal truths, such as Freedom, Justice, etc., that are common to all states of society. But communism abolishes eternal truths, it abolishes all religion, and all morality, instead of constituting them on a new basis; it therefore acts in contradiction to all past historical experience."

What does this accusation reduce itself to? The history of all past society has consisted in the development of class antagonisms, antagonisms that assumed different forms at different epochs.

But whatever form they may have taken, one fact is common to all past ages, viz., the exploitation of one part of society by the other. No wonder, then, that the social consciousness of past ages, despite all the multiplicity and variety it displays, moves within certain common forms, or general ideas, which cannot completely vanish except with the total disappearance of class antagonisms.

The communist revolution is the most radical rupture with traditional relations; no wonder that its development involved the most radical rupture with traditional ideas.

But let us have done with the bourgeois objections to communism.

We have seen above that the first step in the revolution by the working class is to raise the proletariat to the position of ruling class to win the battle of democracy.

The proletariat will use its political supremacy to wrest, by degree, all capital from the bourgeoisie, to centralize all instruments of production in the hands of the state, i.e., of the proletariat organized as the ruling class; and to increase the total productive forces as rapidly as possible.

Of course, in the beginning, this cannot be effected except by means of despotic inroads on the rights of property, and on the conditions of bourgeois production; by means of measures, therefore, which appear economically insufficient and untenable, but which, in the course of the movement, outstrip themselves, necessitate further inroads upon the old social order, and are unavoidable as a means of entirely revolutionizing the mode of production.

These measures will, of course, be different in different countries.

Nevertheless, in most advanced countries, the following will be pretty generally applicable.

Abolition of property in land and application of all rents of land to public purposes.

A heavy progressive or graduated income tax.

Abolition of all rights of inheritance.

Confiscation of the property of all emigrants and rebels.

Centralization of credit in the banks of the state, by means of a national bank with state capital and an exclusive monopoly.

Centralization of the means of communication and transport in the hands of the state.

Extension of factories and instruments of production owned by the state; the bringing into cultivation of waste lands, and the improvement of the soil generally in accordance with a common plan.

Equal obligation of all to work. Establishment of industrial armies, especially for agriculture.

Combination of agriculture with manufacturing industries; gradual abolition of all the distinction between town and country by a more equable distribution of the populace over the country.

Free education for all children in public schools. Abolition of children's factory labor in its present form. Combination of education with industrial production, etc.

When, in the course of development, class distinctions have disappeared, and all production has been concentrated in the hands of a vast association of the whole nation, the public power will lose its political character. Political power, properly so called, is merely the organized power of one class for oppressing another. If the proletariat during its contest with the bourgeoisie is compelled, by the force of circumstances, to organize itself as a class; if, by means of a revolution, it makes itself the ruling class, and, as such, sweeps away by force the old conditions of production, then it will, along with these conditions, have swept away the conditions for the existence of class antagonisms and of classes generally, and will thereby have abolished its own supremacy as a class.

In place of the old bourgeois society, with its classes and class antagonisms, we shall have an association in which the free development of each is the condition for the free development of all.

Chapter III: Socialist and Communist Literature

Owing to their historical position, it became the vocation of the aristocracies of France and England to write pamphlets against modern bourgeois society. In the French Revolution of July 1830, and in the English reform agitation, these aristocracies again succumbed to the hateful upstart. Thenceforth, a serious political struggle was altogether out of the question. A literary battle alone remained possible. But even in the domain of literature, the old cries of the restoration period had become impossible.□

In order to arouse sympathy, the aristocracy was obliged to lose sight, apparently, of its own interests, and to formulate its indictment against the bourgeoisie in the interest of the exploited working class alone. Thus, the aristocracy took their revenge by singing lampoons on their new masters and whispering in his ears sinister prophesies of coming catastrophe.

In this way arose feudal socialism: half lamentation, half lampoon; half an echo of the past, half menace of the future; at times, by its bitter, witty and incisive criticism, striking the bourgeoisie to the very heart's core, but always ludicrous in its effect, through total incapacity to comprehend the march of modern history.

The aristocracy, in order to rally the people to them, waved the proletarian alms-bag in front for a banner. But the people, so often as it joined them, saw on their hindquarters the old feudal coats of arms, and deserted with loud and irreverent laughter.

One section of the French Legitimists and "Young England" exhibited this spectacle.

In pointing out that their mode of exploitation was different to that of the bourgeoisie, the feudalists forget that they exploited under circumstances and conditions that were quite different and that are now antiquated. In showing that, under their rule, the modern proletariat never existed, they forget that the modern bourgeoisie is the necessary offspring of their own form of society.

For the rest, so little do they conceal the reactionary character of their criticism that their chief accusation against the bourgeois amounts to this: that under the bourgeois regime a class is being developed which is destined to cut up, root and branch, the old order of society.

What they upbraid the bourgeoisie with is not so much that it creates a proletariat as that it creates a revolutionary proletariat.

In political practice, therefore, they join in all corrective measures against the working class; and in ordinary life, despite their high-falutin phrases, they stoop to pick up the golden apples dropped from the tree of industry, and to barter truth, love, and honour, for traffic in wool, beetroot-sugar, and potato spirits. □

As the parson has ever gone hand in hand with the landlord, so has clerical socialism with feudal socialism.

Nothing is easier than to give Christian asceticism a socialist tinge. Has not Christianity declaimed against private property, against marriage, against the state? Has it not preached in the place of these, charity and poverty, celibacy and mortification of the flesh, monastic life and Mother Church? Christian socialism is but the holy water with which the priest consecrates the heart-burnings of the aristocrat.

Petty-Bourgeois Socialism

The feudal aristocracy was not the only class that was ruined by the bourgeoisie, not the only class whose conditions of existence pined and perished in the atmosphere of modern bourgeois society. The medieval burgesses and the small peasant proprietors were the precursors of the modern bourgeoisie. In those countries which are but little developed, industrially and commercially, these two classes still vegetate side by side with the rising bourgeoisie.

In countries where modern civilization has become fully developed, a new class of petty bourgeois has been formed, fluctuating between proletariat and bourgeoisie, and ever renewing itself a supplementary part of bourgeois society. The individual members of this class, however, as being constantly hurled down into the proletariat by the action of competition, and, as Modern Industry develops, they even see the moment approaching when they will completely disappear as an independent section of modern society, to be replaced in manufactures, agriculture and commerce, by overlookers, bailiffs and shopmen.

In countries like France, where the peasants constitute far more than half of the population, it was natural that writers who sided with the proletariat against the bourgeoisie should use, in their criticism of the bourgeois régime, the standard of the peasant and petty bourgeois, and from the standpoint of these intermediate classes, should take up the cudgels for the working class. Thus arose petty-bourgeois socialism. Sismondi was the head of this school, not only in France but also in England.

This school of socialism dissected with great acuteness the contradictions in the conditions of modern production. It laid bare the hypocritical apologies of economists. It proved, incontrovertibly, the disastrous effects of machinery and division of labor; the concentration of capital and land in a few hands; overproduction and crises; it pointed out the inevitable ruin of the petty bourgeois and peasant, the misery of the proletariat, the anarchy in production, the crying inequalities in the distribution of wealth, the industrial war of extermination between nations, the dissolution of old moral bonds, of the old family relations, of the old nationalities.

In it positive aims, however, this form of socialism aspires either to restoring the old means of production and of exchange, and with them the old property relations, and the old society, or to cramping the modern means of production and of exchange within the framework of the old property relations that have been, and were bound to be, exploded by those means. In either case, it is both reactionary and Utopian.

Its last words are: corporate guilds for manufacture; patriarchal relations in agriculture.

Ultimately, when stubborn historical facts had dispersed all intoxicating effects of self-deception, this form of socialism ended in a miserable hangover.

German or "True" Socialism

The socialist and communist literature of France, a literature that originated under the pressure of a bourgeoisie in power, and that was the expressions of the struggle against this power, was introduced into Germany at a time when the bourgeoisie in that country had just begun its contest with feudal absolutism.

German philosophers, would-be philosophers, and beaux esprits (men of letters), eagerly seized on this literature, only forgetting that when these writings immigrated from France into Germany, French social conditions had not immigrated along with them. In contact with German social conditions, this French literature lost all its immediate practical significance and assumed a purely literary aspect.

Thus, to the German philosophers of the eighteenth century, the demands of the first French Revolution were nothing more than the demands of "Practical Reason" in general, and the utterance of the will of the revolutionary French bourgeoisie signified, in their eyes, the laws of pure will, of will as it was bound to be, of true human will generally.

The work of the German literati consisted solely in bringing the new French ideas into harmony with their ancient philosophical conscience, or rather, in annexing the French ideas without deserting their own philosophic point of view.

This annexation took place in the same way in which a foreign language is appropriated, namely, by translation.

It is well known how the monks wrote silly lives of Catholic saints over the manuscripts on which the classical works of ancient heathendom had been written. The German literati reversed this process with the profane French literature. They wrote their philosophical nonsense beneath the French original. For instance, beneath the French criticism of the economic functions of money, they wrote "alienation of humanity", and beneath the French criticism of the bourgeois state they wrote "dethronement of the category of the general", and so forth.

The introduction of these philosophical phrases at the back of the French historical criticisms, they dubbed "Philosophy of Action", "True Socialism", "German Science of Socialism", "Philosophical Foundation of Socialism", and so on.

The French socialist and communist literature was thus completely emasculated. And, since it ceased, in the hands of the German, to express the struggle of one class with the other, he felt conscious of having overcome "French one-sidedness" and of representing, not true requirements, but the requirements of truth; not the interests of the proletariat, but the interests of human nature, of man in general, who belongs to no class, has no reality, who exists only in the misty realm of philosophical fantasy.

This German socialism, which took its schoolboy task so seriously and solemnly, and extolled its poor stock-in-trade in such a mountebank fashion, meanwhile gradually lost its pedantic innocence.

The fight of the Germans, and especially of the Prussian bourgeoisie, against feudal aristocracy and absolute monarchy, in other words, the liberal movement, became more earnest.

By this, the long-wished for opportunity was offered to "True" Socialism of confronting the political movement with the socialistic demands, of hurling the traditional anathemas against liberalism, against representative government, against bourgeois competition, bourgeois freedom of the press, bourgeois legislation, bourgeois liberty and equality, and of preaching to the masses that they had nothing to gain, and everything to lose, by this bourgeois movement. German socialism forgot, in the nick of time, that the French criticism, whose silly echo it was, presupposed the existence of modern bourgeois society, with its corresponding economic conditions of existence, and the political constitution adapted thereto, the very things those attainment was the object of the pending struggle in Germany.

To the absolute governments, with their following of parsons, professors, country squires, and officials, it served as a welcome scarecrow against the threatening bourgeoisie.

It was a sweet finish, after the bitter pills of flogging and bullets, with which these same governments, just at that time, dosed the German working-class risings.

While this "True" Socialism thus served the government as a weapon for fighting the German bourgeoisie, it, at the same time, directly represented a reactionary interest, the interest of German philistines. In Germany, the petty-bourgeois class, a relic of the sixteenth century, and since then constantly cropping up again under the various forms, is the real social basis of the existing state of things.

To preserve this class is to preserve the existing state of things in Germany. The industrial and political supremacy of the bourgeoisie threatens it with certain destruction—on the one hand, from the concentration of capital; on the other, from the rise of a revolutionary proletariat. "True" Socialism appeared to kill these two birds with one stone. It spread like an epidemic.

The robe of speculative cobwebs, embroidered with flowers of rhetoric, steeped in the dew of sickly sentiment, this transcendental robe in which the German Socialists wrapped their sorry "eternal truths", all skin and bone, served to wonderfully increase the sale of their goods amongst such a public. And on its part German socialism recognized, more and more, its own calling as the bombastic representative of the petty-bourgeois philistine.

It proclaimed the German nation to be the model nation, and the German petty philistine to be the typical man. To every villainous meanness of this model man, it gave a hidden, higher, socialistic interpretation, the exact contrary of its real character. It went to the extreme length of directly opposing the "brutally destructive" tendency of communism, and of proclaiming its supreme and impartial contempt of all class struggles. With very few exceptions, all the so-called socialist and communist publications that now (1847) circulate in Germany belong to the domain of this foul and enervating literature.

Conservative or Bourgeois Socialism

A part of the bourgeoisie is desirous of redressing social grievances in order to secure the continued existence of bourgeois society.

To this section belong economists, philanthropists, humanitarians, improvers of the condition of the working class, organizers of charity, members of societies for the prevention of cruelty to animals, temperance fanatics, hole-and-corner reformers of every imaginable kind. This form of socialism has, moreover, been worked out into complete systems.

We may cite Proudhon's *Philosophy of Poverty* as an example of this form.

The socialistic bourgeois want all the advantages of modern social conditions without the struggles and dangers necessarily resulting therefrom. They desire the existing state of society, minus its revolutionary and disintegrating elements. They wish for a bourgeoisie without a proletariat. The bourgeoisie naturally conceives the world in which it is supreme to be the best; and bourgeois socialism develops this comfortable conception into various more or less complete systems. In requiring the proletariat to carry out such a system, and thereby to march straightaway into the social New Jerusalem, it but requires in reality that the proletariat should remain within the bounds of existing society, but should cast away all its hateful ideas concerning the bourgeoisie.

A second, and more practical, but less systematic, form of this socialism sought to depreciate every revolutionary movement in the eyes of the working class by showing that no mere political reform, but only a change in the material conditions of existence, in economical relations, could be of any advantage to them. By changes in the material conditions of existence, this form of socialism, however, by no means understands abolition of the bourgeois relations of production, an abolition that can be affected only by a revolution, but administrative reforms, based on the continued existence of these relations; reforms, therefore, that in no respect affect the relations between capital and labor, but, at the best, lessen the cost, and simplify the administrative work of bourgeois government.

Bourgeois socialism attains adequate expression when, and only when, it becomes a mere figure of speech.

Free trade: for the benefit of the working class. Protective duties: for the benefit of the working class. Prison reform: for the benefit of the working class. This is the last word and the only seriously meant word of bourgeois socialism.

It is summed up in the phrase: the bourgeois is a bourgeois—for the benefit of the working class.

Critical-Utopian Socialism and Communism

We do not here refer to that literature which, in every great modern revolution, has always given voice to the demands of the proletariat, such as the writings of Babeuf and others.

The first direct attempts of the proletariat to attain its own ends, made in times of universal excitement, when feudal society was being overthrown, necessarily failed, owing to the then undeveloped state of the proletariat, as well as to the absence of the economic conditions for its emancipation, conditions that had yet to be produced, and could be produced by the impending bourgeois epoch alone. The revolutionary literature that accompanied these first movements of the proletariat had necessarily a reactionary character. It inculcated universal asceticism and social levelling in its crudest form.

The socialist and communist systems, properly so called, those of Saint-Simon, Fourier, Owen, and others, spring into existence in the early undeveloped period, described above, of the struggle between proletariat and bourgeoisie (see Section 1. Bourgeois and Proletarians).

The founders of these systems see, indeed, the class antagonisms, as well as the action of the decomposing elements in the prevailing form of society. But the proletariat, as yet in its infancy, offers to them the spectacle of a class without any historical initiative or any independent political movement.

Since the development of class antagonism keeps even pace with the development of industry, the economic situation, as they find it, does not as yet offer to them the material conditions for the emancipation of the proletariat. They therefore search after a new social science, after new social laws, that are to create these conditions.

Historical action is to yield to their personal inventive action; historically created conditions of emancipation to fantastic ones; and the gradual, spontaneous class organization of the proletariat to an organization of society especially contrived by these inventors. Future history resolves itself, in their eyes, into the propaganda and the practical carrying out of their social plans.

In the formation of their plans, they are conscious of caring chiefly for the interests of the working class, as being the most suffering class. Only from the point of view of being the most suffering class does the proletariat exist for them.

The undeveloped state of the class struggle, as well as their own surroundings, causes Socialists of this kind to consider themselves far superior to all class antagonisms. They want to improve the condition of every member of society, even that of the most favored. Hence, they habitually appeal to society at large, without the distinction of class; nay, by preference, to the ruling class. For how can people when once they understand their system, fail to see in it the best possible plan of the best possible state of society?

Hence, they reject all political, and especially all revolutionary action; they wish to attain their ends by peaceful means, necessarily doomed to failure, and by the force of example, to pave the way for the new social gospel.

Such fantastic pictures of future society, painted at a time when the proletariat is still in a very undeveloped state and has but a fantastic conception of its own position, correspond with the first instinctive yearnings of that class for a general reconstruction of society.

But these socialist and communist publications contain also a critical element. They attack every principle of existing society. Hence, they are full of the most valuable materials for the enlightenment of the working class. The practical measures proposed in them—such as the abolition of the distinction between town and country, of the family, of the carrying on of industries for the account of private individuals, and of the wage system, the proclamation of social harmony, the conversion of the function of the state into a more superintendence of production—all these proposals point solely to the disappearance of class antagonisms which were, at that time, only just cropping up, and which, in these publications, are recognized in their earliest indistinct and undefined forms only. These proposals, therefore, are of a purely utopian character.

The significance of critical-utopian socialism and communism bears an inverse relation to historical development. In proportion as the modern class struggle develops and takes definite shape, this fantastic standing apart from the contest, these fantastic attacks on it, lose all practical value and all theoretical justifications. Therefore, although the originators of these systems were, in many respects, revolutionary, their disciples have, in every case, formed mere reactionary sects. They hold fast by the original views of their masters, in opposition to the progressive historical development of the proletariat. They, therefore, endeavour, and that consistently, to deaden the class struggle and to reconcile the class antagonisms. They still dream of experimental realization of their social utopias, of founding isolated phalansteres, of establishing "Home Colonies", or setting up a "Little Icaria" — pocket editions of the New Jerusalem — and to realise all these castles in the air, they are compelled to appeal to the feelings and purses of the bourgeois. By degrees, they sink into the category of the reactionary conservative socialists depicted above, differing from these only by more systematic pedantry, and by their fanatical and superstitious belief in the miraculous effects of their social science.

They, therefore, violently oppose all political action on the part of the working class; such action, according to them, can only result from blind unbelief in the new gospel.

The Owenites in England, and the Fourierists in France, respectively, oppose the Chartists and the Réformistes.

Chapter IV: Position of the Communists in Relation to the Various Existing Opposition Parties

Section II has made clear the relations of the Communists to the existing working-class parties, such as the Chartists in England and the Agrarian Reformers in America.

The Communists fight for the attainment of the immediate aims, for the enforcement of the momentary interests of the working class; but in the movement of the present, they also represent and take care of the future of that movement. In France, the Communists ally with the Social Democrats against the conservative and radical bourgeoisie, reserving, however, the right to take up a critical position in regard to phases and illusions traditionally handed down from the great Revolution.

In Switzerland, they support the Radicals, without losing sight of the fact that this party consists of antagonistic elements, partly of Democratic Socialists, in the French sense, partly of radical bourgeois.

In Poland, they support the party that insists on an agrarian revolution as the prime condition for national emancipation, that party which fomented the insurrection of Krakow in 1846.

In Germany, they fight with the bourgeoisie whenever it acts in a revolutionary way, against the absolute monarchy, the feudal squirearchy, and the petty-bourgeoisie.

But they never cease, for a single instant, to instill into the working class the clearest possible recognition of the hostile antagonism between bourgeoisie and proletariat, in order that the German workers may straightway use, as so many weapons against the bourgeoisie, the social and political conditions that the bourgeoisie must necessarily introduce along with its supremacy, and in order that, after the fall of the reactionary classes in Germany, the fight against the bourgeoisie itself may immediately begin.

The Communists turn their attention chiefly to Germany, because that country is on the eve of a bourgeois revolution that is bound to be carried out under more advanced conditions of European civilization and with a much more developed proletariat than that of England was in the seventeenth, and France in the eighteenth century, and because the bourgeois revolution in Germany will be but the prelude to an immediately following proletarian revolution.

In short, the Communists everywhere support every revolutionary movement against the existing social and political order of things. In all these movements, they bring to the front, as the leading question in each, the property question, no matter what its degree of development at the time.

Finally, they labor everywhere for the union and agreement of the democratic parties of all countries.

The Communists disdain to conceal their views and aims. They openly declare that their ends can be attained only by the forcible overthrow of all existing social conditions. Let the ruling classes tremble at a communist revolution. The proletarians have nothing to lose but their chains. They have a world to win. Workers Of The World Unite, You Have Nothing To Lose But Your Chains!

Wage Labour and Capital

Introduction
by Frederick Engels

This pamphlet first appeared in the form of a series of leading articles in the *Neue Rheinische Zeitung*, beginning on April 4th, 1849. The text is made up of from lectures delivered by Marx before the German Workingmen's Club of Brussels in 1847. The series was never completed. The promise "to be continued," at the end of the editorial in Number 269 of the newspaper, remained unfulfilled in consequence of the precipitous events of that time: the invasion of Hungary by the Russians, and the uprisings in Dresden, Iserlohn, Elberfeld, the Palatinate, and in Baden, which led to the suppression of the paper on May 19th, 1849. And among the papers left by Marx no manuscript of any continuation of these articles has been found.

"Wage-Labor and Capital" has appeared as an independent publication in several editions, the last of which was issued by the Swiss Co-operative Printing Association, in Hottingen-Zurich, in 1884. Hitherto, the several editions have contained the exact wording of the original articles. But since at least 10,000 copies of the present edition are to be circulated as a propaganda tract, the question necessarily forced itself upon me, would Marx himself, under these circumstance, have approved of an unaltered literal reproduction of the original?

Marx, in the '40s, had not yet completed his criticism of political economy. This was not done until toward the end of the fifties. Consequently, such of his writings as were published before the first installment of his Critique of Political Economy was finished, deviate in some points from those written after 1859, and contain expressions and whole sentences which, viewed from the standpoint of his later writings, appear inexact, and even incorrect. Now, it goes without saying that in ordinary editions, intended for the public in general, this earlier standpoint, as a part of the intellectual development of the author, has its place; that the author as well as the public, has an indisputable right to an unaltered reprint of these older writings. In such a case, I would not have dreamed of changing a single word in it. But it is otherwise when the edition is destined almost exclusively for the purpose of propaganda. In such a case, Marx himself would unquestionably have brought the old work, dating from 1849, into harmony with his new point of view, and I feel sure that I am acting in his spirit when I insert in this edition the few changes and additions which are necessary in order to attain this object in all essential point.

Therefore, I say to the reader at once: this pamphlet is not as Marx wrote it in 1849, but approximately as Marx would have written it in 1891. Moreover, so many copies of the original text are in circulation, that these will suffice until I can publish it again unaltered in a complete edition of Marx's works, to appear at some future time.

My alterations centre about one point. According to the original reading, the worker sells his labor for wages, which he receives from the capitalist; according to the present text, he sells his labor-power. And for this change, I must render an explanation: to the workers, in order that they may understand that we are not quibbling or word-juggling, but are dealing here with one of the most important points in the whole range of political economy; to the bourgeois, in order that they may convince themselves how greatly the uneducated workers, who can be easily made to grasp the most difficult economic analyses, excel our supercilious "cultured" folk, for whom such ticklish problems remain insoluble their whole life long.

Classical political economy borrowed from the industrial practice the current notion of the manufacturer, that he buys and pays for the labor of his employees. This conception had been quite serviceable for the business purposes of the manufacturer, his bookkeeping and price calculation. But naively carried over into political economy, it there produced truly wonderful errors and confusions.

Political economy finds it an established fact that the prices of all commodities, among them the price of the commodity which it calls "labor," continually change; that they rise and fall in consequence of the most diverse circumstances, which often have no connection whatsoever with the production of the commodities themselves, so that prices appear to be determined, as a rule, by pure chance. As soon, therefore, as political economy stepped forth as a science, it was one of its first tasks to search for the law that hid itself behind this chance, which apparently determined the prices of commodities, and which in reality controlled this very chance. Among the prices of commodities, fluctuating and oscillating, now upward, now downward, the fixed central point was searched for around which these fluctuations and oscillations were taking place. In short, starting from the price of commodities, political economy sought for the value of commodities as the regulating law, by means of which all price fluctuations could be explained, and to which they could all be reduced in the last resort.

And so, classical political economy found that the value of a commodity was determined by the labor incorporated in it and requisite to its production. With this explanation, it was satisfied. And we, too, may, for the present, stop at this point. But, to avoid misconceptions, I will remind the reader that today this explanation has become wholly inadequate. Marx was the first to investigate thoroughly into the value-forming quality of labor and to discover that not all labor which is apparently, or even really, necessary to the production of a commodity, imparts under all circumstances to this commodity a magnitude of value corresponding to the quantity of labor used up. If, therefore, we say today in short, with economists like Ricardo, that the value of a commodity is determined by the labor necessary to its production, we always imply the reservations and restrictions made by Marx. Thus much for our present purpose; further information can be found in Marx's Critique of Political Economy, which appeared in 1859, and in the first volume of Capital.

But, as soon as the economists applied this determination of value by labor to the commodity "labor", they fell from one contradiction into another. How is the value of "labor" determined? By the necessary labor embodied in it. But how much labor is embodied in the labor of a laborer of a day a week, a month, a year. If labor is the measure of all values, we can express the "value of labor" only in labor. But we know absolutely nothing about the value of an hour's labor, if all that we know about it is that it is equal to one hour's labor. So, thereby, we have not advanced one hair's breadth nearer our goal; we are constantly turning about in a circle.

Classical economics, therefore, essayed another turn. It said: the value of a commodity is equal to its cost of production. But, what is the cost of production of "labor"? In order to answer this question, the economists are forced to strain logic just a little. Instead of investigating the cost of production of labor itself, which, unfortunately, cannot be ascertained, they now investigate the cost of production of the laborer. And this latter can be ascertained. It changes according to time and circumstances, but for a given condition of society, in a given locality, and in a given branch of production, it, too, is given, at least within quite narrow limits. We live today under the regime of capitalist production, under which a large and steadily growing class of the population can live only on the condition that it works for the owners of the means of production – tools, machines, raw materials, and means of subsistence – in return for wages. On the basis of this mode of production, the laborer's cost of production consists of the sum of the means of subsistence (or their price in money) which on the average are requisite to enable him to work, to maintain in him this capacity for work, and to replace him at his departure, by reason of age, sickness, or death, with another laborer – that is to say, to propagate the working class in required numbers.

Let us assume that the money price of these means of subsistence averages 3 shillings a day. Our laborer gets, therefore, a daily wage of 3 shillings from his employer. For this, the capitalist lets him work, say, 12 hours a day. Our capitalist, moreover, calculates somewhat in the following fashion: Let us assume that our laborer (a machinist) has to make a part of a machine which he finishes in one day. The raw material (iron and brass in the necessary prepared form) costs 20 shillings. The consumption of coal by the steam-engine, the wear-and-tear of this engine itself, of the turning-lathe, and of the other tools with which our laborer works, represent, for one day and one laborer, a value of 1 shilling. The wages for one day are, according to our assumption, 3 shillings. This makes a total of 24 shillings for our piece of a machine.

But, the capitalist calculates that, on an average, he will receive for it a price of 27 shillings from his customers, or 3 shillings over and above his outlay.

Whence do they 3 shillings pocketed by the capitalist come? According to the assertion of classical political economy, commodities are in the long run sold at their values, that is, they are sold at prices which correspond to the necessary quantities of labor contained in them. The average price of our part of a machine – 27 shillings – would therefore equal its value, i.e., equal the amount of labor embodied in it. But, of these 27 shillings, 21 shillings were values were values already existing before the machinist began to work; 20 shillings were contained in the raw material, 1 shilling in the fuel consumed during the work and in the machines and tools used in the process and reduced in their efficiency to the value of this amount. There remains 6 shillings, which have been added to the value of the raw material. But, according to the supposition of our economists, themselves, these 6 shillings can arise only from the labor added to the raw material by the laborer. His 12 hours' labor has created, according to this, a new value of 6 shillings. Therefore, the value of his 12 hours' labor would be equivalent to 6 shillings. So we have at last discovered what the "value of labor" is.

"Hold on there!" cries our machinist. "Six shillings? But I have received only 3 shillings! My capitalist swears high and day that the value of my 12 hours' labor is no more than 3 shillings, and if I were to demand 6, he'd laugh at me. What kind of a story is that?"

If before this we got with our value of labor into a vicious circle, we now surely have driven straight into an insoluble contradiction. We searched for the value of labor, and we found more than we can use. For the laborer, the value of the 12 hours' labor is 3 shillings; for the capitalist, it is 6 shillings, of which he pays the workingman 3 shillings as wages, and pockets the remaining 3 shilling himself. According to this, labor has not one but two values, and, moreover, two very different values!

As soon as we reduce the values, now expressed in money, to labor-time, the contradiction becomes even more absurd. By the 12 hours' labor, a new value of 6 shillings is created. Therefore, in 6 hours, the new value created equals 3 shilling – the amount which the laborer receives for 12 hours' labor. For 12 hours' labor, the workingman receives, as an equivalent, the product of 6 hours' labor. We are, thus, forced to one of two conclusions: either labor has two values, one of which is twice as large as the other, or 12 equals 6! In both cases, we get pure absurdities. Turn and twist as we may, we will not get out of this contradiction as long as we speak of the buying and selling of "labor" and of the "value of labor." And just so it happened to the political economists. The last offshoot of classical political economy – the Ricardian school – was largely wrecked on the insolubility of this contradiction. Classical political economy had run itself into a blind alley. The man who discovered the way out of this blind alley was Karl Marx.

What the economists had considered as the cost of production of "labor" was really the cost of production, not of "labor," but of the living laborer himself. And what this laborer sold to the capitalist was not his labor.

"So soon as his labor really begins," says Marx, "it ceases to belong to him, and therefore can no longer be sold by him."

At the most, he could sell his future labor – i.e., assume the obligation of executing a certain piece of work in a certain time. But, in this way, he does not sell labor (which would first have to be performed), but not for a stipulated payment he places his labor-power at the disposal of the capitalist for a certain time (in case of time-wages), or for the performance of a certain task (in case of piece-wages). He hires out or sells his labor-power. But this labor-power has grown up with his person and is inseparable from it. Its cost of production, therefore, coincides with his own cost of production; what the economist called the cost of production of labor is really the cost of production of the laborer, and therewith of his labor-power. And, thus, we can also go back from the cost of production of labor-power to the value of labor-power, and determine the quantity of social labor that is required for the production of a labor-power of a given quantity, as Marx has done in the chapter on "The Buying and Selling of Labor Power." [Capital, Vol.I]

Now what takes place after the worker has sold his labor-power, i.e., after he has placed his labor-power at the disposal of the capitalist for stipulated-wages – whether time-wages or piece-wages? The capitalist takes the laborer into his workshop or factory, where all the articles required for the work can be found – raw materials, auxiliary materials (coal, dyestuffs, etc.), tools, and machines. Here, the worker begins to work. His daily wages are, as above, 3 shillings, and it makes no difference whether he earns them as day-wages or piece-wages. We again assume that in 12 hours the worker adds by his labor a new value of 6 shillings to the value of the raw materials consumed, which new value the capitalist realizes by the sale of the finished piece of work. Out of this new value, he pays the worker his 3 shillings, and the remaining 3 shillings he keeps for himself. If, now, the laborer creates in 12 hours a value of 6 shilling, in 6 hours he creates a value of 3 shillings. Consequently, after working 6 hours for the capitalist, the laborer has returned to him the equivalent of the 3 shillings received as wages. After 6 hours' work, both are quits, neither one owing a penny to the other.

"Hold on there!" now cries out the capitalist. "I have hired the laborer for a whole day, for 12 hours. But 6 hours are only half-a-day. So work along lively there until the other 6 hours are at an end – only then will we be even." And, in fact, the laborer has to submit to the conditions of the contract upon which he entered of "his own free will", and according to which he bound himself to work 12 whole hours for a product of labor which cost only 6 hours' labor.

Similarly with piece-wages. Let us suppose that in 12 hours our worker makes 12 commodities. Each of these costs a shilling in raw materials and wear-and-tear, and is sold for 2.5 shillings. On our former assumption, the capitalist gives the laborer .25 of a shilling for each piece, which makes a total of 3 shillings for 12 pieces. To earn this, the worker requires 12 hours. The capitalist receives 30 shillings for the 12 pieces; deducting 24 shillings for raw materials and wear-and-tear, there remains 6 shillings, of which he pays 3 shillings in wages and pockets the remaining 3. Just as before! Here, also, the worker labors 6 hours for himself – i.e., to replace his wages (half-an-hour in each of the 12 hours), and 6 hours for the capitalist.

The rock upon which the best economists were stranded, as long as they started out from the value of labor, vanishes as soon as we make our starting-point the value of labor-power. Labor-power is, in our present-day capitalist society, a commodity like every other commodity, but yet a very peculiar commodity. It has, namely, the peculiarity of being a value-creating force, the source of value, and, moreover, when properly treated, the source of more value than it possesses itself. In the present state of production, human labor-power not only produces in a day a greater value than it itself possesses and costs; but with each new scientific discovery, with each new technical invention, there also rises the surplus of its daily production over its daily cost, while as a consequence there diminishes that part of the working-day in which the laborer produces the equivalent of his day's wages, and, on the other hand, lengthens that part of the working-day in which he must present labor gratis to the capitalist.

And this is the economic constitution of our entire modern society: the working class alone produces all values. For value is only another expression for labor, that expression, namely, by which is designated, in our capitalist society of today, the amount of socially necessary labor embodied in a particular commodity. But, these values produced by the workers do not belong to the workers. They belong to the owners of the raw materials, machines, tools, and money, which enable them to buy the labor-power of the working class. Hence, the working class gets back only a part of the entire mass of products produced by it. And, as we have just seen, the other portion, which the capitalist class retains, and which it has to share, at most, only with the landlord class, is increasing with every new discovery and invention, while the share which falls to the working class (per capita) rises but little and very slowly, or not at all, and under certain conditions it may even fall.

But, these discoveries and inventions which supplant one another with ever-increasing speed, this productiveness of human labor which increases from day to day to unheard-of proportions, at last gives rise to a conflict, in which present capitalistic economy must go to ruin. On the one hand, immeasurable wealth and a superfluidity of products with which the buyers cannot cope. On the other hand, the great mass of society proletarianized, transformed into wage-laborers, and thereby disabled from appropriating to themselves that superfluidity of products. The splitting up of society into a small class, immoderately rich, and a large class of wage-laborers devoid of all property, brings it about that this society smothers in its own superfluidity, while the great majority of its members are scarcely, or not at all, protected from extreme want.

This condition becomes every day more absurd and more unnecessary. It must be gotten rid of; it can be gotten rid of. A new social order is possible, in which the class differences of today will have disappeared, and in which – perhaps after a short transition period, which, though somewhat deficient in other respects, will in any case be very useful morally – there will be the means of life, of the enjoyment of life, and of the development and activity of all bodily and mental faculties, through the systematic use and further development of the enormous productive powers of society, which exists with us even now, with equal obligation upon all to work. And that the workers are growing ever more determined to achieve this new social order will be proven on both sides of the ocean on this dawning May Day, and on Sunday, May 3rd.

FREDERICK ENGELS
London, April 30, 1891.

Preliminary

From various quarters we have been reproached for neglecting to portray the economic conditions which form the material basis of the present struggles between classes and nations. With set purpose we have hitherto touched upon these conditions only when they forced themselves upon the surface of the political conflicts.

It was necessary, beyond everything else, to follow the development of the class struggle in the history of our own day, and to prove empirically, by the actual and daily newly created historical material, that with the subjugation of the working class, accomplished in the days of February and March, 1848, the opponents of that class – the bourgeois republicans in France, and the bourgeois and peasant classes who were fighting feudal absolutism throughout the whole continent of Europe – were simultaneously conquered; that the victory of the "moderate republic" in France sounded at the same time the fall of the nations which had responded to the February revolution with heroic wars of independence; and finally that, by the victory over the revolutionary workingmen, Europe fell back into its old double slavery, into the English-Russian slavery. The June conflict in Paris, the fall of Vienna, the tragi-comedy in Berlin in November 1848, the desperate efforts of Poland, Italy, and Hungary, the starvation of Ireland into submission – these were the chief events in which the European class struggle between the bourgeoisie and the working class was summed up, and from which we proved that every revolutionary uprising, however remote from the class struggle its object might appear, must of necessity fail until the revolutionary working class shall have conquered; that every social reform must remain a Utopia until the proletarian revolution and the feudalistic counter-revolution have been pitted against each other in a world-wide war. In our presentation, as in reality, Belgium and Switzerland were tragicomic caricaturish genre pictures in the great historic tableau; the one the model State of the bourgeois monarchy, the other the model State of the bourgeois republic; both of them, States that flatter themselves to be just as free from the class struggle as from the European revolution.

But now, after our readers have seen the class struggle of the year 1848 develop into colossal political proportions, it is time to examine more closely the economic conditions themselves upon which is founded the existence of the capitalist class and its class rule, as well as the slavery of the workers.

We shall present the subject in three great divisions:

The Relation of Wage-Labor to Capital, the Slavery of the Worker, the Rule of the Capitalist.

The Inevitable Ruin of the Middle Classes (petty-bourgeois) and the so-called Commons (peasants) under the present system.

The Commercial Subjugation and Exploitation of the Bourgeois classes of the various European nations by the Despot of the World Market – England.

We shall seek to portray this as simply and popularly as possible, and shall not presuppose a knowledge of even the most elementary notions of political economy. We wish to be understood by the workers. And, moreover, there prevails in Germany the most remarkable ignorance and confusion of ideas in regard to the simplest economic relations, from the patented defenders of existing conditions, down to the socialist wonder-workers and the unrecognized political geniuses, in which divided Germany is even richer than in duodecimo princelings. We therefore proceed to the consideration of the first problem.

What are Wages? How are they Determined?

If several workmen were to be asked: "How much wages do you get?", one would reply, "I get two shillings a day", and so on. According to the different branches of industry in which they are employed, they would mention different sums of money that they receive from their respective employers for the completion of a certain task; for example, for weaving a yard of linen, or for setting a page of type. Despite the variety of their statements, they would all agree upon one point: that wages are the amount of money which the capitalist pays for a certain period of work or for a certain amount of work.

Consequently, it appears that the capitalist buys their labour with money, and that for money they sell him their labour. But this is merely an illusion. What they actually sell to the capitalist for money is their labour-power. This labour-power the capitalist buys for a day, a week, a month, etc. And after he has bought it, he uses it up by letting the worker labour during the stipulated time. With the same amount of money with which the capitalist has bought their labour-power (for example, with two shillings) he could have bought a certain amount of sugar or of any other commodity. The two shillings with which he bought 20 pounds of sugar is the price of the 20 pounds of sugar. The two shillings with which he bought 12 hours' use of labour-power, is the price of 12 hours' labour. Labour-power, then, is a commodity, no more, no less so than is the sugar. The first is measured by the clock, the other by the scales.

Their commodity, labour-power, the workers exchange for the commodity of the capitalist, for money, and, moreover, this exchange takes place at a certain ratio. So much money for so long a use of labour-power. For 12 hours' weaving, two shillings. And these two shillings, do they not represent all the other commodities which I can buy for two shillings? Therefore, actually, the worker has exchanged his commodity, labour-power, for commodities of all kinds, and, moreover, at a certain ratio. By giving him two shillings, the capitalist has given him so much meat, so much clothing, so much wood, light, etc., in exchange for his day's work. The two shillings therefore express the relation in which labour-power is exchanged for other commodities, the exchange-value of labour-power.

The exchange value of a commodity estimated in money is called its price. Wages therefore are only a special name for the price of labour-power, and are usually called the price of labour; it is the special name for the price of this peculiar commodity, which has no other repository than human flesh and blood.

Let us take any worker; for example, a weaver. The capitalist supplies him with the loom and yarn. The weaver applies himself to work, and the yarn is turned into cloth. The capitalist takes possession of the cloth and sells it for 20 shillings, for example. Now are the wages of the weaver a share of the cloth, of the 20 shillings, of the product of the work? By no means. Long before the cloth is sold, perhaps long before it is fully woven, the weaver has received his wages. The capitalist, then, does not pay his wages out of the money which he will obtain from the cloth, but out of money already on hand. Just as little as loom and yarn are the product of the weaver to whom they are supplied by the employer, just so little are the commodities which he receives in exchange for his commodity – labour-power – his product. It is possible that the employer found no purchasers at all for the cloth. It is possible that he did not get even the amount of the wages by its sale. It is possible that he sells it very profitably in proportion to the weaver's wages. But all that does not concern the weaver. With a part of his existing wealth, of his capital, the capitalist buys the labour-power of the weaver in exactly the same manner as, with another part of his wealth, he has bought the raw material – the yarn – and the instrument of labour – the loom. After he has made these purchases, and among them belongs the labour-power necessary to the production of the cloth he produces only with raw materials and instruments of labour belonging to him. For our good weaver, too, is one of the instruments of labour, and being in this respect on a par with the loom, he has no more share in the product (the cloth), or in the price of the product, than the loom itself has.

Wages, therefore, are not a share of the worker in the commodities produced by himself. Wages are that part of already existing commodities with which the capitalist buys a certain amount of productive labour-power.

Consequently, labour-power is a commodity which its possessor, the wage-worker, sells to the capitalist. Why does he sell it? It is in order to live.

But the putting of labour-power into action – i.e., the work – is the active expression of the labourer's own life. And this life activity he sells to another person in order to secure the necessary means of life. His life-activity, therefore, is but a means of securing his own existence. He works that he may keep alive. He does not count the labour itself as a part of his life; it is rather a sacrifice of his life. It is a commodity that he has auctioned off to another. The product of his activity, therefore, is not the aim of his activity. What he produces for himself is not the silk that he weaves, not the gold that he draws up the mining shaft, not the palace that he builds. What he produces for himself is wages; and the silk, the gold, and the palace are resolved for him into a certain quantity of necessaries of life, perhaps into a cotton jacket, into copper coins, and into a basement dwelling. And the labourer who for 12 hours long, weaves, spins, bores, turns, builds, shovels, breaks stone, carries hods, and so on – is this 12 hours' weaving, spinning, boring, turning, building, shovelling, stone-breaking, regarded by him as a manifestation of life, as life? Quite the contrary. Life for him begins where this activity ceases, at the table, at the tavern, in bed. The 12 hours' work, on the other hand, has no meaning for him as weaving, spinning, boring, and so on, but only as earnings, which enable him to sit down at a table, to take his seat in the tavern, and to lie down in a bed. If the silk-worm's object in spinning were to prolong its existence as caterpillar, it would be a perfect example of a wage-worker.

Labour-power was not always a commodity (merchandise). Labour was not always wage-labour, i.e., free labour. The slave did not sell his labour-power to the slave-owner, any more than the ox sells his labour to the farmer. The slave, together with his labour-power, was sold to his owner once for all. He is a commodity that can pass from the hand of one owner to that of another. He himself is a commodity, but his labour-power is not his commodity. The serf sells only a portion of his labour-power. It is not he who receives wages from the owner of the land; it is rather the owner of the land who receives a tribute from him. The serf belongs to the soil, and to the lord of the soil he brings its fruit. The free labourer, on the other hand, sells his very self, and that by fractions. He auctions off eight, 10, 12, 15 hours of his life, one day like the next, to the highest bidder, to the owner of raw materials, tools, and the means of life – i.e., to the capitalist. The labourer belongs neither to an owner nor to the soil, but eight, 10, 12, 15 hours of his daily life belong to whomsoever buys them. The worker leaves the capitalist, to whom he has sold himself, as often as he chooses, and the capitalist discharges him as often as he sees fit, as soon as he no longer gets any use, or not the required use, out of him. But the worker, whose only source of income is the sale of his labour-power, cannot leave the whole class of buyers, i.e., the capitalist class, unless he gives up his own existence. He does not belong to this or that capitalist, but to the capitalist class; and it is for him to find his man – i.e., to find a buyer in this capitalist class.

Before entering more closely upon the relation of capital to wage-labour, we shall present briefly the most general conditions which come into consideration in the determination of wages.

Wages, as we have seen, are the price of a certain commodity, labour-power. Wages, therefore, are determined by the same laws that determine the price of every other commodity. The question then is, How is the price of a commodity determined?

By what is the price of a commodity determined?

By the competition between buyers and sellers, by the relation of the demand to the supply, of the call to the offer. The competition by which the price of a commodity is determined is threefold.

The same commodity is offered for sale by various sellers. Whoever sells commodities of the same quality most cheaply, is sure to drive the other sellers from the field and to secure the greatest market for himself. The sellers therefore fight among themselves for the sales, for the market. Each one of them wishes to sell, and to sell as much as possible, and if possible to sell alone, to the exclusion of all other sellers. Each one sells cheaper than the other. Thus there takes place a competition among the sellers which forces down the price of the commodities offered by them.

But there is also a competition among the buyers; this upon its side causes the price of the proffered commodities to rise.

Finally, there is competition between the buyers and the sellers: these wish to purchase as cheaply as possible, those to sell as dearly as possible. The result of this competition between buyers and sellers will depend upon the relations between the two above-mentioned camps of competitors – i.e., upon whether the competition in the army of sellers is stronger. Industry leads two great armies into the field against each other, and each of these again is engaged in a battle among its own troops in its own ranks. The army among whose troops there is less fighting, carries off the victory over the opposing host.

Let us suppose that there are 100 bales of cotton in the market and at the same time purchasers for 1,000 bales of cotton. In this case, the demand is 10 times greater than the supply. Competition among the buyers, then, will be very strong; each of them tries to get hold of one bale, if possible, of the whole 100 bales. This example is no arbitrary supposition. In the history of commerce we have experienced periods of scarcity of cotton, when some capitalists united together and sought to buy up not 100 bales, but the whole cotton supply of the world. In the given case, then, one buyer seeks to drive the others from the field by offering a relatively higher price for the bales of cotton. The cotton sellers, who perceive the troops of the enemy in the most violent contention among themselves, and who therefore are fully assured of the sale of their whole 100 bales, will beware of pulling one another's hair in order to force down the price of cotton at the very moment in which their opponents race with one another to screw it up high. So, all of a sudden, peace reigns in the army of sellers. They stand opposed to the buyers like one man, fold their arms in philosophic contentment and their claims would find no limit did not the offers of even the most importunate of buyers have a very definite limit.

If, then, the supply of a commodity is less than the demand for it, competition among the sellers is very slight, or there may be none at all among them. In the same proportion in which this competition decreases, the competition among the buyers increases. Result: a more or less considerable rise in the prices of commodities.

It is well known that the opposite case, with the opposite result, happens more frequently. Great excess of supply over demand; desperate competition among the sellers, and a lack of buyers; forced sales of commodities at ridiculously low prices.

But what is a rise, and what a fall of prices? What is a high and what a low price? A grain of sand is high when examined through a microscope, and a tower is low when compared with a mountain. And if the price is determined by the relation of supply and demand, by what is the relation of supply and demand determined?

Let us turn to the first worthy citizen we meet. He will not hesitate one moment, but, like Alexander the Great, will cut this metaphysical knot with his multiplication table. He will say to us: "If the production of the commodities which I sell has cost me 100 pounds, and out of the sale of these goods I make 110 pounds – within the year, you understand – that's an honest, sound, reasonable profit. But if in the exchange I receive 120 or 130 pounds, that's a higher profit; and if I should get as much as 200 pounds, that would be an extraordinary, and enormous profit." What is it, then, that serves this citizen as the standard of his profit? The cost of the production of his commodities. If in exchange for these goods he receives a quantity of other goods whose production has cost less, he has lost. If he receives in exchange for his goods a quantity of other goods whose production has cost more, he has gained. And he reckons the falling or rising of the profit according to the degree at which the exchange value of his goods stands, whether above or below his zero – the cost of production.

We have seen how the changing relation of supply and demand causes now a rise, now a fall of prices; now high, now low prices. If the price of a commodity rises considerably owing to a failing supply or a disproportionately growing demand, then the price of some other commodity must have fallen in proportion; for of course the price of a commodity only expresses in money the proportion in which other commodities will be given in exchange for it. If, for example, the price of a yard of silk rises from two to three shillings, the price of silver has fallen in relation to the silk, and in the same way the prices of all other commodities whose prices have remained stationary have fallen in relation to the price of silk. A large quantity of them must be given in exchange in order to obtain the same amount of silk. Now, what will be the consequence of a rise in the price of a particular commodity? A mass of capital will be thrown into the prosperous branch of industry, and this immigration of capital into the provinces of the favored industry will continue until it yields no more than the customary profits, or, rather until the price of its products, owning to overproduction, sinks below the cost of production.

Conversely: if the price of a commodity falls below its cost of production, then capital will be withdrawn from the production of this commodity. Except in the case of a branch of industry which has become obsolete and is therefore doomed to disappear, the production of such a commodity (that is, its supply), will, owning to this flight of capital, continue to decrease until it corresponds to the demand, and the price of the commodity rises again to the level of its cost of production; or, rather, until the supply has fallen below the demand and its price has risen above its cost of production, for the current price of a commodity is always either above or below its cost of production.

We see how capital continually emigrates out of the province of one industry and immigrates into that of another. The high price produces an excessive immigration, and the low price an excessive emigration.

We could show, from another point of view, how not only the supply, but also the demand, is determined by the cost of production. But this would lead us too far away from our subject.

We have just seen how the fluctuation of supply and demand always bring the price of a commodity back to its cost of production. The actual price of a commodity, indeed, stands always above or below the cost of production; but the rise and fall reciprocally balance each other, so that, within a certain period of time, if the ebbs and flows of the industry are reckoned up together, the commodities will be exchanged for one another in accordance with their cost of production. Their price is thus determined by their cost of production.

The determination of price by the cost of production is not to be understood in the sense of the bourgeois economists. The economists say that the average price of commodities equals the cost of production: that is the law. The anarchic movement, in which the rise is compensated for by a fall and the fall by a rise, they regard as an accident. We might just as well consider the fluctuations as the law, and the determination of the price by cost of production as an accident – as is, in fact, done by certain other economists. But it is precisely these fluctuations which, viewed more closely, carry the most frightful devastation in their train, and, like an earthquake, cause bourgeois society to shake to its very foundations – it is precisely these fluctuations that force the price to conform to the cost of production. In the totality of this disorderly movement is to be found its order. In the total course of this industrial anarchy, in this circular movement, competition balances, as it were, the one extravagance by the other.

We thus see that the price of a commodity is indeed determined by its cost of production, but in such a manner that the periods in which the price of these commodities rises above the costs of production are balanced by the periods in which it sinks below the cost of production, and vice versa. Of course this does not hold good for a single given product of an industry, but only for that branch of industry. So also it does not hold good for an individual manufacturer, but only for the whole class of manufacturers.

The determination of price by cost of production is tantamount to the determination of price by the labor-time requisite to the production of a commodity, for the cost of production consists, first of raw materials and wear and tear of tools, etc., i.e., of industrial products whose production has cost a certain number of work-days, which therefore represent a certain amount of labor-time, and, secondly, of direct labor, which is also measured by its duration.

By what are wages determined?

Now, the same general laws which regulate the price of commodities in general, naturally regulate wages, or the price of labor-power. Wages will now rise, now fall, according to the relation of supply and demand, according as competition shapes itself between the buyers of labor-power, the capitalists, and the sellers of labor-power, the workers. The fluctuations of wages correspond to the fluctuation in the price of commodities in general. But within the limits of these fluctuations the price of labor-power will be determined by the cost of production, by the labor-time necessary for production of this commodity: labor-power.

What, then, is the cost of production of labor-power?

It is the cost required for the maintenance of the laborer as a laborer, and for his education and training as a laborer.

Therefore, the shorter the time required for training up to a particular sort of work, the smaller is the cost of production of the worker, the lower is the price of his labor-power, his wages. In those branches of industry in which hardly any period of apprenticeship is necessary and the mere bodily existence of the worker is sufficient, the cost of his production is limited almost exclusively to the commodities necessary for keeping him in working condition. The price of his work will therefore be determined by the price of the necessary means of subsistence.

Here, however, there enters another consideration. The manufacturer who calculates his cost of production and, in accordance with it, the price of the product, takes into account the wear and tear of the instruments of labor. If a machine costs him, for example, 1,000 shillings, and this machine is used up in 10 years, he adds 100 shillings annually to the price of the commodities, in order to be able after 10 years to replace the worn-out machine with a new one. In the same manner, the cost of production of simple labor-power must include the cost of propagation, by means of which the race of workers is enabled to multiply itself, and to replace worn-out workers with new ones. The wear and tear of the worker, therefore, is calculated in the same manner as the wear and tear of the machine.

Thus, the cost of production of simple labor-power amounts to the cost of the existence and propagation of the worker. The price of this cost of existence and propagation constitutes wages. The wages thus determined are called the minimum of wages. This minimum wage, like the determination of the price of commodities in general by cost of production, does not hold good for the single individual, but only for the race. Individual workers, indeed, millions of workers, do not receive enough to be able to exist and to propagate themselves; but the wages of the whole working class adjust themselves, within the limits of their fluctuations, to this minimum.

Now that we have come to an understanding in regard to the most general laws which govern wages, as well as the price of every other commodity, we can examine our subject more particularly.

The Nature and Growth of Capital

Capital consists of raw materials, instruments of labor, and means of subsistence of all kinds, which are employed in producing new raw materials, new instruments, and new means of subsistence. All these components of capital are created by labor, products of labor, accumulated labor. Accumulated labor that serves as a means to new production is capital.

So says the economists.

What is a Negro slave? A man of the black race. The one explanation is worthy of the other.

A Negro is a Negro. Only under certain conditions does he become a slave. A cotton-spinning machine is a machine for spinning cotton. Only under certain conditions does it become capital. Torn away from these conditions, it is as little capital as gold is itself money, or sugar is the price of sugar.

In the process of production, human beings work not only upon nature, but also upon one another. They produce only by working together in a specified manner and reciprocally exchanging their activities. In order to produce, they enter into definite connections and relations to one another, and only within these social connections and relations does their influence upon nature operate – i.e., does production take place.

These social relations between the producers, and the conditions under which they exchange their activities and share in the total act of production, will naturally vary according to the character of the means of production. With the discover of a new instrument of warfare, the firearm, the whole internal organization of the army was necessarily altered, the relations within which individuals compose an army and can work as an army were transformed, and the relation of different armies to another was likewise changed.

We thus see that the social relations within which individuals produce, the social relations of production, are altered, transformed, with the change and development of the material means of production, of the forces of production. The relations of production in their totality constitute what is called the social relations, society, and, moreover, a society at a definite stage of historical development, a society with peculiar, distinctive characteristics. Ancient society, feudal society, bourgeois (or capitalist) society, are such totalities of relations of production, each of which denotes a particular stage of development in the history of mankind.

Capital also is a social relation of production. It is a bourgeois relation of production, a relation of production of bourgeois society. The means of subsistence, the instruments of labor, the raw materials, of which capital consists – have they not been produced and accumulated under given social conditions, within definite special relations? Are they not employed for new production, under given special conditions, within definite social relations? And does not just the definite social character stamp the products which serve for new production as capital?

Capital consists not only of means of subsistence, instruments of labor, and raw materials, not only as material products; it consists just as much of exchange values. All products of which it consists are commodities. Capital, consequently, is not only a sum of material products, it is a sum of commodities, of exchange values, of social magnitudes. Capital remains the same whether we put cotton in the place of wool, rice in the place of wheat, steamships in the place of railroads, provided only that the cotton, the rice, the steamships – the body of capital – have the same exchange value, the same price, as the wool, the wheat, the railroads, in which it was previously embodied. The bodily form of capital may transform itself continually, while capital does not suffer the least alteration.

But though every capital is a sum of commodities – i.e., of exchange values – it does not follow that every sum of commodities, of exchange values, is capital.

Every sum of exchange values is an exchange value. Each particular exchange value is a sum of exchange values. For example: a house worth 1,000 pounds is an exchange value of 1,000 pounds: a piece of paper worth one penny is a sum of exchange values of 100 1/100ths of a penny. Products which are exchangeable for others are commodities. The definite proportion in which they are exchangeable forms their exchange value, or, expressed in money, their price. The quantity of these products can have no effect on their character as commodities, as representing an exchange value , as having a certain price. Whether a tree be large or small, it remains a tree. Whether we exchange iron in pennyweights or in hundredweights, for other products, does this alter its character: its being a commodity, or exchange value? According to the quantity, it is a commodity of greater or of lesser value, of higher or of lower price.

How then does a sum of commodities, of exchange values, become capital?

Thereby, that as an independent social power – i.e., as the power of a part of society – it preserves itself and multiplies by exchange with direct, living labor-power.

The existence of a class which possess nothing but the ability to work is a necessary presupposition of capital.

It is only the dominion of past, accumulated, materialized labor over immediate living labor that stamps the accumulated labor with the character of capital.

Capital does not consist in the fact that accumulated labor serves living labor as a means for new production. It consists in the fact that living labor serves accumulated labor as the means of preserving and multiplying its exchange value.

Relation of Wage-Labour to Capital

What is it that takes place in the exchange between the capitalist and the wage-labor?

The laborer receives means of subsistence in exchange for his labor-power; the capitalist receives, in exchange for his means of subsistence, labor, the productive activity of the laborer, the creative force by which the worker not only replaces what he consumes, but also gives to the accumulated labor a greater value than it previously possessed. The laborer gets from the capitalist a portion of the existing means of subsistence. For what purpose do these means of subsistence serve him? For immediate consumption. But as soon as I consume means of subsistence, they are irrevocably lost to me, unless I employ the time during which these means sustain my life in producing new means of subsistence, in creating by my labor new values in place of the values lost in consumption. But it is just this noble reproductive power that the laborer surrenders to the capitalist in exchange for means of subsistence received. Consequently, he has lost it for himself.

Let us take an example. For one shilling a laborer works all day long in the fields of a farmer, to whom he thus secures a return of two shillings. The farmer not only receives the replaced value which he has given to the day laborer, he has doubled it. Therefore, he has consumed the one shilling that he gave to the day laborer in a fruitful, productive manner. For the one shilling he has bought the labor-power of the day-laborer, which creates products of the soil of twice the value, and out of one shilling makes two. The day-laborer, on the contrary, receives in the place of his productive force, whose results he has just surrendered to the farmer, one shilling, which he exchanges for means of subsistence, which he consumes more or less quickly. The one shilling has therefore been consumed in a double manner – reproductively for the capitalist, for it has been exchanged for labor-power, which brought forth two shillings; unproductively for the worker, for it has been exchanged for means of subsistence which are lost for ever, and whose value he can obtain again only by repeating the same exchange with the farmer. Capital therefore presupposes wage-labor; wage-labor presupposes capital. They condition each other; each brings the other into existence.

Does a worker in a cotton factory produce only cotton? No. He produces capital. He produces values which serve anew to command his work and to create by means of it new values.

Capital can multiply itself only by exchanging itself for labor-power, by calling wage-labor into life. The labor-power of the wage-laborer can exchange itself for capital only by increasing capital, by strengthening that very power whose slave it is. Increase of capital, therefore, is increase of the proletariat, i.e., of the working class.

And so, the bourgeoisie and its economists maintain that the interest of the capitalist and of the laborer is the same. And in fact, so they are! The worker perishes if capital does not keep him busy. Capital perishes if it does not exploit labor-power, which, in order to exploit, it must buy. The more quickly the capital destined for production – the productive capital – increases, the more prosperous industry is, the more the bourgeoisie enriches itself, the better business gets, so many more workers does the capitalist need, so much the dearer does the worker sell himself. The fastest possible growth of productive capital is, therefore, the indispensable condition for a tolerable life to the laborer.

But what is growth of productive capital? Growth of the power of accumulated labor over living labor; growth of the rule of the bourgeoisie over the working class. When wage-labor produces the alien wealth dominating it, the power hostile to it, capital, there flow back to it its means of employment – i.e., its means of subsistence, under the condition that it again become a part of capital, that is become again the lever whereby capital is to be forced into an accelerated expansive movement.

To say that the interests of capital and the interests of the workers are identical, signifies only this: that capital and wage-labor are two sides of one and the same relation. The one conditions the other in the same way that the usurer and the borrower condition each other.

As long as the wage-laborer remains a wage-laborer, his lost is dependent upon capital. That is what the boasted community of interests between worker and capitalists amounts to.

If capital grows, the mass of wage-labor grows, the number of wage-workers increases; in a word, the sway of capital extends over a greater mass of individuals.

Let us suppose the most favorable case: if productive capital grows, the demand for labor grows. It therefore increases the price of labor-power, wages.

A house may be large or small; as long as the neighboring houses are likewise small, it satisfies all social requirement for a residence. But let there arise next to the little house a palace, and the little house shrinks to a hut. The little house now makes it clear that its inmate has no social position at all to maintain, or but a very insignificant one; and however high it may shoot up in the course of civilization, if the neighboring palace rises in equal of even in greater measure, the occupant of the relatively little house will always find himself more uncomfortable, more dissatisfied, more cramped within his four walls.

An appreciable rise in wages presupposes a rapid growth of productive capital. Rapid growth of productive capital calls forth just as rapid a growth of wealth, of luxury, of social needs and social pleasures. Therefore, although the pleasures of the laborer have increased, the social gratification which they afford has fallen in comparison with the increased pleasures of the capitalist, which are inaccessible to the worker, in comparison with the stage of development of society in general. Our wants and pleasures have their origin in society; we therefore measure them in relation to society; we do not measure them in relation to the objects which serve for their gratification. Since they are of a social nature, they are of a relative nature.

But wages are not at all determined merely by the sum of commodities for which they may be exchanged. Other factors enter into the problem. What the workers directly receive for their labor-power is a certain sum of money. Are wages determined merely by this money price?

In the 16th century, the gold and silver circulation in Europe increased in consequence of the discovery of richer and more easily worked mines in America. The value of gold and silver, therefore, fell in relation to other commodities. The workers received the same amount of coined silver for their labor-power as before. The money price of their work remained the same, and yet their wages had fallen, for in exchange for the same amount of silver they obtained a smaller amount of other commodities. This was one of the circumstances which furthered the growth of capital, the rise of the bourgeoisie, in the 18th century.

Let us take another case. In the winter of 1847, in consequence of bad harvest, the most indispensable means of subsistence – grains, meat, butter, cheese, etc. – rose greatly in price. Let us suppose that the workers still received the same sum of money for their labor-power as before. Did not their wages fall? To be sure. For the same money they received in exchange less bread, meat, etc. Their wages fell, not because the value of silver was less, but because the value of the means of subsistence had increased.

Finally, let us suppose that the money price of labor-power remained the same, while all agricultural and manufactured commodities had fallen in price because of the employment of new machines, of favorable seasons, etc. For the same money the workers could now buy more commodities of all kinds. Their wages have therefore risen, just because their money value has not changed.

The money price of labor-power, the nominal wages, do not therefore coincide with the actual or real wages – i.e., with the amount of commodities which are actually given in exchange for the wages. If then we speak of a rise or fall of wages, we have to keep in mind not only the money price of labor-power, the nominal wages, but also the real wages.

But neither the nominal wages – i.e., the amount of money for which the laborer sells himself to the capitalist – nor the real wages – i.e., the amount of commodities which he can buy for this money – exhausts the relations which are comprehended in the term wages.

Wages are determined above all by their relations to the gain, the profit, of the capitalist. In other words, wages are a proportionate, relative quantity.

Real wages express the price of labor-power in relation to the price of commodities; relative wages, on the other hand, express the share of immediate labor in the value newly created by it, in relation to the share of it which falls to accumulated labor, to capital.

The General Law that Determines the Rise and Fall of Wages and Profits

We have said: "Wages are not a share of the worker in the commodities produced by him. Wages are that part of already existing commodities with which the capitalist buys a certain amount of productive labor-power." But the capitalist must replace these wages out of the price for which he sells the product made by the worker; he must so replace it that, as a rule, there remains to him a surplus above the cost of production expended by him, that is, he must get a profit.

The selling price of the commodities produced by the worker is divided, from the point of view of the capitalist, into three parts:

First, the replacement of the price of the raw materials advanced by him, in addition to the replacement of the wear and tear of the tools, machines, and other instruments of labor likewise advanced by him;

Second, the replacement of the wages advanced; and

Third, the surplus leftover – i.e., the profit of the capitalist.

While the first part merely replaces previously existing values, it is evident that the replacement of the wages and the surplus (the profit of capital) are as a whole taken out of the new value, which is produced by the labor of the worker and added to the raw materials. And in this sense we can view wages as well as profit, for the purpose of comparing them with each other, as shares in the product of the worker.

Real wages may remain the same, they may even rise, nevertheless the relative wages may fall. Let us suppose, for instance, that all means of subsistence have fallen 2/3rds in price, while the day's wages have fallen but 1/3rd – for example, from three to two shillings. Although the worker can now get a greater amount of commodities with these two shillings than he formerly did with three shillings, yet his wages have decreased in proportion to the gain of the capitalist. The profit of the capitalist – the manufacturer's for instance – has increased one shilling, which means that for a smaller amount of exchange values, which he pays to the worker, the latter must produce a greater amount of exchange values than before. The share of capitals in proportion to the share of labor has risen. The distribution of social wealth between capital and labor has become still more unequal. The capitalist commands a greater amount of labor with the same capital. The power of the capitalist class over the working class has grown, the social position of the worker has become worse, has been forced down still another degree below that of the capitalist.

What, then, is the general law that determines the rise and fall of wages and profit in their reciprocal relation?

They stand in inverse proportion to each other. The share of (profit) increases in the same proportion in which the share of labor (wages) falls, and vice versa. Profit rises in the same degree in which wages fall; it falls in the same degree in which wages rise.

It might perhaps be argued that the capitalist class can gain by an advantageous exchange of his products with other capitalists, by a rise in the demand for his commodities, whether in consequence of the opening up of new markets, or in consequence of temporarily increased demands in the old market, and so on; that the profit of the capitalist, therefore, may be multiplied by taking advantage of other capitalists, independently of the rise and fall of wages, of the exchange value of labor-power; or that the profit of the capitalist may also rise through improvements in the instruments of labor, new applications of the forces of nature, and so on.

But in the first place it must be admitted that the result remains the same, although brought about in an opposite manner. Profit, indeed, has not risen because wages have fallen, but wages have fallen because profit has risen. With the same amount of another man's labor the capitalist has bought a larger amount of exchange values without having paid more for the labor on that account – i.e., the work is paid for less in proportion to the net gain which it yields to the capitalist.

In the second place, it must be borne in mind that, despite the fluctuations in the prices of commodities, the average price of every commodity, the proportion in which it exchanges for other commodities, is determined by its cost of production. The acts of overreaching and taking advantage of one another within the capitalist ranks necessarily equalize themselves. The improvements of machinery, the new applications of the forces of nature in the service of production, make it possible to produce in a given period of time, with the same amount of labor and capital, a larger amount of products, but in no wise a larger amount of exchange values. If by the use of the spinning-machine I can furnish twice as much yarn in an hour as before its invention – for instance, 100 pounds instead of 50 pounds – in the long run I receive back, in exchange for this 100 pounds no more commodities than I did before for 50; because the cost of production has fallen by ½, or because I can furnish double the product at the same cost.

Finally, in whatsoever proportion the capitalist class, whether of one country or of the entire world-market, distribute the net revenue of production among themselves, the total amount of this net revenue always consists exclusively of the amount by which accumulated labor has been increased from the proceeds of direct labor. This whole amount, therefore, grows in the same proportion in which labor augments capital – i.e., in the same proportion in which profit rises as compared with wages.

The interests of Capital and Wage-Labour are diametrically opposed.

Effect of growth of productive Capital on Wages

We thus see that, even if we keep ourselves within the relation of capital and wage-labor, the interests of capitals and the interests of wage-labor are diameterically opposed to each other.

A rapid growth of capital is synonymous with a rapid growth of profits. Profits can grow rapidly only when the price of labor – the relative wages – decrease just as rapidly. Relative wages may fall, although real wages rise simultaneously with nominal wages, with the money value of labor, provided only that the real wage does not rise in the same proportion as the profit. If, for instance, in good business years wages rise 5 per cent, while profits rise 30 per cent, the proportional, the relative wage has not increased, but decreased.

If, therefore, the income of the worker increased with the rapid growth of capital, there is at the same time a widening of the social chasm that divides the worker from the capitalist, and increase in the power of capital over labor, a greater dependence of labor upon capital.

To say that "the worker has an interest in the rapid growth of capital", means only this: that the more speedily the worker augments the wealth of the capitalist, the larger will be the crumbs which fall to him, the greater will be the number of workers than can be called into existence, the more can the mass of slaves dependent upon capital be increased.

We have thus seen that even the most favorable situation for the working class, namely, the most rapid growth of capital, however much it may improve the material life of the worker, does not abolish the antagonism between his interests and the interests of the capitalist. Profit and wages remain as before, in inverse proportion.

If capital grows rapidly, wages may rise, but the profit of capital rises disproportionately faster. The material position of the worker has improved, but at the cost of his social position. The social chasm that separates him from the capitalist has widened.

Finally, to say that "the most favorable condition for wage-labor is the fastest possible growth of productive capital", is the same as to say: the quicker the working class multiplies and augments the power inimical to it – the wealth of another which lords over that class – the more favorable will be the conditions under which it will be permitted to toil anew at the multiplication of bourgeois wealth, at the enlargement of the power of capital, content thus to forge for itself the golden chains by which the bourgeoisie drags it in its train.

Growth of productive capital and rise of wages, are they really so indissolubly united as the bourgeois economists maintain? We must not believe their mere words. We dare not believe them even when they claim that the fatter capital is the more will its slave be pampered. The bourgeoisie is too much enlightened, it keeps its accounts much too carefully, to share the prejudices of the feudal lord, who makes an ostentatious display of the magnificence of his retinue. The conditions of existence of the bourgeoisie compel it to attend carefully to its bookkeeping. We must therefore examine more closely into the following question:

In what manner does the growth of productive capital affect wages?

If as a whole, the productive capital of bourgeois society grows, there takes place a more many-sided accumulation of labor. The individual capitals increase in number and in magnitude. The multiplications of individual capitals increases the competition among capitalists. The increasing magnitude of increasing capitals provides the means of leading more powerful armies of workers with more gigantic instruments of war upon the industrial battlefield.

The one capitalist can drive the other from the field and carry off his capital only by selling more cheaply. In order to sell more cheaply without ruining himself, he must produce more cheaply – i.e., increase the productive forces of labor as much as possible.

But the productive forces of labor is increased above all by a greater division of labor and by a more general introduction and constant improvement of machinery. The larger the army of workers among whom the labor is subdivided, the more gigantic the scale upon which machinery is introduced, the more in proportion does the cost of production decrease, the more fruitful is the labor. And so there arises among the capitalists a universal rivalry for the increase of the division of labor and of machinery and for their exploitation upon the greatest possible scale.

If, now, by a greater division of labor, by the application and improvement of new machines, by a more advantageous exploitation of the forces of nature on a larger scale, a capitalist has found the means of producing with the same amount of labor (whether it be direct or accumulated labor) a larger amount of products of commodities than his competitors – if, for instance, he can produce a whole yard of linen in the same labor-time in which his competitors weave half-a-yard – how will this capitalist act?

He could keep on selling half-a-yard of linen at old market price; but this would not have the effect of driving his opponents from the field and enlarging his own market. But his need of a market has increased in the same measure in which his productive power has extended. The more powerful and costly means of production that he has called into existence enable him, it is true, to sell his wares more cheaply, but they compel him at the same time to sell more wares, to get control of a very much greater market for his commodities; consequently, this capitalist will sell his half-yard of linen more cheaply than his competitors.

But the capitalist will not sell the whole yard so cheaply as his competitors sell the half-yard, although the production of the whole yard costs him no more than does that of the half-yard to the others. Otherwise, he would make no extra profit, and would get back in exchange only the cost of production. He might obtain a greater income from having set in motion a larger capital, but not from having made a greater profit on his capital than the others. Moreover, he attains the object he is aiming at if he prices his goods only a small percentage lower than his competitors. He drives them off the field, he wrests from them at least part of their market, by underselling them.

And finally, let us remember that the current price always stands either above or below the cost of production, according as the sale of a commodity takes place in the favorable or unfavorable period of the industry. According as the market price of the yard of linen stands above or below its former cost of production, will the percentage vary at which the capitalist who has made use of the new and more faithful means of production sell above his real cost of production.

But the privilege of our capitalist is not of long duration. Other competing capitalists introduce the same machines, the same division of labor, and introduce them upon the same or even upon a greater scale. And finally this introduction becomes so universal that the price of the linen is lowered not only below its old, but even below its new cost of production.

The capitalists therefore find themselves, in their mutual relations, in the same situation in which they were before the introduction of the new means of production; and if they are by these means enabled to offer double the product at the old price, they are now forced to furnish double the product for less than the old price. Having arrived at the new point, the new cost of production, the battle for supremacy in the market has to be fought out anew. Given more division of labor and more machinery, and there results a greater scale upon which division of labor and machinery are exploited. And competition again brings the same reaction against this result.

Effect of Capitalist Competition on the Capitalist Class, the Middle Class and the Working Class

We thus see how the method of production and the means of production are constantly enlarged, revolutionized, how division of labor necessarily draws after it greater division of labor, the employment of machinery greater employment of machinery, work upon a large scale work upon a still greater scale. This is the law that continually throws capitalist production out of its old ruts and compels capital to strain ever more the productive forces of labor for the very reason that it has already strained them – the law that grants it no respite, and constantly shouts in its ear: March! march! This is no other law than that which, within the periodical fluctuations of commerce, necessarily adjusts the price of a commodity to its cost of production.

No matter how powerful the means of production which a capitalist may bring into the field, competition will make their adoption general; and from the moment that they have been generally adopted, the sole result of the greater productiveness of his capital will be that he must furnish at the same price, 10, 20, 100 times as much as before. But since he must find a market for, perhaps, 1,000 times as much, in order to outweigh the lower selling price by the greater quantity of the sale; since now a more extensive sale is necessary not only to gain a greater profit, but also in order to replace the cost of production (the instrument of production itself grows always more costly, as we have seen), and since this more extensive sale has become a question of life and death not only for him, but also for his rivals, the old struggle must begin again, and it is all the more violent the more powerful the means of production already invented are. The division of labor and the application of machinery will therefore take a fresh start, and upon an even greater scale.

Whatever be the power of the means of production which are employed, competition seeks to rob capital of the golden fruits of this power by reducing the price of commodities to the cost of production; in the same measure in which production is cheapened - i.e., in the same measure in which more can be produced with the same amount of labor - it compels by a law which is irresistible a still greater cheapening of production, the sale of ever greater masses of product for smaller prices. Thus the capitalist will have gained nothing more by his efforts than the obligation to furnish a greater product in the same labor-time; in a word, more difficult conditions for the profitable employment of his capital. While competition, therefore, constantly pursues him with its law of the cost of production and turns against himself every weapon that he forges against his rivals, the capitalist continually seeks to get the best of competition by restlessly introducing further subdivision of labor and new machines, which, though more expensive, enable him to produce more cheaply, instead of waiting until the new machines shall have been rendered obsolete by competition.

If we now conceive this feverish agitation as it operates in the market of the whole world, we shall be in a position to comprehend how the growth, accumulation, and concentration of capital bring in their train an ever more detailed subdivision of labor, an ever greater improvement of old machines, and a constant application of new machine - a process which goes on uninterruptedly, with feverish haste, and upon an ever more gigantic scale.

But what effect do these conditions, which are inseparable from the growth of productive capital, have upon the determination of wages?

The greater division of labor enables one laborer to accomplish the work of five, 10, or 20 laborers; it therefore increases competition among the laborers fivefold, tenfold, or twentyfold. The laborers compete not only by selling themselves one cheaper than the other, but also by one doing the work of five, 10, or 20; and they are forced to compete in this manner by the division of labor, which is introduced and steadily improved by capital.

Furthermore, to the same degree in which the division of labor increases, is the labor simplified. The special skill of the laborer becomes worthless. He becomes transformed into a simple monotonous force of production, with neither physical nor mental elasticity. His work becomes accessible to all; therefore competitors press upon him from all sides. Moreover, it must be remembered that the more simple, the more easily learned the work is, so much the less is its cost to production, the expense of its acquisition, and so much the lower must the wages sink – for, like the price of any other commodity, they are determined by the cost of production. Therefore, in the same manner in which labor becomes more unsatisfactory, more repulsive, do competition increase and wages decrease.

The laborer seeks to maintain the total of his wages for a given time by performing more labor, either by working a great number of hours, or by accomplishing more in the same number of hours. Thus, urged on by want, he himself multiplies the disastrous effects of division of labor. The result is: the more he works, the less wages he receives. And for this simple reason: the more he works, the more he competes against his fellow workmen, the more he compels them to compete against him, and to offer themselves on the same wretched conditions as he does; so that, in the last analysis, he competes against himself as a member of the working class.

Machinery produces the same effects, but upon a much larger scale. It supplants skilled laborers by unskilled, men by women, adults by children; where newly introduced, it throws workers upon the streets in great masses; and as it becomes more highly developed and more productive it discards them in additional though smaller numbers.

We have hastily sketched in broad outlines the industrial war of capitalists among themselves. This war has the peculiarity that the battles in it are won less by recruiting than by discharging the army of workers. The generals (the capitalists) vie with one another as to who can discharge the greatest number of industrial soldiers.

The economists tell us, to be sure, that those laborers who have been rendered superfluous by machinery find new venues of employment. They dare not assert directly that the same laborers that have been discharged find situations in new branches of labor. Facts cry out too loudly against this lie. Strictly speaking, they only maintain that new means of employment will be found for other sections of the working class; for example, for that portion of the young generation of laborers who were about to enter upon that branch of industry which had just been abolished. Of course, this is a great satisfaction to the disabled laborers. There will be no lack of fresh exploitable blood and muscle for the Messrs. Capitalists – the dead may bury their dead. This consolation seems to be intended more for the comfort of the capitalists themselves than their laborers. If the whole class of the wage-laborer were to be annihilated by machinery, how terrible that would be for capital, which, without wage-labor, ceases to be capital!

But even if we assume that all who are directly forced out of employment by machinery, as well as all of the rising generation who were waiting for a chance of employment in the same branch of industry, do actually find some new employment – are we to believe that this new employment will pay as high wages as did the one they have lost? If it did, it would be in contradiction to the laws of political economy. We have seen how modern industry always tends to the substitution of the simpler and more subordinate employments for the higher and more complex ones. How, then, could a mass of workers thrown out of one branch of industry by machinery find refuge in another branch, unless they were to be paid more poorly?

An exception to the law has been adduced, namely, the workers who are employed in the manufacture of machinery itself. As soon as there is in industry a greater demand for and a greater consumption of machinery, it is said that the number of machines must necessarily increase; consequently, also, the manufacture of machines; consequently, also, the employment of workers in machine manufacture; – and the workers employed in this branch of industry are skilled, even educated, workers.

Since the year 1840 this assertion, which even before that date was only half-true, has lost all semblance of truth; for the most diverse machines are now applied to the manufacture of the machines themselves on quite as extensive a scale as in the manufacture of cotton yarn, and the laborers employed in machine factories can but play the role of very stupid machines alongside of the highly ingenious machines.

But in place of the man who has been dismissed by the machine, the factory may employ, perhaps, three children and one woman! And must not the wages of the man have previously sufficed for the three children and one woman? Must not the minimum wages have sufficed for the preservation and propagation of the race? What, then, do these beloved bourgeois phrases prove? Nothing more than that now four times as many workers' lives are used up as there were previously, in order to obtain the livelihood of one working family.

To sum up: the more productive capital grows, the more it extends the division of labor and the application of machinery; the more the division of labor and the application of machinery extend, the more does competition extend among the workers, the more do their wages shrink together.

In addition, the working class is also recruited from the higher strata of society; a mass of small business men and of people living upon the interest of their capitals is precipitated into the ranks of the working class, and they will have nothing else to do than to stretch out their arms alongside of the arms of the workers. Thus the forest of outstretched arms, begging for work, grows ever thicker, while the arms themselves grow every leaner.

It is evident that the small manufacturer cannot survive in a struggle in which the first condition of success is production upon an ever greater scale. It is evident that the small manufacturers and thereby increasing the number of candidates for the proletariat – all this requires no further elucidation.

Finally, in the same measure in which the capitalists are compelled, by the movement described above, to exploit the already existing gigantic means of production on an ever-increasing scale, and for this purpose to set in motion all the mainsprings of credit, in the same measure do they increase the industrial earthquakes, in the midst of which the commercial world can preserve itself only by sacrificing a portion of its wealth, its products, and even its forces of production, to the gods of the lower world – in short, the crises increase. They become more frequent and more violent, if for no other reason, than for this alone, that in the same measure in which the mass of products grows, and there the needs for extensive markets, in the same measure does the world market shrink ever more, and ever fewer markets remain to be exploited, since every previous crisis has subjected to the commerce of the world a hitherto unconquered or but superficially exploited market.

But capital not only lives upon labor. Like a master, at once distinguished and barbarous, it drags with it into its grave the corpses of its slaves, whole hecatombs of workers, who perish in the crises.

We thus see that if capital grows rapidly, competition among the workers grows with even greater rapidity – i.e., the means of employment and subsistence for the working class decrease in proportion even more rapidly; but, this notwithstanding, the rapid growth of capital is the most favorable condition for wage-labor.

Critique of the Gotha Programme

Foreword

The manuscript published here—the covering letter to Bracke as well as the critique of the draft programme—was sent in 1875, shortly before the Gotha Unity Congress, to Bracke for communication to Geib, Auer, Bebel, and Liebknecht and subsequent return to Marx. Since the Halle Party Congress has put the discussion of the Gotha Programme on the agenda of the Party, I think I would be guilty of suppression if I any longer withheld from publicity this important—perhaps the most important—document relevant to this discussion.

But the manuscript has yet another and more far-reaching significance. Here for the first time Marx's attitude to the line adopted by Lassalle in his agitation from the very beginning is clearly and firmly set forth, both as regards Lassalle's economic principles and his tactics.

The ruthless severity with which the draft programme is dissected here, the mercilessness with which the results obtained are enunciated and the shortcomings of the draft laid bare—all this today, after fifteen years, can no longer give offence. Specific Lassalleans now exist only abroad as isolated ruins, and in Halle the Gotha Programme was given up even by its creators as altogether inadequate.

Nevertheless, I have omitted a few sharp personal expressions and judgments where these were immaterial, and replaced them by dots. Marx himself would have done so if he had published the manuscript today. The violence of the language in some passages was provoked by two circumstances. In the first place, Marx and I had been more intimately connected with the German movement than with any other; we were, therefore, bound to be particularly perturbed by the decidedly retrograde step manifested by this draft programme. And secondly, we were at that time, hardly two years after the Hague Congress of the International, engaged in the most violent struggle against Bakunin and his anarchists, who made us responsible for everything that happened in the labour movement in Germany; hence we had to expect that we would also be addled with the secret paternity of this programme. These considerations do not now exist and so there is no necessity for the passages in question.

For reasons arising form the Press Law, also, a few sentences have been indicated only by dots. Where I have had to choose a milder expression this has been enclosed in square brackets. Otherwise the text has been reproduced word for word.

Friedrich Engels
London, January 6, 1891

Marx to W. Bracke In Brunswick

London, 5 May 1875 Dear Bracke,

When you have read the following critical marginal notes on the Unity Programme, would you be so good as to send them on to Geib and Auer, Bebel and Liebknecht for examination. I am exceedingly busy and have to overstep by far the limit of work allowed me by the doctors. Hence it was anything but a "pleasure" to write such a lengthy creed. It was, however, necessary so that the steps to be taken by me later on would not be misinterpreted by our friends in the Party for whom this communication is intended.

After the Unity Congress has been held, Engels and I will publish a short statement to the effect that our position is altogether remote from the said programme of principle and that we have nothing to do with it.

This is indispensable because the opinion – the entirely erroneous opinion – is held abroad and assiduously nurtured by enemies of the Party that we secretly guide from here the movement of the so-called

Eisenach Party. In a Russian book [Statism and Anarchy] that has recently appeared, Bakunin still makes me responsible, for example, not only for all the programmes, etc., of that party but even for every step taken by Liebknecht from the day of his cooperation with the People's Party.

Apart from this, it is my duty not to give recognition, even by diplomatic silence, to what in my opinion is a thoroughly objectionable programme that demoralises the Party.

Every step of real movement is more important than a dozen programmes. If, therefore, it was not possible – and the conditions of the item did not permit it – to go beyond the Eisenach programme, one should simply have concluded an agreement for action against the common enemy. But by drawing up a programme of principles (instead of postponing this until it has been prepared for by a considerable period of common activity) one sets up before the whole world landmarks by which it measures the level of the Party movement.

The Lassallean leaders came because circumstances forced them to. If they had been told in advance that there would be haggling about principles, they would have had to be content with a programme of action or a plan of organisation for common action. Instead of this, one permits them to arrive armed with mandates, recognises these mandates on one's part as binding, and thus surrenders unconditionally to those who are themselves in need of help. To crown the whole business, they are holding a congress before the Congress of Compromise, while one's own party is holding its congress post festum. One had obviously had a desire to stifle all criticism and to give one's own party no opportunity for reflection. One knows that the mere fact of unification is satisfying to the workers, but it is a mistake to believe that this momentary success is not bought too dearly.

For the rest, the programme is no good, even apart from its sanctification of the Lassallean articles of faith.

I shall be sending you in the near future the last parts of the French edition of Capital. The printing was held up for a considerable time by a ban of the French Government. The thing will be ready this week or the beginning of next week. Have you received the previous six parts? Please let me have the address of Bernhard Becker, to whom I must also send the final parts.

The bookshop of the Volksstaat has peculiar ways of doing things. Up to this moment, for example, I have not been sent a single copy of the Cologne Communist Trial.

With best regards,

Yours,

Karl Marx

Engels to August Bebel In Zwickau

London, March 18-28, 1875 Dear Bebel,

I have received your letter of February 23 and am glad to hear that you are in such good bodily health.

You ask me what we think of the unification affair. We are, unfortunately, in exactly the same boat as yourself. Neither Liebknecht nor anyone else has let us have any kind of information, and hence we too know only what is in the papers — not that there was anything in them until a week or so ago, when the draft programme appeared. That astonished us not a little, I must say.

Our party had so often held out a conciliatory hand to the Lassalleans, or at least proffered co-operation, only to be rebuffed so often and so contemptuously by the Hasenclevers, Hasselmanns and Tolckes as to lead any child to the conclusion that, should these gentlemen now come and themselves proffer conciliation, they must be in a hell of a dilemma. Knowing full well what these people are like, however, it behoves us to make the most of that dilemma and insist on every conceivable guarantee that might prevent these people from restoring, at our party's expense, their shattered reputation in general working-class opinion. They should be given an exceedingly cool and cautious reception, and union be made dependent on the degree of their readiness to abandon their sectarian slogans and their state aid, and to accept in its essentials the Eisenach Programme of 1869 or an improved edition of it adapted to the present day. Our party has absolutely nothing to learn from the Lassalleans in the theoretical sphere, i.e. the crux of the matter where the programme is concerned, but the Lassalleans doubtless have something to learn from the party; the first prerequisite for union was that they cease to be sectarians, Lassalleans, i.e. that, first and foremost, they should, if not wholly relinquish the universal panacea of state aid, at least admit it to be a secondary provisional measure alongside and amongst many others recognised as possible. The draft programme shows that our people, while infinitely superior to the Lassallean leaders in matters of theory, are far from being a match for them where political guile is concerned; once again the "honest men" have been cruelly done in the eye by the dishonest.

To begin with, they adopt the high-sounding but historically false Lassallean dictum: in relation to the working class all other classes are only one reactionary mass. This proposition is true only in certain exceptional instances, for example in the case of a revolution by the proletariat, e.g. the Commune, or in a country in which not only has the bourgeoisie constructed state and society after its own image but the democratic petty bourgeoisie, in its wake, has already carried that reconstruction to its logical conclusion. If, for instance, in Germany, the democratic petty bourgeoisie were part of this reactionary mass, then how could the Social-Democratic Workers' Party have gone hand in hand with it, with the People's Party, for years on end? How could the Volksstaat derive virtually all its political content from the petty-bourgeois democratic Frankfurter Zeitung? And how can one explain the adoption in this same programme of no less than seven demands that coincide exactly and word for word with the programme of the People's Party and of petty-bourgeois democracy? I mean the seven political demands, 1 to 5 and 1 to 2, of which there is not one that is not bourgeois-democratic.

Secondly, the principle that the workers' movement is an international one is, to all intents and purposes, utterly denied in respect of the present, and this by men who, for the space of five years and under the most difficult conditions, upheld that principle in the most laudable manner. The German workers' position in the van of the European movement rests essentially on their genuinely international attitude during the war; no other proletariat would have behaved so well. And now this principle is to be denied by them at a moment when, everywhere abroad, workers are stressing it all the more by reason of the efforts made by governments to suppress every attempt at its practical application in an organisation! And what is left of the internationalism of the workers' movement? The dim prospect — not even of subsequent co-operation among European workers with a view to their liberation — nay, but of a future "international brotherhood of peoples" — of your Peace League bourgeois "United States of Europe"!

There was, of course, no need whatever to mention the International as such. But at the very least there should have been no going back on the programme of 1869, and some sort of statement to the effect that, though first of all the German workers' party is acting within the limits set by its political frontiers (it has no right to speak in the name of the European proletariat, especially when what it says is wrong), it is nevertheless conscious of its solidarity with the workers of all other countries and will, as before, always be ready to meet the obligations that solidarity entails. Such obligations, even if one does not definitely proclaim or regard oneself as part of the "International," consist for example in aid, abstention from blacklegging during strikes, making sure that the party organs keep German workers informed of the movement abroad, agitation against impending or incipient dynastic wars and, during such wars, an attitude such as was exemplarily maintained in 1870 and 1871, etc.

Thirdly, our people have allowed themselves to be saddled with the Lassallean "iron law of wages" which is based on a completely outmoded economic view, namely that on average the workers receive only the minimum wage because, according to the Malthusian theory of population, there are always too many workers (such was Lassalle's reasoning). Now in Capital Marx has amply demonstrated that the laws governing wages are very complex, that, according to circumstances, now this law, now that, holds sway, that they are therefore by no means iron but are, on the contrary, exceedingly elastic, and that the subject really cannot be dismissed in a few words, as Lassalle imagined. Malthus' argument, upon which the law Lassalle derived from him and Ricardo (whom he misinterpreted) is based, as that argument appears, for instance, on p. 5 of the Arbeiterlesebuch, where it is quoted from another pamphlet of Lassalle's, is exhaustively refuted by Marx in the section on "Accumulation of Capital." Thus, by adopting the Lassallean "iron law" one commits oneself to a false proposition and false reasoning in support of the same.

Fourthly, as its one and only social demand, the programme puts forward — Lassallean state aid in its starkest form, as stolen by Lassalle from Buchez. And this, after Bracke has so ably demonstrated the sheer futility of that demand; after almost all if not all, of our party speakers have, in their struggle against the Lassalleans, been compelled to make a stand against this "state aid"! Our party could hardly demean itself further. Internationalism sunk to the level of Amand Goegg, socialism to that of the bourgeois republican Buchez, who confronted the socialists with this demand in order to supplant them!

But "state aid" in the Lassallean sense of the word is, after all, at most only one measure among many others for the attainment of an end here lamely described as "paving the way for the solution of the social question," as though in our case there were still a social question that remained unsolved in theory! Thus, if you were to say: The German workers' party strives to abolish wage labour and hence class distinctions by introducing co-operative production into industry and agriculture, and on a national scale; it is in favour of any measure calculated to attain that end! — then no Lassallean could possibly object.

Fifthly, there is absolutely no mention of the organisation of the working class as a class through the medium of trade unions. And that is a point of the utmost importance, this being the proletariat's true class organisation in which it fights its daily battles with capital, in which it trains itself and which nowadays can no longer simply be smashed, even with reaction at its worst (as presently in Paris). Considering the importance this organisation is likewise assuming in Germany, it would in our view be indispensable to accord it some mention in the programme and, possibly, to leave some room for it in the organisation of the party.

All these things have been done by our people to oblige the Lassalleans. And what have the others conceded? That a host of somewhat muddled and purely democratic demands should figure in the programme, some of them being of a purely fashionable nature — for instance "legislation by the people" such as exists in Switzerland and does more harm than good, if it can be said to do anything at all. Administration by the people — that would at least be something. Similarly omitted is the first prerequisite of all liberty — that all officials be responsible for all their official actions to every citizen before the ordinary courts and in accordance with common law. That demands such as freedom of science and freedom of conscience figure in every liberal bourgeois programme and seem a trifle out of place here is something I shall not enlarge upon.

The free people's state is transformed into the free state. Grammatically speaking, a free state is one in which the state is free vis-à-vis its citizens, a state, that is, with a despotic government. All the palaver about the state ought to be dropped, especially after the Commune, which had ceased to be a state in the true sense of the term. The people's state has been flung in our teeth ad nauseam by the anarchists, although Marx's anti-Proudhon piece and after it the

Communist Manifesto declare outright that, with the introduction of the socialist order of society, the state will dissolve of itself and disappear. Now, since the state is merely a transitional institution of which use is made in the struggle, in the revolution, to keep down one's enemies by force, it is utter nonsense to speak of a free people's state; so long as the proletariat still makes use of the state, it makes use of it, not for the purpose of freedom, but of keeping down its enemies and, as soon as there can be any question of freedom, the state as such ceases to exist. We would therefore suggest that Gemeinwesen ["commonalty"] be universally substituted for state; it is a good old German word that can very well do service for the French "Commune."

"The elimination of all social and political inequality," rather than "the abolition of all class distinctions," is similarly a most dubious expression. As between one country, one province and even one place and another, living conditions will always evince a certain inequality which may be reduced to a minimum but never wholly eliminated. The living conditions of Alpine dwellers will always be different from those of the plainsmen. The concept of a socialist society as a realm of equality is a one-sided French concept deriving from the old "liberty, equality, fraternity," a concept which was justified in that, in its own time and place, it signified a phase of development, but which, like all the one-sided ideas of earlier socialist schools, ought now to be superseded, since they produce nothing but mental confusion, and more accurate ways of presenting the matter have been discovered.

I shall desist, although almost every word in this programme, a programme which is, moreover, insipidly written, lays itself open to criticism. It is such that, should it be adopted, Marx and I could never recognise a new party set up on that basis and shall have to consider most seriously what attitude — public as well as private — we should adopt towards it. Remember that abroad we are held responsible for any and every statement and action of the German Social-Democratic Workers' Party. E.g. by Bakunin in his work Statehood and Anarchy, in which we are made to answer for every injudicious word spoken or written by Liebknecht since the inception of the Demokratisches Wochenblatt. People imagine that we run the whole show from here, whereas you know as well as I do that we have hardly ever interfered in the least with internal party affairs, and then only in an attempt to make good, as far as possible, what we considered to have been blunders — and only theoretical blunders at that. But, as you yourself will realise, this programme marks a turning-point which may very well force us to renounce any kind of responsibility in regard to the party that adopts it.

Generally speaking, less importance attaches to the official programme of a party than to what it does. But a new programme is after all a banner planted in public, and the outside world judges the party by it. Hence, whatever happens there should be no going-back, as there is here, on the Eisenach programme. It should further be considered what the workers of other countries will think of this programme; what impression will be created by this genuflection on the part of the entire German socialist proletariat before Lassalleanism.

I am, moreover, convinced that a union on this basis would not last a year. Are the best minds of our party to descend to repeating, parrot-fashion, Lassallean maxims concerning the iron law of wages and state aid? I'd like to see you, for one, thus employed! And were they to do so, their audiences would hiss them off the stage. And I feel sure that it is precisely on these bits of the programme that the Lassalleans are insisting, like Shylock the Jew on his pound of flesh. The split will come; but we shall have "made honest men" again of Hasselmann, Hasenclever and Tolcke and Co.; we shall emerge from the split weaker and the Lassalleans stronger; our party will have lost its political virginity and will never again be able to come out whole-heartedly against the Lassallean maxims which for a time it inscribed on its own banner; and then, should the Lassalleans again declare themselves to be the sole and most genuine workers' party and our people to be bourgeois, the programme would be there to prove it. All the socialist measures in it are theirs, and our party has introduced nothing save the demands of that petty-bourgeois democracy which it has itself described in that same programme as part of the "reactionary mass"!

I had held this letter back in view of the fact that you would only be released on April 1, in honour of Bismarck's birthday, not wanting to expose it to the risk of interception in the course of an attempt to smuggle it in. Well, I have just had a letter from Bracke, who has also felt grave doubts about the programme and asks for our opinion. I shall therefore send this letter to him for forwarding, so that he can read it without my having to write the whole thing over again. I have, by the way, also spoken my mind to Ramm; to Liebknecht I wrote but briefly. I cannot forgive his not having told us a single word about the whole business (whereas Ramm and others believed he had given us exact information) until it was, in a manner of speaking, too late. True, this has always been his wont — hence the large amount of disagreeable correspondence which we, both Marx and myself, have had with him, but this time it really is too bad, and we definitely shan't act in concert with him.

Do see that you manage to come here in the summer; you would, of course, stay with me and, if the weather is fine, we might spend a day or two taking sea baths, which would really do you good after your long spell in jail.

Ever your friend,

F. E.

Marx has just moved house. He is living at 41 Maitland Park Crescent, NW London.

Critique of the Gotha Programme

I

1. "Labor is the source of wealth and all culture, and since useful labor is possible only in society and through society, the proceeds of labor belong undiminished with equal right to all members of society."

First part of the paragraph: "Labor is the source of all wealth and all culture."

Labor is not the source of all wealth. Nature is just as much the source of use values (and it is surely of such that material wealth consists!) as labor, which itself is only the manifestation of a force of nature, human labor power. the above phrase is to be found in all children's primers and is correct insofar as it is implied that labor is performed with the appurtenant subjects and instruments. But a socialist program cannot allow such bourgeois phrases to pass over in silence the conditions that lone give them meaning. And insofar as man from the beginning behaves toward nature, the primary source of all instruments and subjects of labor, as an owner, treats her as belonging to him, his labor becomes the source of use values, therefore also of wealth. The bourgeois have very good grounds for falsely ascribing supernatural creative power to labor; since precisely from the fact that labor depends on nature it follows that the man who possesses no other property than his labor power must, in all conditions of society and culture, be the slave of other men who have

---

made themselves the owners of the material conditions of labor. He can only work with their permission, hence live only with their permission.

Let us now leave the sentence as it stands, or rather limps. What could one have expected in conclusion? Obviously this:

"Since labor is the source of all wealth, no one in society can appropriate wealth except as the product of labor. Therefore, if he himself does not work, he lives by the labor of others and also acquires his culture at the expense of the labor of others."

Instead of this, by means of the verbal river "and since", a proposition is added in order to draw a conclusion from this and not from the first one.

Second part of the paragraph: "Useful labor is possible only in society and through society."

According to the first proposition, labor was the source of all wealth and all culture; therefore no society is possible without labor. Now we learn, conversely, that no "useful" labor is possible without society.

One could just as well have said that only in society can useless and even socially harmful labor become a branch of gainful occupation, that only in society can one live by being idle, etc., etc. — in short, once could just as well have copied the whole of Rousseau.

And what is "useful" labor? Surely only labor which produces the intended useful result. A savage — and man was a savage after he had ceased to be an ape — who kills an animal with a stone, who collects fruit, etc., performs "useful" labor.

Thirdly, the conclusion: "Useful labor is possible only in society and through society, the proceeds of labor belong undiminished with equal right to all members of society."

A fine conclusion! If useful labor is possible only in society and through society, the proceeds of labor belong to society — and only so much therefrom accrues to the individual worker as is not required to maintain the "condition" of labor, society.

In fact, this proposition has at all times been made use of by the champions of the state of society prevailing at any given time. First comes the claims of the government and everything that sticks to it, since it is the social organ for the maintenance of the social order; then comes the claims of the various kinds of private property, for the various kinds of private property are the foundations of society, etc. One sees that such hollow phrases are the foundations of society, etc.

One sees that such hollow phrases can be twisted and turned as desired.

The first and second parts of the paragraph have some intelligible connection only in the following wording:

"Labor becomes the source of wealth and culture only as social labor", or, what is the same thing, "in and through society".

This proposition is incontestably correct, for although isolated labor (its material conditions presupposed) can create use value, it can create neither wealth nor culture.

But equally incontestable is this other proposition:

"In proportion as labor develops socially, and becomes thereby a source of wealth and culture, poverty and destitution develop among the workers, and wealth and culture among the nonworkers."

This is the law of all history hitherto. What, therefore, had to be done here, instead of setting down general phrases about "labor" and "society", was to prove concretely how in present capitalist society the material, etc., conditions have at last been created which enable and compel the workers to lift this social curse.

In fact, however, the whole paragraph, bungled in style and content, is only there in order to inscribe the Lassallean catchword of the "undiminished proceeds of labor" as a slogan at the top of the party banner. I shall return later to the "proceeds of labor", "equal right", etc., since the same thing recurs in a somewhat different form further on.

2. "In present-day society, the instruments of labor are the monopoly of the capitalist class; the resulting dependence of the working class is the cause of misery and servitude in all forms."

This sentence, borrowed from the Rules of the International, is incorrect in this "improved" edition.

In present-day society, the instruments of labor are the monopoly of the landowners (the monopoly of property in land is even the basis of the monopoly of capital) and the capitalists. In the passage in question, the Rules of the International do not mention either one or the other class of monopolists. They speak of the "monopolizer of the means of labor, that is, the sources of life." The addition, "sources of life", makes it sufficiently clear that land is included in the instruments of labor.

The correction was introduced because Lassalle, for reasons now generally known, attacked only the capitalist class and not the landowners. In England, the capitalist class is usually not even the owner of the land on which his factory stands.

3. "The emancipation of labor demands the promotion of the instruments of labor to the common property of society and the co-operative regulation of the total labor, with a fair distribution of the proceeds of labor.

"Promotion of the instruments of labor to the common property" ought obviously to read their "conversion into the common property"; but this is only passing.

What are the "proceeds of labor"? The product of labor, or its value? And in the latter case, is it the total value of the product, or only that part of the value which labor has newly added to the value of the means of production consumed?

"Proceeds of labor" is a loose notion which Lassalle has put in the place of definite economic conceptions.

What is "a fair distribution"?

Do not the bourgeois assert that the present-day distribution is "fair"? And is it not, in fact, the only "fair" distribution on the basis of the present-day mode of production? Are economic relations regulated by legal conceptions, or do not, on the contrary, legal relations arise out of economic ones? Have not also the socialist sectarians the most varied notions about "fair" distribution?

To understand what is implied in this connection by the phrase "fair distribution", we must take the first paragraph and this one together. The latter presupposes a society wherein the instruments of labor are common property and the total labor is co-operatively regulated, and from the first paragraph we learn that "the proceeds of labor belong undiminished with equal right to all members of society."

"To all members of society"? To those who do not work as well? What remains then of the "undiminished" proceeds of labor? Only to those members of society who work? What remains then of the "equal right" of all members of society?

But "all members of society" and "equal right" are obviously mere phrases. The kernel consists in this, that in this communist society every worker must receive the "undiminished" Lassallean "proceeds of labor".

Let us take, first of all, the words "proceeds of labor" in the sense of the product of labor; then the co-operative proceeds of labor are the total social product.

From this must now be deducted: First, cover for replacement of the means of production used up. Second, additional portion for expansion of production. Third, reserve or insurance funds to provide against accidents, dislocations caused by natural calamities, etc.

These deductions from the "undiminished" proceeds of labor are an economic necessity, and their magnitude is to be determined according to available means and forces, and partly by computation of probabilities, but they are in no way calculable by equity.

There remains the other part of the total product, intended to serve as means of consumption.

Before this is divided among the individuals, there has to be deducted again, from it: First, the general costs of administration not belonging to production. This part will, from the outset, be very considerably restricted in comparison with present-day society, and it diminishes in proportion as the new society develops. Second, that which is intended for the common satisfaction of needs, such as schools, health services, etc. From the outset, this part grows considerably in comparison with present-day society, and it grows in proportion as the new society develops. Third, funds for those unable to work, etc., in short, for what is included under so-called official poor relief today.

Only now do we come to the "distribution" which the program, under Lassallean influence, alone has in view in its narrow fashion — namely, to that part of the means of consumption which is divided among the individual producers of the co-operative society.

The "undiminished" proceeds of labor have already unnoticeably become converted into the "diminished" proceeds, although what the producer is deprived of in his capacity as a private individual benefits him directly or indirectly in his capacity as a member of society.

Just as the phrase of the "undiminished" proceeds of labor has disappeared, so now does the phrase of the "proceeds of labor" disappear altogether.

Within the co-operative society based on common ownership of the means of production, the producers do not exchange their products; just as little does the labor employed on the products appear here as the value of these products, as a material quality possessed by them, since now, in contrast to capitalist society, individual labor no longer exists in an indirect fashion but directly as a component part of total labor. The phrase "proceeds of labor", objectionable also today on account of its ambiguity, thus loses all meaning.

What we have to deal with here is a communist society, not as it has developed on its own foundations, but, on the contrary, just as it emerges from capitalist society; which is thus in every respect, economically, morally, and intellectually, still stamped with the birthmarks of the old society from whose womb it emerges. Accordingly, the individual producer receives back from society — after the deductions have been made — exactly what he gives to it. What he has given to it is his individual quantum of labor. For example, the social working day consists of the sum of the individual hours of work; the individual labor time of the individual producer is the part of the social working day contributed by him, his share in it. He receives a certificate from society that he has furnished such-and-such an amount of labor (after deducting his labor for the common funds); and with this certificate, he draws from the social stock of means of consumption as much as the same amount of labor cost. The same amount of labor which he has given to society in one form, he receives back in another.

Here, obviously, the same principle prevails as that which regulates the exchange of commodities, as far as this is exchange of equal values. Content and form are changed, because under the altered circumstances no one can give anything except his labor, and because, on the other hand, nothing can pass to the ownership of individuals, except individual means of consumption. But as far as the distribution of the latter among the individual producers is concerned, the same principle prevails as in the exchange of commodity equivalents: a given amount of labor in one form is exchanged for an equal amount of labor in another form.

Hence, equal right here is still in principle — bourgeois right, although principle and practice are no longer at loggerheads, while the exchange of equivalents in commodity exchange exists only on the average and not in the individual case.

In spite of this advance, this equal right is still constantly stigmatized by a bourgeois limitation. The right of the producers is proportional to the labor they supply; the equality consists in the fact that measurement is made with an equal standard, labor.

But one man is superior to another physically, or mentally, and supplies more labor in the same time, or can labor for a longer time; and labor, to serve as a measure, must be defined by its duration or intensity, otherwise it ceases to be a standard of measurement. This equal right is an unequal right for unequal labor. It recognizes no class differences, because everyone is only a worker like everyone else; but it tacitly recognizes unequal individual endowment, and thus productive capacity, as a natural privilege. It is, therefore, a right of inequality, in its content, like every right. Right, by its very nature, can consist only in the application of an equal standard; but unequal individuals (and they would not be different individuals if they were not unequal) are measurable only by an equal standard insofar as they are brought under an equal point of view, are taken from one definite side only — for instance, in the present case, are regarded only as workers and nothing more is seen in them, everything else being ignored. Further, one worker is married, another is not; one has more children than another, and so on and so forth. Thus, with an equal performance of labor, and hence an equal in the social consumption fund, one will in fact receive more than another, one will be richer than another, and so on. To avoid all these defects, right, instead of being equal, would have to be unequal.

But these defects are inevitable in the first phase of communist society as it is when it has just emerged after prolonged birth pangs from capitalist society. Right can never be higher than the economic structure of society and its cultural development conditioned thereby.

In a higher phase of communist society, after the enslaving subordination of the individual to the division of labor, and therewith also the antithesis between mental and physical labor, has vanished; after labor has become not only a means of life but life's prime want; after the productive forces have also increased with the all-around development of the individual, and all the springs of co-operative wealth flow more abundantly — only then can the narrow horizon of bourgeois right be crossed in its entirety and society inscribe on its banners: From each according to his ability, to each according to his needs!

I have dealt more at length with the "undiminished" proceeds of labor, on the one hand, and with "equal right" and "fair distribution", on the other, in order to show what a crime it is to attempt, on the one hand, to force on our Party again, as dogmas, ideas which in a certain period had some meaning but have now become obsolete verbal rubbish, while again perverting, on the other, the realistic outlook, which it cost so much effort to instill into the Party but which has now taken root in it, by means of ideological nonsense about right and other trash so common among the democrats and French socialists.

Quite apart from the analysis so far given, it was in general a mistake to make a fuss about so-called distribution and put the principal stress on it.

Any distribution whatever of the means of consumption is only a consequence of the distribution of the conditions of production themselves. The latter distribution, however, is a feature of the mode of production itself. The capitalist mode of production, for example, rests on the fact that the material conditions of production are in the hands of nonworkers in the form of property in capital and land, while the masses are only owners of the personal condition of production, of labor power. If the elements of production are so distributed, then the present-day distribution of the means of consumption results automatically. If the material conditions of production are the co-operative property of the workers themselves, then there likewise results a distribution of the means of consumption different from the present one. Vulgar socialism (and from it in turn a section of the democrats) has taken over from the bourgeois economists the consideration and treatment of distribution as independent of the mode of production and hence the presentation of socialism as turning principally on distribution. After the real relation has long been made clear, why retrogress again?

4. "The emancipation of labor must be the work of the working class, relative to which all other classes are only one reactionary mass."

The first strophe is taken from the introductory words of the Rules of the International, but "improved". There it is said: "The emancipation of the working class must be the act of the workers themselves"; here, on the contrary, the "working class" has to emancipate — what? "Labor." Let him understand who can.

In compensation, the antistrophe, on the other hand, is a Lassallean quotation of the first water: "relative to which" (the working class) "all other classes are only one reactionary mass."

In the Communist Manifesto it is said:

"Of all the classes that stand face-to-face with the bourgeoisie today, the proletariat alone is a really revolutionary class. The other classes decay and finally disappear in the face of modern industry; the proletariat is its special and essential product."

The bourgeoisie is here conceived as a revolutionary class—as the bearer of large-scale industry—relative to the feudal lords and the lower middle class, who desire to maintain all social positions that are the creation of obsolete modes of production. thus, they do not form together with the bourgeoisie "only one reactionary mass".

On the other hand, the proletariat is revolutionary relative to the bourgeoisie because, having itself grown up on the basis of large-scale industry, it strives to strip off from production the capitalist character that the bourgeoisie seeks to perpetuate. But the Manifesto adds that the "lower middle class" is becoming revolutionary "in view of [its] impending transfer to the proletariat".

From this point of view, therefore, it is again nonsense to say that it, together with the bourgeoisie, and with the feudal lords into the bargain, "form only one reactionary mass" relative to the working class.

Has one proclaimed to the artisan, small manufacturers, etc., and peasants during the last elections: Relative to us, you, together with the bourgeoisie and feudal lords, form one reactionary mass?

Lassalle knew the Communist Manifesto by heart, as his faithful followers know the gospels written by him. If, therefore, he has falsified it so grossly, this has occurred only to put a good color on his alliance with absolutist and feudal opponents against the bourgeoisie.

In the above paragraph, moreover, his oracular saying is dragged in by main force without any connection with the botched quotation from the Rules of the International. Thus, it is simply an impertinence, and indeed not at all displeasing to Herr Bismarck, one of those cheap pieces of insolence in which the Marat of Berlin deals. [Marat of Berlin a reference to Hasselmann, cheif editor of the Neuer Social-Demokrat]

5. "The working class strives for its emancipation first of all within the framework of the present-day national states, conscious that the necessary result of its efforts, which are common to the workers of all civilized countries, will be the international brotherhood of peoples."

Lassalle, in opposition to the Communist Manifesto and to all earlier socialism, conceived the workers' movement from the narrowest national standpoint. He is being followed in this—and that after the work of the International!

It is altogether self-evident that, to be able to fight at all, the working class must organize itself at home as a class and that its own country is the immediate arena of its struggle—insofar as its class struggle is national, not in substance, but, as the Communist Manifesto says, "in form". But the "framework of the present-day national state", for instance, the German Empire, is itself, in its turn, economically "within the framework" of the world market, politically "within the framework" of the system of states. Every businessman knows that German trade is at the same time foreign trade, and the greatness of Herr Bismarck consists, to be sure, precisely in his pursuing a kind of international policy.

And to what does the German Workers' party reduce its internationalism? To the consciousness that the result of its efforts will be "the international brotherhood of peoples"—a phrase borrowed from the bourgeois League of Peace and Freedom, which is intended to pass as equivalent to the international brotherhood of working classes in the joint struggle against the ruling classes and their governments. Not a word, therefore, about the international functions of the German working class! And it is thus that it is to challenge its own bourgeoisie—which is already linked up in brotherhood against it with the bourgeois of all other countries—and Herr Bismarck's international policy of conspiracy.

In fact, the internationalism of the program stands even infinitely below that of the Free Trade party. The latter also asserts that the result of its efforts will be "the international brotherhood of peoples". But it also does something to make trade international and by no means contents itself with the consciousness that all people are carrying on trade at home.

The international activity of the working classes does not in any way depend on the existence of the International Working Men's Association. This was only the first attempt to create a central organ for the activity; an attempt which was a lasting success on account of the impulse which it gave but which was no longer realizable in its historical form after the fall of the Paris Commune.

Bismarck's Norddeutsche was absolutely right when it announced, to the satisfaction of its master, that the German Workers' party had sworn off internationalism in the new program.

II

"Starting from these basic principles, the German workers' party strives by all legal means for the free state—and—socialist society: that abolition of the wage system together with the iron law of wages—and—exploitation in every form; the elimination of all social and political inequality."

I shall return to the "free" state later.

So, in future, the German Workers' party has got to believe in Lassalle's "iron law of wages"! That this may not be lost, the nonsense is perpetrated of speaking of the "abolition of the wage system" (it should read: system of wage labor), "together with the iron law of wages". If I abolish wage labor, then naturally I abolish its laws also, whether they are of "iron" or sponge. But Lassalle's attack on wage labor turns almost solely on this so-called law. In order, therefore, to prove that Lassalle's sect has conquered, the "wage system" must be abolished "together with the iron law of wages" and not without it.

It is well known that nothing of the "iron law of wages" is Lassalle's except the word "iron" borrowed from Goethe's "great, eternal iron laws". The word "iron" is a label by which the true believers recognize one another. But if I take the law with Lassalle's stamp on it, and consequently in his sense, then I must also take it with his substantiation for it. And what is that? As Lange already showed, shortly after Lassalle's death, it is the Malthusian theory of population (preached by Lange himself). But if this theory is correct, then again I cannot abolish the law even if I abolish wage labor a hundred times over, because the law then governs not only the system of wage labor but every social system. Basing themselves directly on this, the economists have been proving for 50 years and more that socialism cannot abolish poverty, which has its basis in nature, but can only make it general, distribute it simultaneously over the whole surface of society!

But all this is not the main thing. Quite apart from the false Lassallean formulation of the law, the truly outrageous retrogression consists in the following:

Since Lassalle's death, there has asserted itself in our party the scientific understanding that wages are not what they appear to be— namely, the value, or price, of labor—but only a masked form for the value, or price, of labor power. Thereby, the whole bourgeois conception of wages hitherto, as well as all the criticism hitherto directed against this conception, was thrown overboard once and for all. It was made clear that the wage worker has permission to work for his own subsistence—that is, to live, only insofar as he works for a certain time gratis for the capitalist (and hence also for the latter's co-consumers of surplus value); that the whole capitalist system of production turns on the increase of this gratis labor by extending the working day, or by developing the productivity — that is, increasing the intensity or labor power, etc.; that, consequently, the system of wage labor is a system of slavery, and indeed of a slavery which becomes more severe in proportion as the social productive forces of labor develop, whether the worker receives better or worse payment. And after this understanding has gained more and more ground in our party, some return to Lassalle's dogma although they must have known that Lassalle did not know what wages were, but, following in the wake of the bourgeois economists, took the appearance for the essence of the matter.

It is as if, among slaves who have at last got behind the secret of slavery and broken out in rebellion, a slave still in thrall to obsolete notions were to inscribe on the program of the rebellion: Slavery must be abolished because the feeding of slaves in the system of slavery cannot exceed a certain low maximum!

Does not the mere fact that the representatives of our party were capable of perpetrating such a monstrous attack on the understanding that has spread among the mass of our party prove, by itself, with what criminal levity and with what lack of conscience they set to work in drawing up this compromise program!

Instead of the indefinite concluding phrase of the paragraph, "the elimination of all social and political inequality", it ought to have been said that with the abolition of class distinctions all social and political inequality arising from them would disappear of itself.

III

"The German Workers' party, in order to pave the way to the solution of the social question, demands the establishment of producers' co-operative societies with state aid under the democratic control of the toiling people. The producers' co-operative societies are to be called into being for industry and agriculture on such a scale that the socialist organization of the total labor will arise from them."

After the Lassallean "iron law of wages", the physic of the prophet. The way to it is "paved" in worthy fashion. In place of the existing class struggle appears a newspaper scribbler's phrase: "the social question", to the "solution" of which one "paves the way".

Instead of arising from the revolutionary process of transformation of society, the "socialist organization of the total labor" "arises" from the "state aid" that the state gives to the producers' co-operative societies and which the state, not the workers, "calls into being". It is worthy of Lassalle's imagination that with state loans one can build a new society just as well as a new railway!

From the remnants of a sense of shame, "state aid" has been put— under the democratic control of the "toiling people".

In the first place, the majority of the "toiling people" in Germany consists of peasants, not proletarians.

Second, "democratic" means in German "Volksherrschaftlich" [by the rule of the people]. But what does "control by the rule of the people of the toiling people" mean? And particularly in the case of a toiling people which, through these demands that it puts to the state, expresses its full consciousness that it neither rules nor is ripe for ruling!

It would be superfluous to deal here with the criticism of the recipe prescribed by Buchez in the reign of Louis Philippe, in opposition to the French socialists and accepted by the reactionary workers, of the Atelier. The chief offense does not lie in having inscribed this specific nostrum in the program, but in taking, in general, a retrograde step from the standpoint of a class movement to that of a sectarian movement.

That the workers desire to establish the conditions for co-operative production on a social scale, and first of all on a national scale, in their own country, only means that they are working to revolutionize the present conditions of production, and it has nothing in common with the foundation of co-operative societies with state aid. But as far as the present co-operative societies are concerned, they are of value only insofar as they are the independent creations of the workers and not protégés either of the governments or of the bourgeois.

IV

I come now to the democratic section.

A. "The free basis of the state."

First of all, according to II, the German Workers' party strives for "the free state".

Free state — what is this?

It is by no means the aim of the workers, who have got rid of the narrow mentality of humble subjects, to set the state free. In the German Empire, the "state" is almost as "free" as in Russia. Freedom consists in converting the state from an organ superimposed upon society into one completely subordinate to it; and today, too, the forms of state are more free or less free to the extent that they restrict the "freedom of the state".

The German Workers' party — at least if it adopts the program — shows that its socialist ideas are not even skin-deep; in that, instead of treating existing society (and this holds good for any future one) as the basis of the existing state (or of the future state in the case of future society), it treats the state rather as an independent entity that possesses its own intellectual, ethical, and libertarian bases.

And what of the riotous misuse which the program makes of the words "present-day state", "present-day society", and of the still more riotous misconception it creates in regard to the state to which it addresses its demands?

"Present-day society" is capitalist society, which exists in all civilized countries, more or less free from medieval admixture, more or less modified by the particular historical development of each country, more or less developed. On the other hand, the "present-day state" changes with a country's frontier. It is different in the Prusso-German Empire from what it is in Switzerland, and different in England from what it is in the United States. The "present-day state" is therefore a fiction.

Nevertheless, the different states of the different civilized countries, in spite or their motley diversity of form, all have this in common: that they are based on modern bourgeois society, only one more or less capitalistically developed. They have, therefore, also certain essential characteristics in common. In this sense, it is possible to speak of the "present-day state" in contrast with the future, in which its present root, bourgeois society, will have died off.

The question then arises: What transformation will the state undergo in communist society? In other words, what social functions will remain in existence there that are analogous to present state functions? This question can only be answered scientifically, and one does not get a flea-hop nearer to the problem by a thousand-fold combination of the word 'people' with the word 'state'.

Between capitalist and communist society there lies the period of the revolutionary transformation of the one into the other. Corresponding to this is also a political transition period in which the state can be nothing but the revolutionary dictatorship of the proletariat.

Now the program does not deal with this nor with the future state of communist society.

Its political demands contain nothing beyond the old democratic litany familiar to all: universal suffrage, direct legislation, popular rights, a people's militia, etc. They are a mere echo of the bourgeois People's party, of the League of Peace and Freedom. They are all demands which, insofar as they are not exaggerated in fantastic presentation, have already been realized. Only the state to which they belong does not lie within the borders of the German Empire, but in Switzerland, the United States, etc. This sort of "state of the future" is a present-day state, although existing outside the "framework" of the German Empire.

But one thing has been forgotten. Since the German Workers' party expressly declares that it acts within "the present-day national state", hence within its own state, the Prusso-German Empire — its demands would indeed be otherwise largely meaningless, since one only demands what one has not got — it should not have forgotten the chief thing, namely, that all those pretty little gewgaws rest on the recognition of the so-called sovereignty of the people and hence are appropriate only in a democratic republic.

Since one has not the courage — and wisely so, for the circumstances demand caution — to demand the democratic republic, as the French workers' programs under Louis Philippe and under Louis Napoleon did, one should not have resorted, either, to the subterfuge, neither "honest" nor decent, of demanding things which have meaning only in a democratic republic from a state which is nothing but a police-guarded military despotism, embellished with parliamentary forms, alloyed with a feudal admixture, already influenced by the bourgeoisie, and bureaucratically carpentered, and then to assure this state into the bargain that one imagines one will be able to force such things upon it "by legal means".

Even vulgar democracy, which sees the millennium in the democratic republic, and has no suspicion that it is precisely in this last form of state of bourgeois society that the class struggle has to be fought out to a conclusion — even it towers mountains above this kind of democratism, which keeps within the limits of what is permitted by the police and not permitted by logic.

That, in fact, by the word "state" is meant the government machine, or the state insofar as it forms a special organism separated from society through division of labor, is shown by the words "the

German Workers' party demands as the economic basis of the state: a single progressive income tax", etc. Taxes are the economic basis of the government machinery and of nothing else. In the state of the future, existing in Switzerland, this demand has been pretty well fulfilled. Income tax presupposes various sources of income of the various social classes, and hence capitalist society. It is, therefore, nothing remarkable that the Liverpool financial reformers — bourgeois headed by Gladstone's brother — are putting forward the same demand as the program.

B. "The German Workers' party demands as the intellectual and ethical basis of the state: "1. Universal and equal elementary education by the state. Universal compulsory school attendance. Free instruction."

"Equal elementary education"? What idea lies behind these words? Is it believed that in present-day society (and it is only with this one has to deal) education can be equal for all classes? Or is it demanded that the upper classes also shall be compulsorily reduced to the modicum of education — the elementary school — that alone is compatible with the economic conditions not only of the wage-workers but of the peasants as well?

"Universal compulsory school attendance. Free instruction." The former exists even in Germany, the second in Switzerland and in the United States in the case of elementary schools. If in some states of the latter country higher education institutions are also "free", that only means in fact defraying the cost of education of the upper classes from the general tax receipts. Incidentally, the same holds good for "free administration of justice" demanded under A, 5. The administration of criminal justice is to be had free everywhere; that of civil justice is concerned almost exclusively with conflicts over property and hence affects almost exclusively the possessing classes. Are they to carry on their litigation at the expense of the national coffers?

This paragraph on the schools should at least have demanded technical schools (theoretical and practical) in combination with the elementary school.

"Elementary education by the state" is altogether objectionable. Defining by a general law the expenditures on the elementary schools, the qualifications of the teaching staff, the branches of instruction, etc., and, as is done in the United States, supervising the fulfillment of these legal specifications by state inspectors, is a very different thing from appointing the state as the educator of the people! Government and church should rather be equally excluded from any influence on the school. Particularly, indeed, in the Prusso-German Empire (and one should not take refuge in the rotten subterfuge that one is speaking of a "state of the future"; we have seen how matters stand in this respect) the state has need, on the contrary, of a very stern education by the people.

But the whole program, for all its democratic clang, is tainted through and through by the Lassallean sect's servile belief in the state, or, what is no better, by a democratic belief in miracles; or rather it is a compromise between these two kinds of belief in miracles, both equally remote from socialism.

"Freedom of science" says paragraph of the Prussian Constitution. Why, then, here?.

"Freedom of conscience"! If one desired, at this time of the Kulturkampf to remind liberalism of its old catchwords, it surely could have been done only in the following form: Everyone should be able to attend his religious as well as his bodily needs without the police sticking their noses in. But the Workers' party ought, at any rate in this connection, to have expressed its awareness of the fact that bourgeois "freedom of conscience" is nothing but the toleration of all possible kinds of religious freedom of conscience, and that for its part it endeavours rather to liberate the conscience from the witchery of religion. But one chooses not to transgress the "bourgeois" level.

I have now come to the end, for the appendix that now follows in the program does not constitute a characteristic component part of it. Hence, I can be very brief.

Appendix
"2. Normal working day."

In no other country has the workers' party limited itself to such an indefinite demand, but has always fixed the length of the working day that it considers normal under the given circumstances.

"3. Restriction of female labor and prohibition of child labor."

The standardization of the working day must include the restriction of female labor, insofar as it relates to the duration, intermissions, etc., of the working day; otherwise, it could only mean the exclusion of female labor from branches of industry that are especially unhealthy for the female body, or are objectionable morally for the female sex. If that is what was meant, it should have been said so.

"Prohibition of child labor." Here it was absolutely essential to state the age limit.

A general prohibition of child labor is incompatible with the existence of large-scale industry and hence an empty, pious wish. Its realization — if it were possible — would be reactionary, since, with a strict regulation of the working time according to the different age groups and other safety measures for the protection of children, an early combination of productive labor with education is one of the most potent means for the transformation of present-day society.

"4. State supervision of factory, workshop, and domestic industry."

In consideration of the Prusso-German state, it should definitely have been demanded that the inspectors are to be removable only by a court of law; that any worker can have them prosecuted for neglect of duty; that they must belong to the medical profession.

"5. Regulation of prison labor."

A petty demand in a general workers' program. In any case, it should have been clearly stated that there is no intention from fear of competition to allow ordinary criminals to be treated like beasts, and especially that there is no desire to deprive them of their sole means of betterment, productive labor. This was surely the least one might have expected from socialists.

"6. An effective liability law."

It should have been stated what is meant by an "effective" liability law.

Be it noted, incidentally, that, in speaking of the normal working day, the part of factory legislation that deals with health regulations and safety measures, etc., has been overlooked. The liability law comes into operation only when these regulations are infringed.

In short, this appendix also is distinguished by slovenly editing.

Dixi et salvavi animam meam. ("I have spoken and saved my soul.")